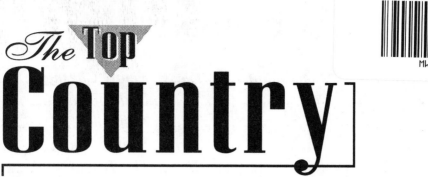

The Top Country Hits of the 90's

Project Manager: Carol Cuellar
Cover Design: Joseph Klucar

CONTENTS

THE KEEPER OF THE STARS

Words and Music by
KAREN STALEY, DANNY MAYO and DICKEY LEE

D A/C♯ Bm

Now, I just can't be - lieve you're in my
I know I don't de - serve a trea - sure like

G D/F♯

life. Heav-en's smil-in' down on me
you. There real - ly are no words

Em A7sus A N.C. D/F♯

as I look at you to - night.
to show my grat - i - tude.
I tip my

mf

Chorus:

G A F♯m

hat to the keep - er of the stars.

G
Em
A7
He sure knew what he was do - in'
when he joined these two
D
D/F♯
G
hearts.
I hold ev - 'ry - thing
A
F♯m
G
D/F♯
Em
when I hold you in my arms.
I've got all I'll ev-er need
1.
A
G
D
A7sus
thanks to the keep-er of the stars.
dim.
mp

2.

A D

thanks to the keep - er of___ the stars.___

dim.

A/C♯ Bm

mp

It was_ no ac - ci - dent,_ me find - ing

G D/F♯

you. Some-one had a hand_ in it___

Em A7sus D A7sus D

long be - fore_ we_ ev - er knew.

a tempo *dim. e rit.* ***p***

ANGELS AMONG US

Words and Music by
BECKY HOBBS and DON GOODMAN

Db(add Eb)
Cm7
3fr
Db(add Eb)
Eb7
Sung: Ma-ma could - n't see him, but he was stand - ing there. But
Db(add Eb)
Ab/C
Db(add Eb)
Eb7
Play first time only
I knew in my heart he was the an-swer to my prayer. Oh,
Ab(add Bb)
Fm7
Bbm7
Eb7
Ab(add Bb)
Fm7
I be-lieve there are an-gels a-mong us, sent down to us from
Db(add Eb)
Eb7
Ab(add Bb)
Fm7
Db
4fr
Eb7
some-where up a-bove. They come to you and me in our dark-est hours to
To Coda
Db(add Eb)
Cm7
3fr
Db(add Eb)
Eb7
Db(add Eb)
Eb7
show us how to live, to teach us how to give to guide us with a light of

1.
Ab
Cm7
Db(add Eb)
Eb7
love.
When
2.
Ab
Db(add Eb)
Cm7
love.
They wear so man - y fa - ces,
Db(add Eb)
Cm7
Db(add Eb)
Cm7
show up in the strang - est plac - es. They grace us with their mer - cies
Bbm7
Eb7
D.S. al Coda
in our time of need.
Oh,
Coda
Ab
No Chord
love.
To guide us with a light of
love.

Additional lyrics

When life held troubled times and had me down on my knees,
There's always been someone to come along and comfort me.
A kind word from a stranger, to lend a helping hand,
A phone call from a friend just to say I understand.
Now, ain't it kind of funny, at the dark end of the road,
Someone lights the way with just a single ray of hope.

(To Chorus)

I WILL ALWAYS LOVE YOU

Words and Music by
DOLLY PARTON

Chorus:
F
Dm
B♭
C
F
Dm
I will al - ways love you. I will
B♭
C
F2
B♭m7/E♭
E♭7
al - ways love you.
Dolly:
Bit - ter -
Verse 2:
A♭
A♭sus
A♭
E♭/G
Fm
A♭/E♭
sweet mem-o - ries, that is all I am tak - ing with
D♭
E♭
E♭7
A♭
E♭/G
me. Good-bye, please don't you cry, 'cause we both

Fm Ab/Eb Db Eb

know___ I'm not what___ you need.___ But

Chorus:

Ab Fm Db Eb Ab Fm

I___ will al - ways_ love___ you.___ I___ will_

Db Eb Ab Db/Ab Ab

al - ways_ love___ you.___ *Vince:* I hope_

Verse 3:

Eb/G Fm Ab/Eb

Dolly: *V.:* *D.:* *Both:*

— life — I hope life treats you kind, treats you kind. and I hope_ you have all you_ dream

Db Eb Ab Eb/G

Dolly: *Vince:* *D.:* *V.:* *Both:*

of. — I wish you joy. Wish you joy and — hap-pi - ness. and hap - pi - ness. — But a-

Fm Ab/Eb Db Eb Bm7/E E7

bove — all this I wish you — love. — Oh, — and

Chorus:
A
F♯m
D
E
A
F♯m
I will al - ways love you. I will
D
E
A
F♯m
D
E
al - ways love you. you. Yes. I will al - ways love
A
F♯m
D
E
you. I will al - ways love
rit. e dim.
N.C.
A(9)
A
you.
mp
a tempo
rit.

I LIKE IT, I LOVE IT

Words and Music by
MARK HALL, STEVE DUKES
and JEB ANDERSON

Moderately ♩ = 100
C7
mf
F7
G7
C7
G7
Verse:
C7
1. Spent for - ty - eight dol - lars last night at the coun - ty fair.
2. See additional lyrics

I throwed out my shoulder-er but I
won her that ted - dy bear.
G7
She's got me
F7
say - in' sug - ar pie, hon - ey, dar - lin' and dear. I
C7
ain't seen the Braves play a game all year. I'm
G7
gon - na get fired if I don't get some sleep. My
long, lost bud - dies say I'm get - tin' in too deep. But I
Chorus:
C7
like it, I love it, I

F7
want some more of it. I
try___ so hard,___ I
can't___ rise a - bove it. I
G7
To Coda
1.
C7
N.C.
don't know what it is 'bout that
lit - tle gal's lov - in', but I
like it, I love it, I
want some more of it.
C7
Inst. solo ad. lib....
F7
G7
C7
G7
2. My

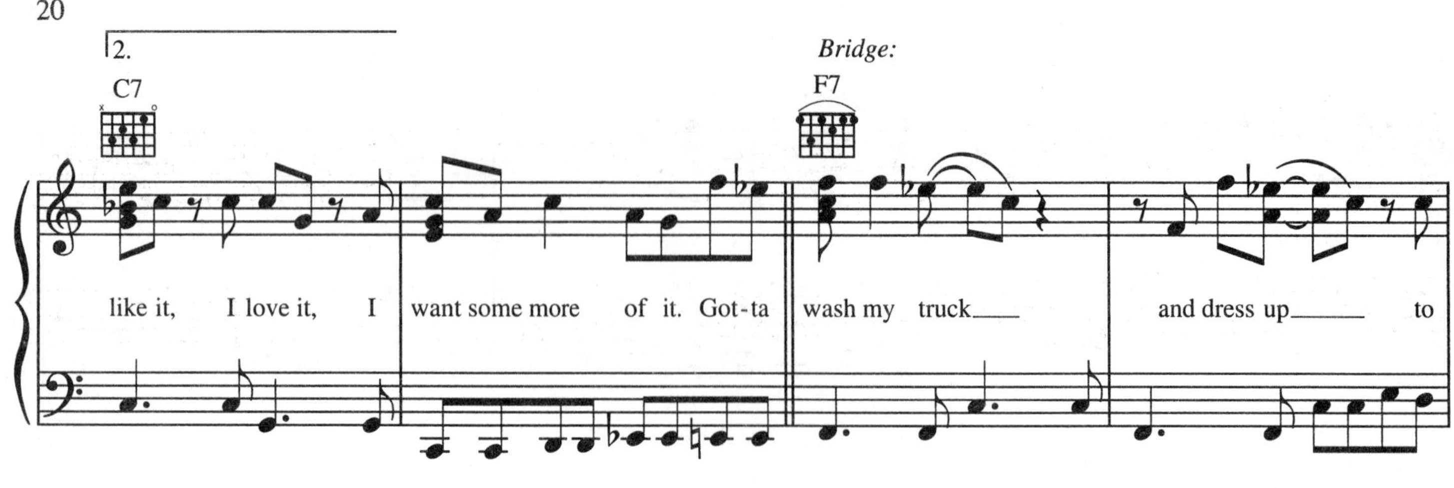
2.
Bridge:
C7
F7
like it, I love it, I want some more of it. Got-ta wash my truck and dress up to

C7
F7
pick her up to watch T. V. If she sits down on the so - fa, she'll

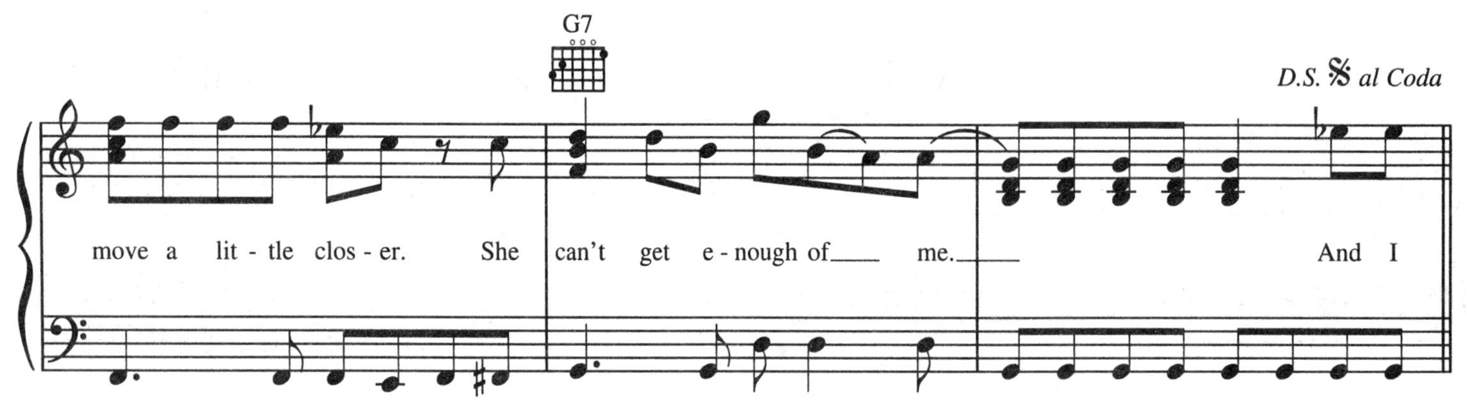
G7
D.S. 𝄋 al Coda
move a lit - tle clos - er. She can't get e - nough of me. And I

Coda
C7
N.C.
C7
like it, I love it, I want some more of it.

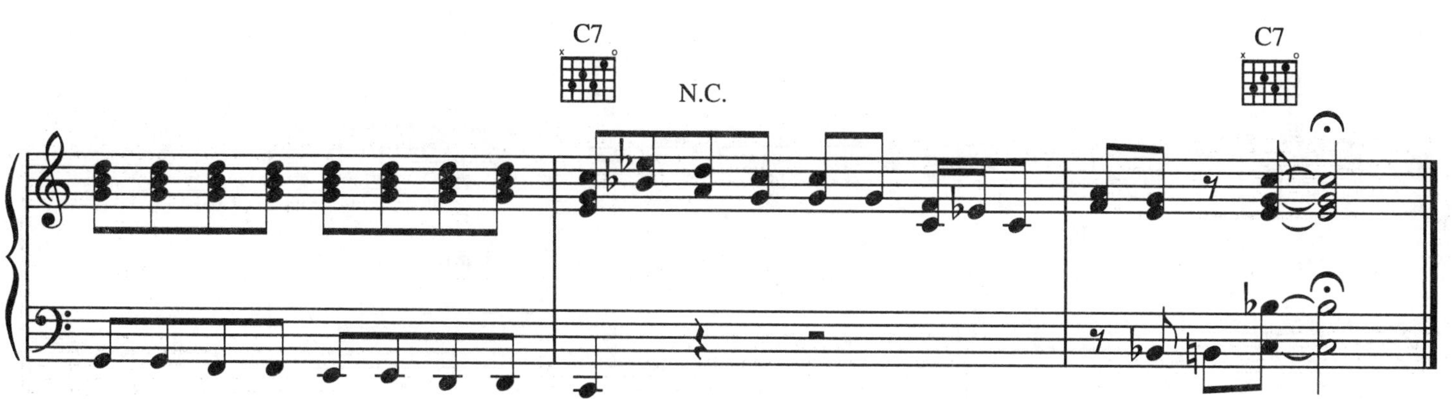

Verse 2:
My mama and daddy tried to teach me courtesy,
But it never sank in till that girl got a hold of me.
Now I'm holdin' up umbrellas and I'm openin' up doors,
I'm takin' out trash and I'm sweepin' my floor.
I'm crossin' my fingers and countin' every kiss,
And prayin' that it keeps on goin' on like this, 'cause I...
(To Chorus:)

ANY MAN OF MINE

Words and Music by
SHANIA TWAIN and
ROBERT JOHN "MUTT" LANGE

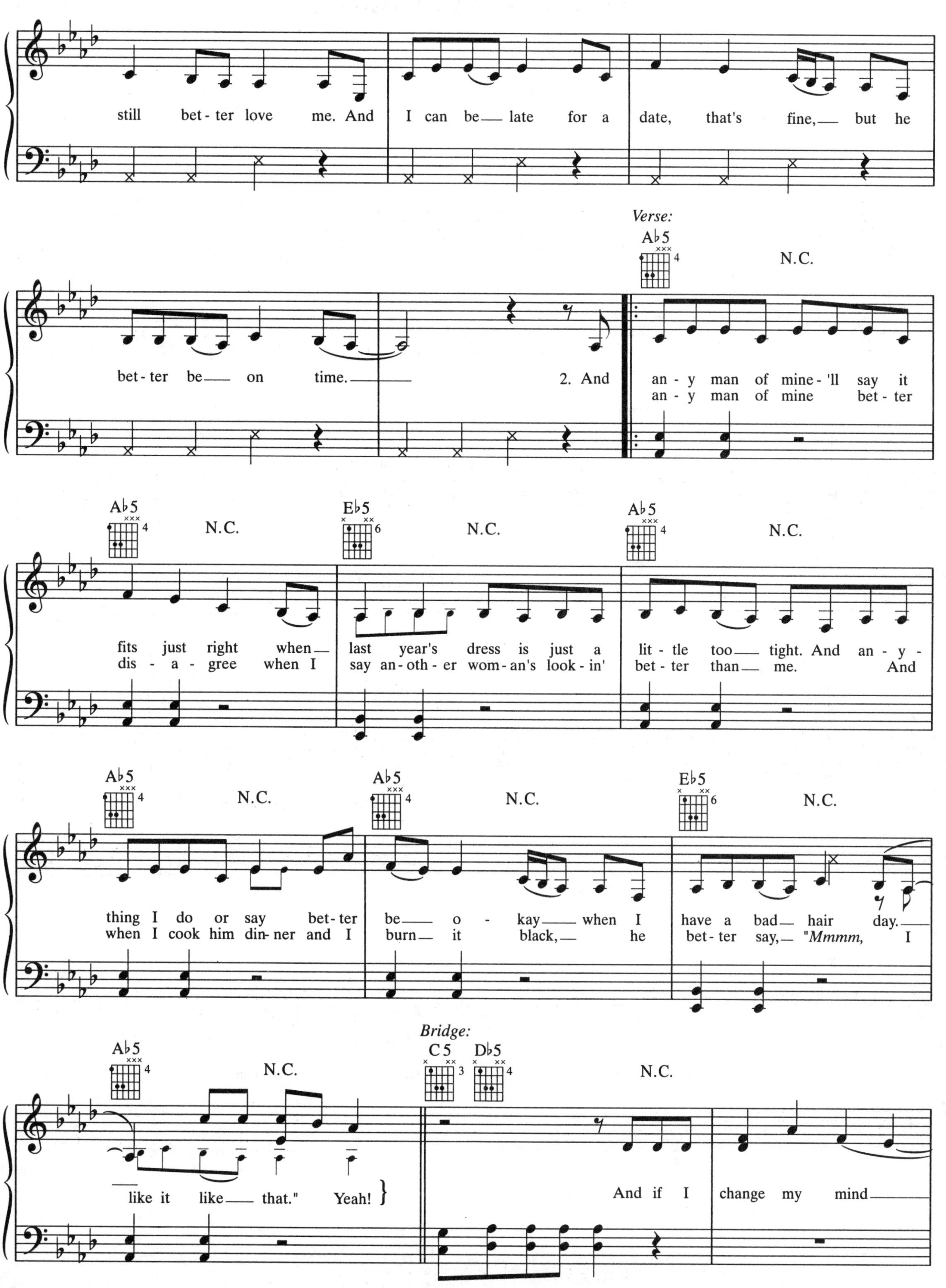
still bet - ter love me. And
I can be late for a date, that's fine, but he
bet - ter be on time.
2. And
Verse:
A♭5
N.C.
an - y man of mine - 'll say it
an - y man of mine bet - ter
fits just right when
dis - a - gree when I
E♭5
last year's dress is just a
say an - oth - er wom - an's look - in'
lit - tle too tight. And an - y -
bet - ter than me. And
thing I do or say bet - ter
when I cook him din - ner and I
be o - kay when I
burn it black, he
have a bad hair day.
bet - ter say, "Mmmm, I
like it like that." Yeah!
Bridge:
C5
D♭5
And if I change my mind

G5 A♭5 N.C. C5 D♭5 N.C.
a mil - lion times, I wan - na
E♭5 N.C. E♭5 N.C.
hear him say, "Yeah, yeah, yeah, yeah,
E♭5 N.C. E♭5 N.C.
yeah, I like it that way!" An - y man of
Country two-beat
Chorus:
D♭ A♭
mine bet - ter walk the line. Bet - ter show me a
E♭ A♭
teas - in', squeez - in', pleas - in' kind of time. I need a man who

D♭
A♭
knows
how the sto - ry
goes.
He's got-ta be a
G♭
D♭
E♭
heart - beat-in', fine treat-in',
breath - tak-in', earth - quak-in'
kind,
1.
N.C.
A♭5
N.C.
A♭5
N.C.
an-y man of
mine.
E♭5
N.C.
A♭5
N.C.
2.
N.C.
an - y man of

D♭
A♭
mine. (Instrumental solo...
D♭
E♭
Let me hear you say, ... end solo)
"Yeah, yeah,
yeah, yeah,
E♭7
N.C.
yeah, I like it that way!"
An-y man, an-y man, an-y man...
Chorus:
B♭
N.C.
E♭
B♭
An-y man of mine bet-ter walk the line.
F
B♭
Bet-ter show me a teas-in', squeez-in', pleas-in' kind of time.

E♭ B♭

I need a man who knows how the sto - ry goes.

A♭ E♭

He's got - ta be a heart - beat - in', fine treat - in', breath - tak - in', earth - quak - in'

F N.C.

kind, an - y man of

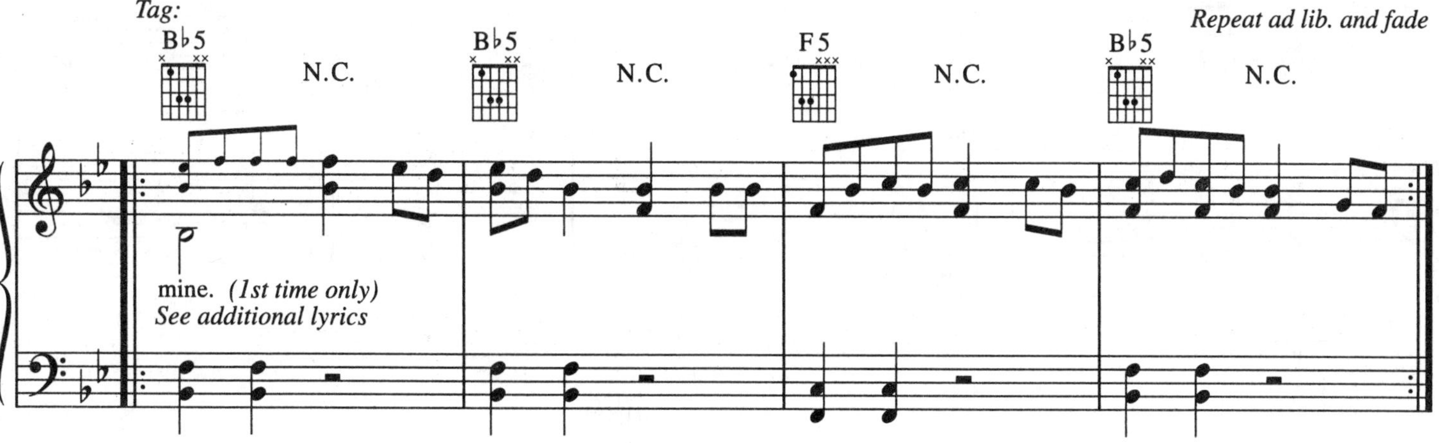

Tag:
You gotta shimmy shake, make the earth quake.
Kick, turn, stomp, stomp, then you jump heel to toe, Do Si Do
'Til your boots wanna break, 'til your feet and your back ache
Keep it movin' 'til you just can't take anymore.
Come on, everybody on the floor, a-one two, a-three four.
Hup two, hup if you wanna be a man of mine, that's right.
This is what a woman wants...

BETTER THINGS TO DO

Words and Music by
TOM SHAPIRO, CHRIS WATERS
and TERRI CLARK

E♭ F

to say I'm bare - ly hang - in' on. Well, may-

E♭ F E♭ F

- be that was true for a night or two, but now

A♭ E♭ B♭

I got bet - ter things to do. I could

Chorus:

E♭

wash my car in the rain, change my new gui-tar strings,

B♭

mow the yard just the same as I did yes - ter-day.

E♭
B♭
I don't need to waste my time cry - in' o - ver you.
F
A♭
1.
E♭
I got bet - ter things to do.
B♭
2. May -
2.
E♭
bet - ter things to do.
Check the air in my tires, straight-en my
B♭
ste - re - o wires, count the stars in the sky, or just get

E♭ B♭

on with my life. I don't need to waste my time cry -

F A♭

-in' o - ver you. I got

E♭ B♭ A♭

bet - ter things to do. I got

E♭ B♭ N.C. B♭

bet-ter things to do.

Verse 2:
Maybe when I don't have so much going,
Or quite so many irons in the fire,
I'll take the time to miss you like you're hopin',
But now, I can't put forth the effort it requires.
Well, I'd love to talk to you, but then I'd miss Donahue.
That's right, I got better things to do.
(To Chorus:)

WHEN LOVE FINDS YOU

Words and Music by
VINCE GILL and MICHAEL OMARTIAN

B♭
B♭/D
B♭maj7/D
B♭7/D
E♭
pain. And with ev - ery e - mo - tion
E♭m6/G♭
4fr.
B♭
Gm7
3fr.
love puts us through, there's noth - ing you can
C9
A♭9
4fr.
1.
B♭
E♭
B♭/D
B♭
say, when love finds you.
F/G
Cm7/F
8fr.
2.
B♭
E♭/B♭
B♭
F
Gm7
3fr.
you. Give it all you can

F/A
E♭/B♭
B♭
F/G
Gm
3fr.
give it, when your love comes a - round. If you
F
Gm7
3fr.
F/A
E♭
B♭/D
B♭
put your heart in it, then it won't let you
F/G
Gm
3fr.
E♭
B♭/F
E♭/G
To Coda
down.___ You'll find out it's true, { ba- by / I'll } some- day / prom- ise when / you
D.S. (no repeat) al Coda
B♭/F
F7
B♭
E♭
B♭/D
B♭
F/G
Cm7/F
8fr.
love finds you.

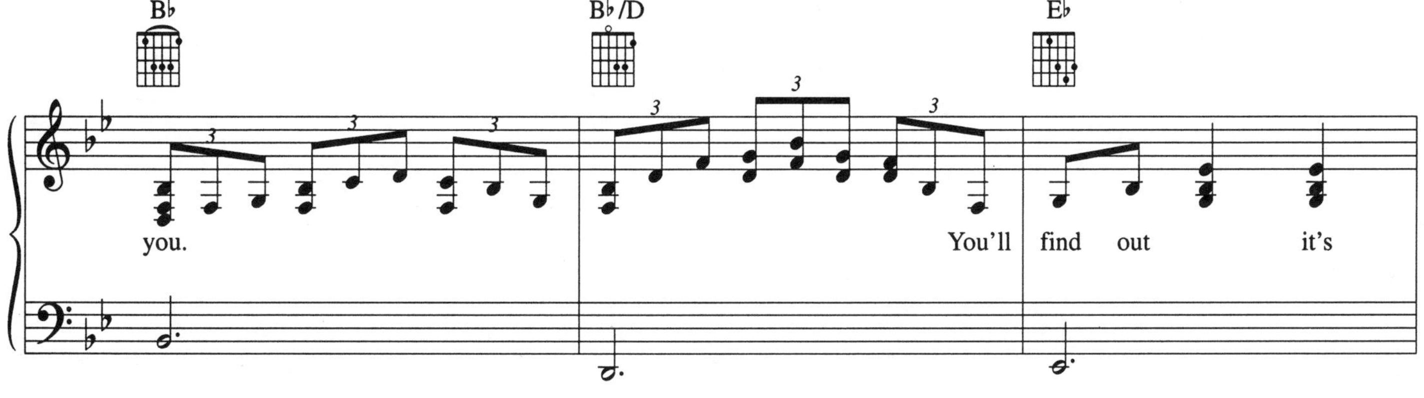

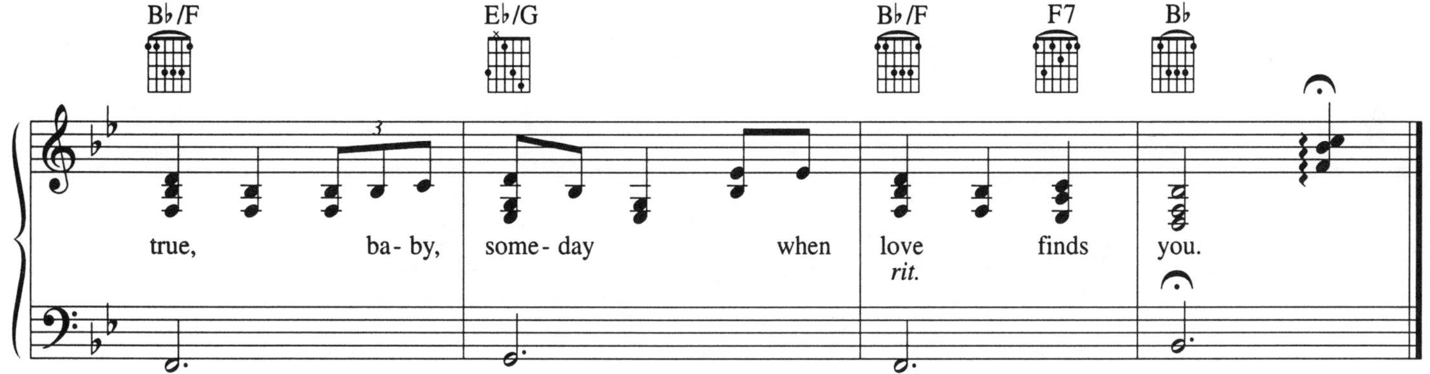

Additional lyrics

2. Love is the power that makes your heart beat,
   It can make you move mountains, make you drop to your knees.
   When it finally hits you, you won't know what to do,
   There's nothing you can say when love finds you.

3. *Instrumental*
   And when you least expect it, it will finally come true,
   There's nothing you can say when love finds you.

ALL I NEED TO KNOW

Words and Music by
STEVE SESKIN and
MARK ALAN SPRINGER

Slowly ♩ = 76

Em7 D/F♯ G G/A A7 D

mp

(with pedal)

Verse:

D G

1. With a lit-tle luck, this ole truck_ will get me home_ to-day._ With a

G/A A7 D G/A A7 D

lit-tle more, I'll still have this job_ to - mor-row. Weath-er-man says wet week - end,_

G G/A A7

he just might_ be right._ But rain or shine, you'll be mine_ to -

Chorus:
D D/F♯ G A7 D
night.__ That's all I need to know____ in a
cresc. mf
G/A A7 D D/F♯ Em7 D/F♯
world where_ most things come and go. I'll al-ways have you__ to hold,_
G G/A A7
1. D Bm7 G G/A
_ and that's all_ I need_ to know.
dim.
2. D
Bridge:
A7sus A7 D/F♯ G
know. Dar - ling,___ say it one more time.____
A7sus A7 D/F♯ G A7sus A7 D/F♯
You will____ for - ev - er be mine.____ That's

Verse 2:
Heaven knows I ain't even close
To being God's gift to women,
But in your arms, I feel like I am.
I don't know it all and I sure can't solve
The problems of the human race,
But I know how to bring a smile to your face.
(To Chorus:)

AMY'S BACK IN AUSTIN

Written by
BRADY SEALS and
STEPHEN ALLEN DAVIS

Moderately ♩ = 116
G
C(9)
mf
Verse:
G
C(9)
1. We left Tex - as on a wind - y night___ in a
G
Em
beat up Chev - y___ van.___ We load - ed it up with our in -
C(9)
D
- no - cent dreams_ and all the love_ we had.___ We

G
C(9)
G
did - n't know then how hard it was, liv - in' on our own.
2. See additional lyrics

Em
C(9)
I'd find her cry - ing late at night

D
Am
talk - in' to the folks back home. I won - der what went wrong

Em
C(9)
D
and where is she now. I'd love to know.

Chorus:

G

I bet Am - y's back in Aus - tin work-in' at La

f *(Instrumental solo 3rd time...*

C(9) G

Zo - na Ro - sa Ca - fe. I re - mem-ber the night we lost

D

it, and the day she went a - way. Was it the an -

...end solo 3rd time)

G C(9)

- gry words or did she miss her mom-ma? I don't know, but it don't feel right.

Em7
C(9)
To Coda
I bet Am - y's back in Aus - tin, and I'm
D
1.
G
miss - ing her to - night.
C(9)
2.
G
Could this
Bridge:
C(9)
Em7
des - ert wind car - ry me back a - gain? With my
mf

Verse 2:
Workin' ten hours in a West Coast sun,
Can make the day so long.
Watchin' the moon crashin' into the ocean
Alone sure gets old.
I remember how sweet it was,
And where is she now, I need to know.
(To Chorus:)

DOCTOR TIME

Words and Music by
LONNIE WILSON and
SUSAN LONGACRE

Moderate country two-beat ♩ = 69

E♭ B♭ E♭ F

mf

(with pedal)

E♭ F

B♭

Verse:

1. May - be the juke - box can heal up a heart - ache,
2. *See additional lyrics*

A♭ B♭

but I'd go in - to debt.

May - be the whis - ky can wipe out a mem - 'ry,

A♭
E♭
F
B♭
but it on - ly hurts my__ head.
May - be some danc - in'-'ll pick me up, but the
B♭7
E♭
B♭
best song al - ways ends.
Now I'm down_ to tell - ing my - self__
F
B♭
E♭
time__ is a fool's best friend._
Doc - tor
Chorus:
B♭
E♭
F
Time,________ have mer - cy on me.
Don't wait
E♭
F
E♭
too long to set me__ free.
Doc - tor

B♭
E♭
F
Time, I'm count-ing on you, 'cause you're the on -
To Coda
1.
E♭
F
B♭
E♭
- ly one who can pull me through.
2.
Bridge:
B♭
Gm
through.
Time, tell the truth, you're the on -
E♭
F
B♭
Cm
- ly one I trust. How man - y weeks un -

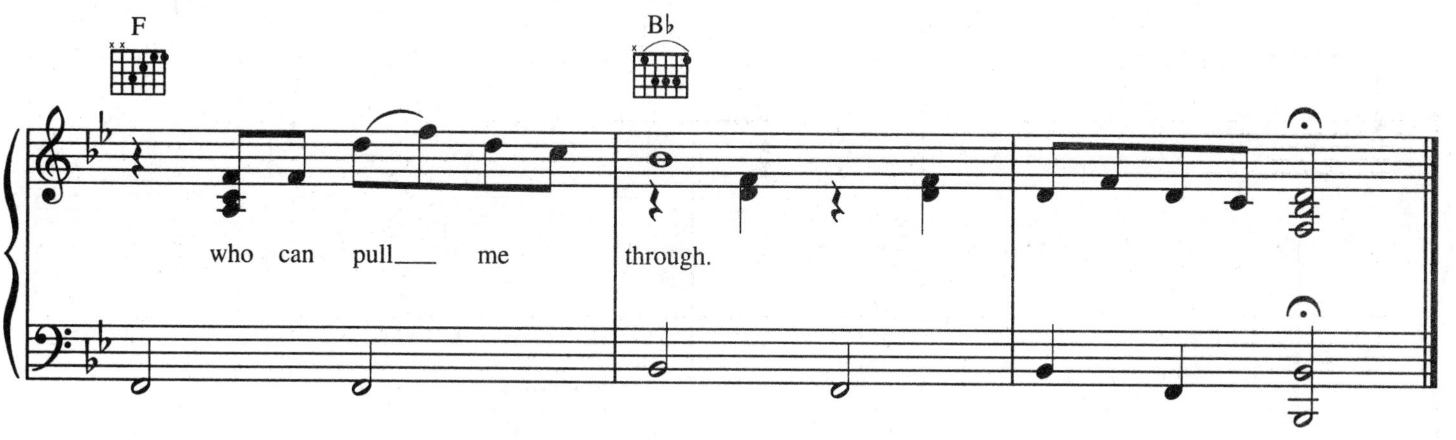

Verse 2:
Friends tell me hard work can fill up the hours,
But it don't fill this bed.
A quarter says a phone call can bring forgiveness,
She'd hang up again.
Gotta give me something to forget her
Everytime I lay down.
There ain't a night goes by I don't wish
I'd wake up a year from now.
(To Chorus:)

I DON'T EVEN KNOW YOUR NAME

Words and Music by
ALAN JACKSON, RON JACKSON
and ANDY LOFTIN

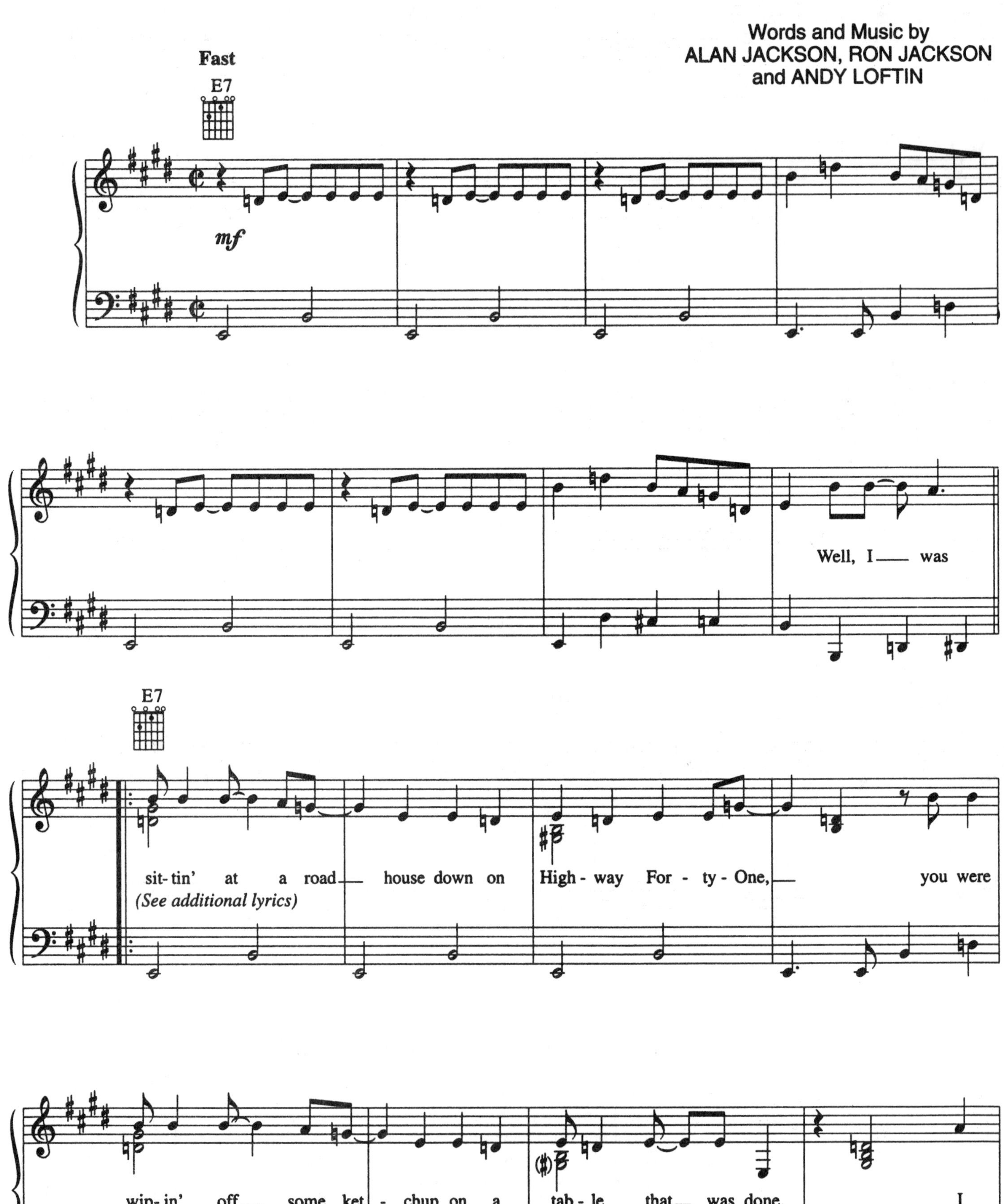
Fast
E7
mf
Well, I was
E7
sit- tin' at a road house down on High - way For - ty - One, you were
(See additional lyrics)
wip- in' off some ket - chup on a tab - le that was done. I

A7
knew you did- n't see me, I was in a cor - ner booth,
E7
of course you weren't my wait - ress, mine was miss- ing her front
B7
tooth. So I flagged you down for cof - fee, but I
E
No Chord
could- n't say a thing. But I'm in love with you, ba -

B
E
F♯m7
G°7
E7/G♯
by, and I don't ev - en know your name. I'm in
A
love with you, ba - by, I don't ev - en know your name. I've
E
F♯m7
nev - er been too good at all those sex - u - al games.
G°7
E7/G♯
A
So may - be it's just bet - ter if we

E
N.C.
leave it this way. I'm in love with you, ba -
B
E
F♯m7
G°7
E7/G♯
by and I don't ev - en know your name.
A7
Instrumental
E7

A7
E7
To Coda
1.
B7
E7
So I
2.
G°7/B♭
F♯m7/A
E
5fr.
The
Slow Shuffle feel
E7
next thing I re-mem-ber I was hear-in' wed-ding bells,

A7
E7
B7
stand- in' by a wom- an in a long_ white la - cy veil. I
raised the veil, she smiled at me with - out her left front tooth, and I said,
"Where the hell am I and just who the hell are you?" She
said, "I was your wait- ress and our last name's now the same, 'cause I'm

D.S. al Coda
E
N.C.
E
F♯m7
G°7
E7/G♯
mar- ried to you, ba - by, and I don't ev - en know your name."
Coda
B7
E
F♯m7
G°7
E7/G♯
A7
(Instrumental solos)
E7

Additional Lyrics

2. So I ordered straight tequilla, a little courage in a shot.
   I asked you for a date and then I asked to tie the knot.
   I got a little wasted, yeah, I went a little far.
   But I finally got to hug you when you helped me to my car.
   The last thing I remember I heard myself say:
   I'm in love with you, baby, and I don't even know your name.
   (To Chorus)

2nd Chorus:
Yeah, I'm married to a waitress; I don't even know her name,
I've never been too good at all those sexual games.
I never thought my love life would quite turn out this way,
Hey, I'm married to a waitress and I don't even know her name.

BABY LIKES TO ROCK IT

Words and Music by
STEVE RIPLEY and W. RICHMOND

C7
F7
Verse:
B♭7
1. You know she likes to take me danc - in' on the out - skirts of town, where the
F7
B♭7
mu - sic's turned up and the lights are turned down. Shake it, shake it, shake it on the
C7
dance, dance floor, crowd, crowd scream-in', scream-in' more, more, more, (She) Got the

Bridge:
F7
B♭7
boog - ie woog - ie woog - ie spread all o - ver the place, got it stacked to the ceil - in', got it
F
C7
stick - in' in your face. You know my ba - by likes to rock it like a boog - ie woog - ie choo - choo train.
F
1.
2.3.
2. John -
Ba -
Chorus:
B♭7
F7
- by likes to rock it. Ba - by likes to rock it.

B♭7

Ba - by likes to rock it like a boog-ie woog-ie choo-choo train.

C7 F

She got the boog-ie woog-ie woog-ie spread all

B♭7

o - ver the place, got it stacked to the ceil - in', got it stick-in' in your face. You know my

F C7 F7

ba - by likes to rock it like a boog-ie woog-ie choo - choo train.

Verse 2:
Johnny's in the back room suckin' on his gin,
Police are at the front door, screamin, "Let me in!"
Go-go-go-go dancer busy showin' off her chest,
She don't know what she doin' but she tries her best.
(To Bridge & Chorus:)

Verse 3:
She said her name was "Emergency" and asked to see my gun,
Said her telephone number was 9-1-1.
Got Brother Jimmy on the TV, Keillor on a stereo,
Said, "If you wanna get it, you got to let it go."
(To Bridge & Chorus:)

DARNED IF I DON'T (DANGED IF I DO)

Words and Music by
DEAN DILLON and RONNIE DUNN

Chorus:
C
run___ or stay?___ On
...end solo 3rd time)
one hand I'm think-in' that I
f
bet-ter lay low,___ but
G
then on the oth-er what a
way to go.___
C
What kind of fix___ have I
got me in - to?___
G
Well, I'm darned___ if I don't,___
D
danged___
G
___ if I do.
mf
1.
2. She's got me
2.

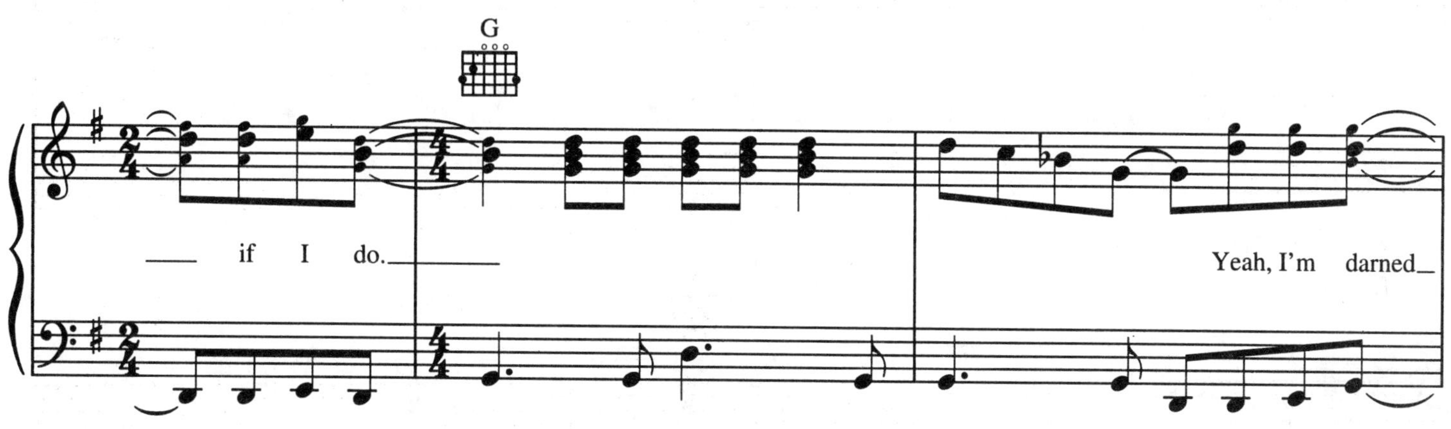

Verse 2:
She's got me wide eyed, tongue tied, beside myself;
I'm tore up, talk me down, I might need help.
Hold me back boys, I ain't thinkin' straight,
My head's cryin' run but my heart's sayin' wait.
(To Chorus:)

THE HEART IS A LONELY HUNTER

Words and Music by
MARK D. SANDERS, KIM WILLIAMS
and ED HILL

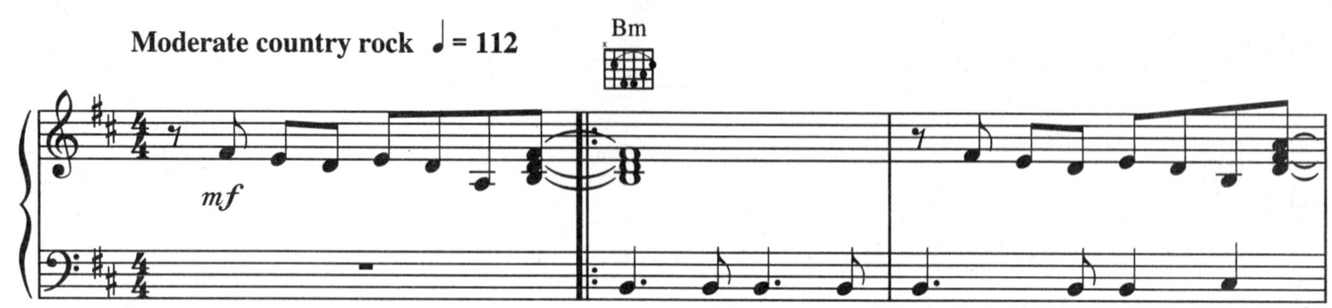
Moderate country rock ♩ = 112
Bm
mf

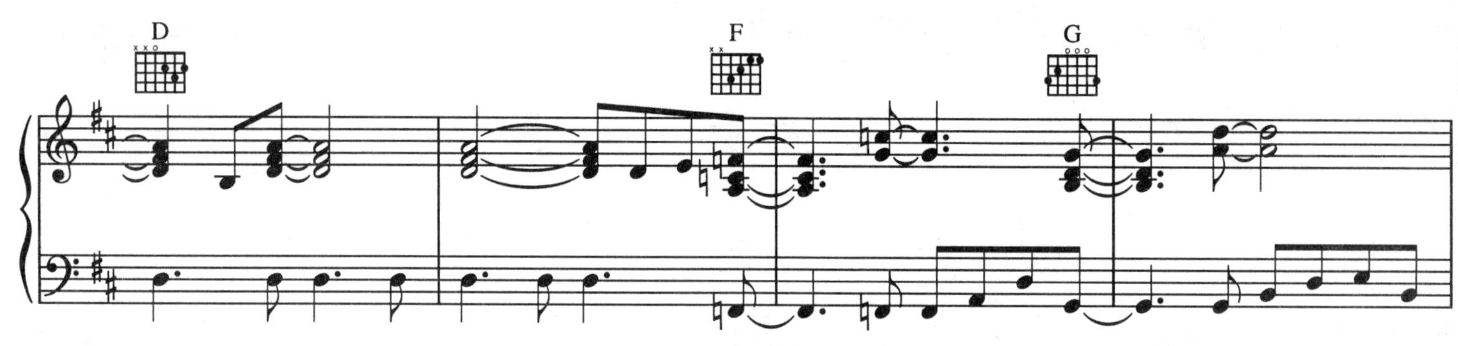
D
F
G

Verse:
D
G
1. She came in look - in' good___ and look-in' a -
2. She hears him say, "Hey, can___ I buy you a

D
G
round.
drink?"
She's check-in' out ev - 'ry man__ in the room right
And sees the pale white__ cir - cle where he wears his
D
Em
G
D
now.__
ring.__
Don't go tell - in' her a-bout right or wrong;
She knows he's deal-in' her a dan-ger-ous hand,
Em
G
A
Asus
A
she's been a - lone__ for way too__ long.__
the con-se-quenc-es of a one-night stand.__
Well,
But,
the heart_
Chorus:
D
D/F♯
__ is a lone - ly hunt - er with on - ly one__ de - sire:__

G
to find some last - in' com - fort in the arms
Asus
A
D
of a lov - er's fire.
Driv - en by a des - per - ate
3
Bm7
hun - ger to the dark of the ne - on light.
Oh, the heart
G
A
is a lone - ly hunt - er when there's no sign of love in

1. D N.C.

sight.

2. D

sight.

Bridge:

Bm A G

From some-where deep in - side___ she tells_ him no.___

Bm A Gmaj9 A N.C.

Be-fore she starts to cry,___ she turns_ to go.___ Oh, the heart_

Chorus:

D D/F♯

___ is a lone - ly hun - ter with on - ly one___ de - sire:__

G
to find some last - in' com - fort in the arms
Asus
Bbsus
Eb
of a lov-er's fire. Driv - en by a des-per-ate
3
Cm7
hun - ger to the dark of the ne - on light, oh, the heart
Ab
Bb
is a lone - ly hunt - er when there's no sign of love in

E♭
A♭
sight. Oh, the heart is a lone - ly hunt - er when there's no
B♭
E♭
N.C.
Cm
sign of love in sight.
E♭
G♭
E♭

I THINK ABOUT IT ALL THE TIME

Words and Music by
BILLY LIVSEY and DON SCHLITZ

I Think about It All the Time - 3 - 1

Bridge:

F C F C

wasn't supposed to hap - pen to me. I'm used to how it used to be. It's

f

F C Am Dm G

not like I've got noth - in' to do, but I can't keep my mind off you, no I

Dm G

1. *D.S.* 𝄋 F/G F C

2. *D.S.* 𝄋 *al Coda* F/G C/G

can-not keep my mind off you. 3. You're not a 5. The way you

𝄌 *Coda* G Am F C G Am

think a - bout it all the time. I'm just a man, I can't de -

mp

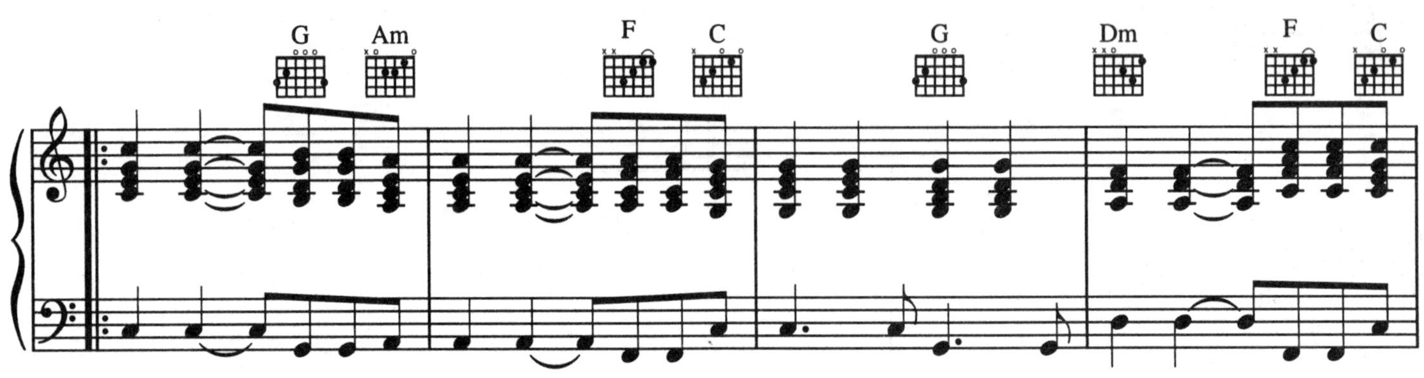

Verse 2:
The day we met, the dress you wore,
You didn't know I was watchin' you.
I've seen your face somewhere before,
And I think about it all the time.
(To Bridge:)

Verse 3:
You're not a thought that comes and goes,
You're more than a dream or a fantasy.
Where it will lead, love only knows
But I think about it all the time.

Verse 4:
(Instrumental solo ad lib.)

Verse 5:
The way you laugh, the way you cry,
The way that you smile without meanin' to.
I'm just a man, I can't deny
And I think about it all the time.
(To Coda)

FEMALE BONDING

Words and Music by
BRETT JAMES

A7
E7
A7
E7
for an - y man.
But I can test - i - fy that ev-en if they're right, there's on-ly
B7
A5
G5
E7
N.C.
so much I can stand.
I need some fe - male bond -
Chorus:
A7
E7
- ing,
I need a wom - an's touch.
B7
You know I like just hang - in' with the boys, but this man can on - ly

A7
E7
A7
stand_ so___ much.___ I want some fem - i - nine com - pan - y,___
E7
To Coda
I need a heart that's true.___ And girl,__
B7
A7
1.
E7
___ if you'll bond with me,___ I'll bond___ with you.___
N.C.
2.
E7
2. Now, too_ ___

A7
E7
A7
B7
D.S. 𝄋 al Coda
Coda
B7
A7
(Inst. solo ad lib. . . .
. . . end solo)
I need some fe - male bond-
if you'll bond with me,
I said, girl,

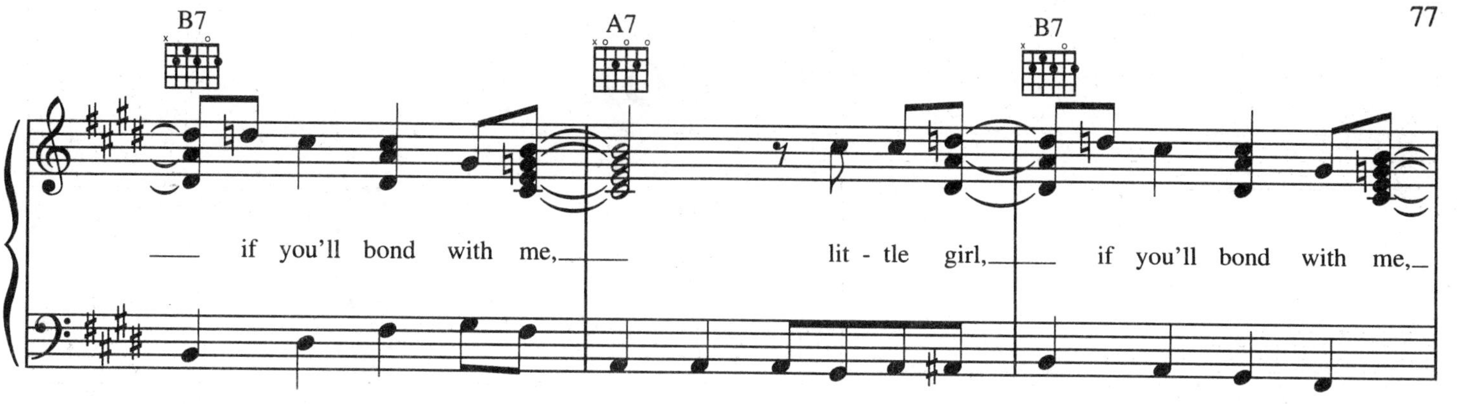

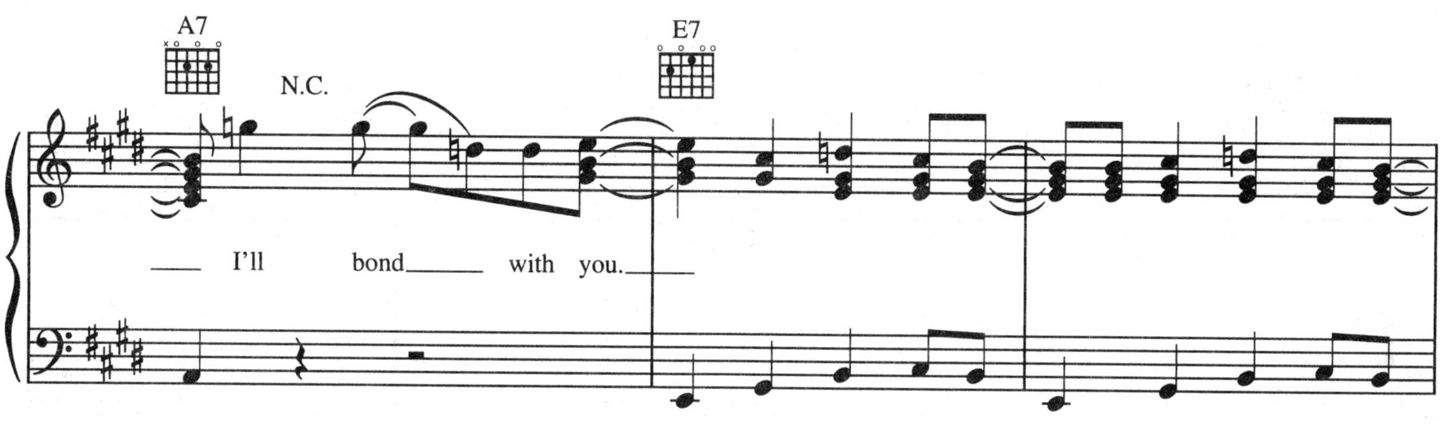

Verse 2:
Now, too much of a good thing
Can drive a man insane.
I got nothin' against my buddies,
And I sure hate to complain.
But male bonding ain't worth nothin'
On a lonesome summer night.
I might even trade my bass boat
For a woman that'll treat me right.
(To Chorus:)

THE BOX

Words and Music by
RANDY TRAVIS and BUCK MOORE

D
E
— that I had nev - er no - ticed till that
A
D
night. Then we set it on the ta -
ble and care - ful - ly we o - pened up the top,
A
E
— and stared in - to the mem -
'ry that he kept in - side the box.

A
D
There was a let - ter from ma -
ma when she went out to Re - no to
A
help her sis - ter out in 'six - ty - two.
E
And a flo - wer from Haw - ai - i; when
they went on va - ca - tion, it was the first time that my

A
dad - dy ev - er flew. And the
D
pock - et knife I gave to him on Fa - ther's
Day; years a - go I thought it had been
A
E
lost. We all thought his heart was made
of so - lid rock, but

1.
A
that was long before we found the box.
I
2.
A
E
box.
We all thought his heart was made
of sol - id rock,
but
A
that was long before we found the box.

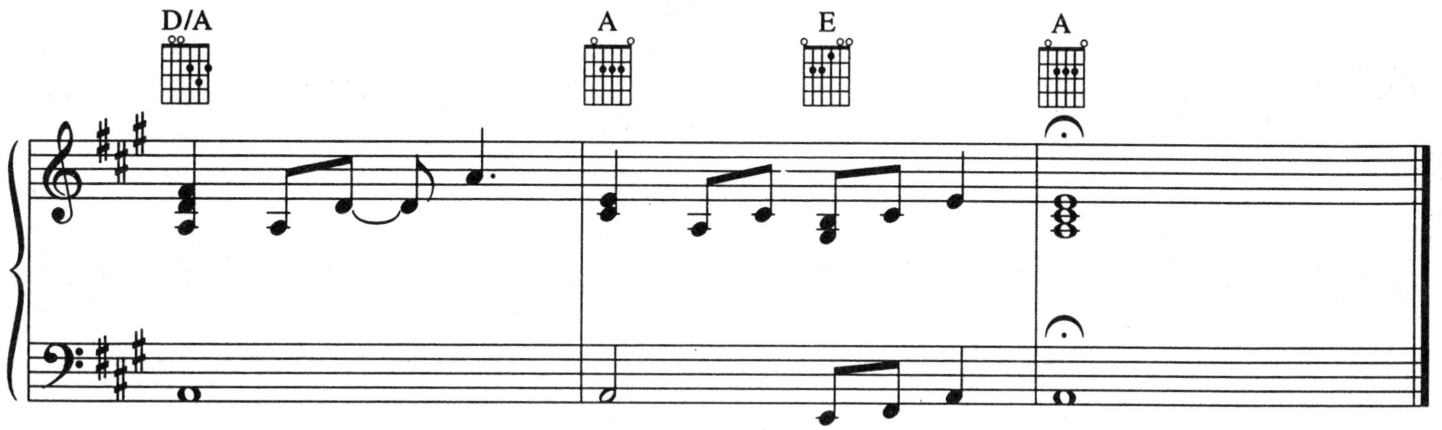

Additional lyrics

2. I guess we always knew it,
But "I love you" was hard for him to say.
Some men show it easily,
And some just never seem to find the way.
But that night I began to see
A softer side of someone I had lost.
I saw the love he kept inside the first time,
When we opened up the box.

2nd Chorus: There was a picture that was taken,
When he and mom were dating
Standing by his 1944.
And a faded leather bible
He got when he was baptized,
I guess no one understood him like the Lord.
And a poem that he had written
All about his wife and children,
The tender words he wrote were quite a shock.
We all thought his heart was made of solid rock,
But that was long before we found the box.

CAIN'S BLOOD

Words and Music by
MICHAEL JOHNSON and JACK SUNDRUD

Am G/A Am G/A Fmaj7

Sun - day choir.______ On her head was a ha - lo,______ she spoke

Am G/A Am Am7(4) G Gsus

brim - stone and fire.______ Dad-dy lived by the bot - tle,______

G Am G

Dad - dy died by the barn. Well, he froze one___ night. Ma - ma

F E7sus E7

said, "Serves him right! The dev - il can keep__ him__ warm."______

Chorus:

A5 Am7 A5 G5 A5

Half of my blood is Cain's blood,_ half of my blood is A - bel's._

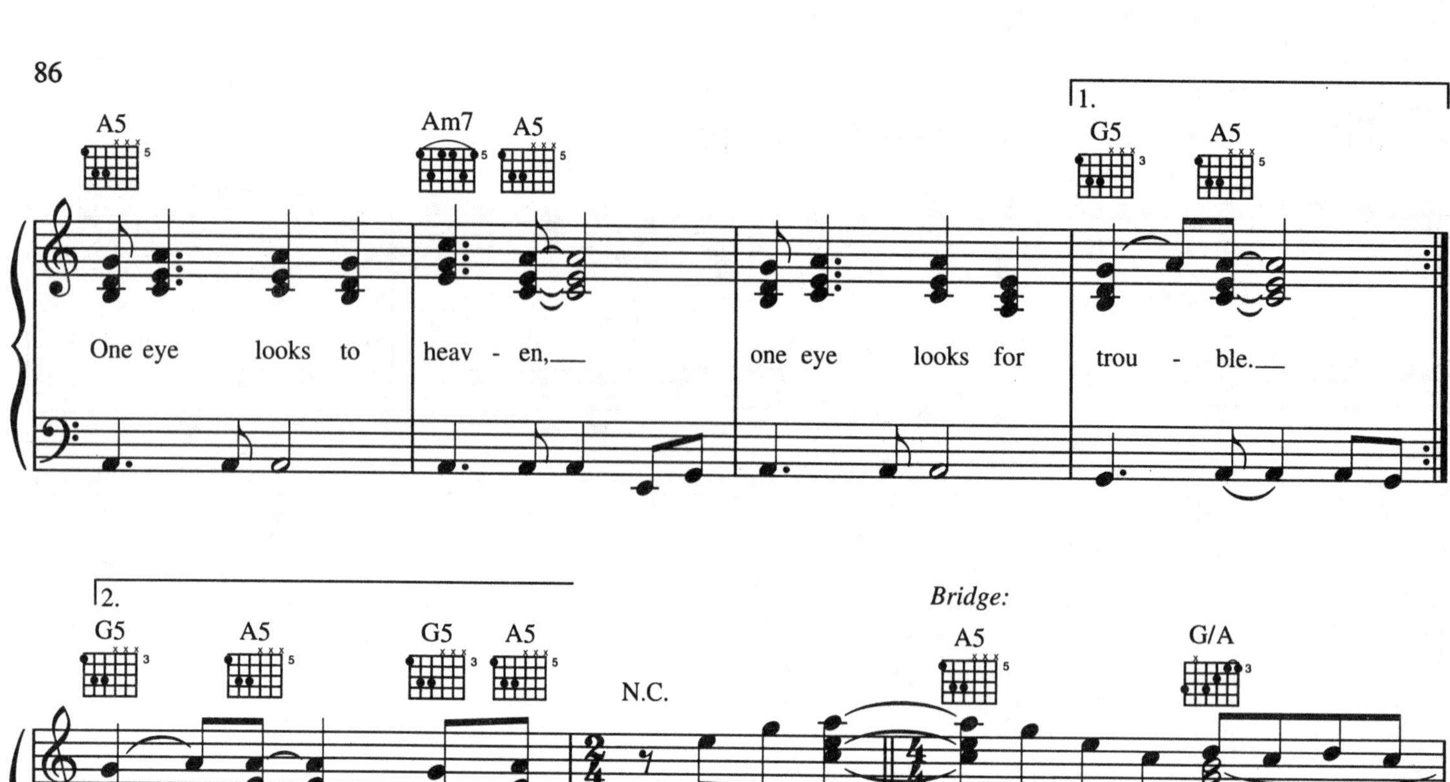
A5
Am7
A5
1.
G5
A5
One eye looks to heav - en,
one eye looks for trou - ble.

2.
G5
A5
G5
A5
N.C.
Bridge:
A5
G/A
trou - ble.
cresc.
There's an an - gel and a dev - il play - ing
mf

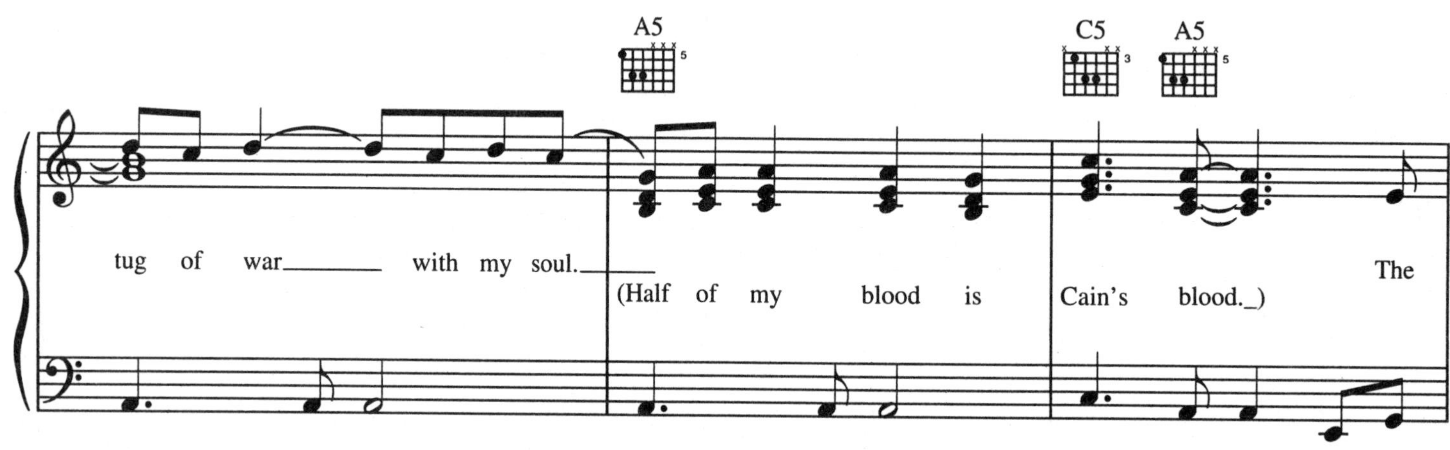
A5
C5
A5
tug of war with my soul.
(Half of my blood is Cain's blood.)
The

bat - tle rag - es on each and ev - 'ry day.
(Half of my blood is

G5
A5
A5
G/A
It's all I can do just to try and main - tain con - trol.
A - bel's.)
A5
C5
A5
Am
My one and on - ly hope is to
(Half of my blood is Cain's blood.)
E7sus
E7
Am
hit my knees and pray.
F
G/F
Fmaj7
Am

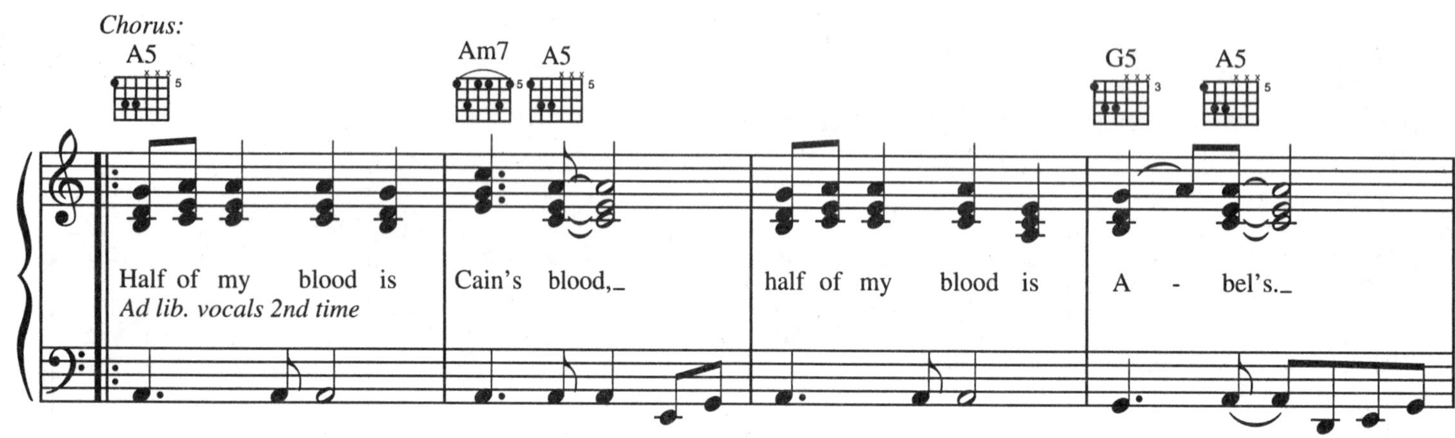

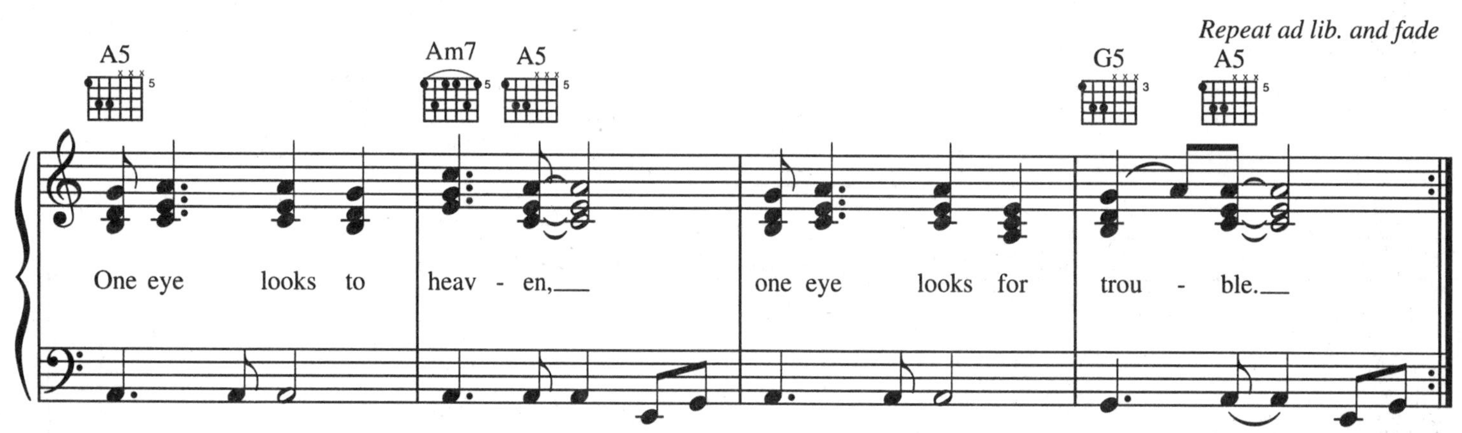

Verse 2:
Guess I always saw myself as a simple man.
But there's a man in the mirror I don't understand.
Every day I fight it, but I know down deep
It's the secrets I've been keeping,
Rising from their sleep.
(To Chorus:)

DEJA BLUE

Words and Music by
CRAIG WISEMAN and DONNIE LOWERY

F♯
A dif - ferent time, an - oth - er frame,
B7
N.C.
still it's spook-y how it seems the same. De - ja
Chorus:
E
B
E
blue,
de - ja blue.
A
I'm feel-in' pret-ty cer-tain that this cry - in' and a-hurt-in' is
E
A
some-thing I've al - read - y been through.
Oh, Lord - y, here I go a - gain.

E
C#7
Tell me will it nev - er end.
Same ol'
F#7(b9)
B7
To Coda
1.
E
fool, noth - in' new, de - ja blue.
E7
B
2.
E
2. Now it

E7

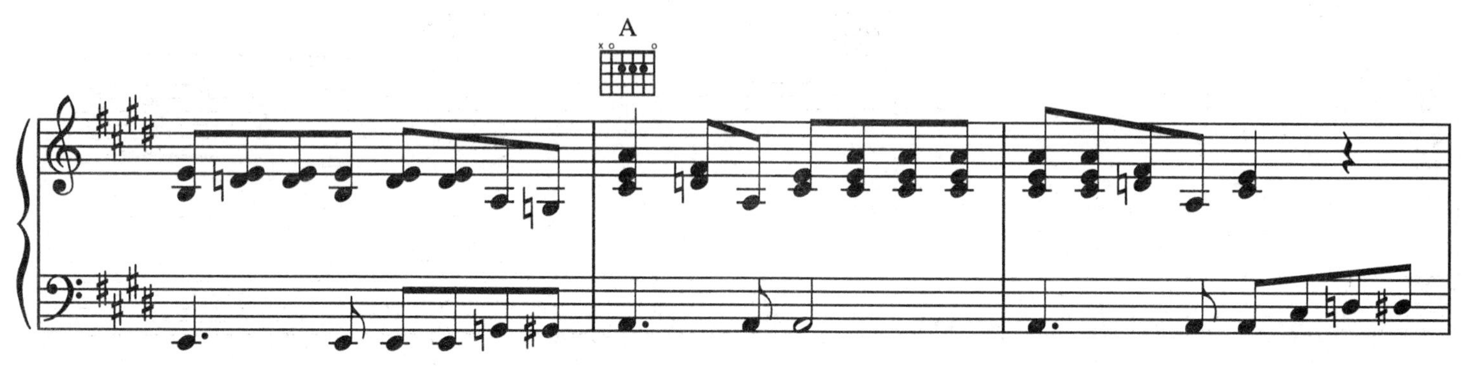
A

E
B

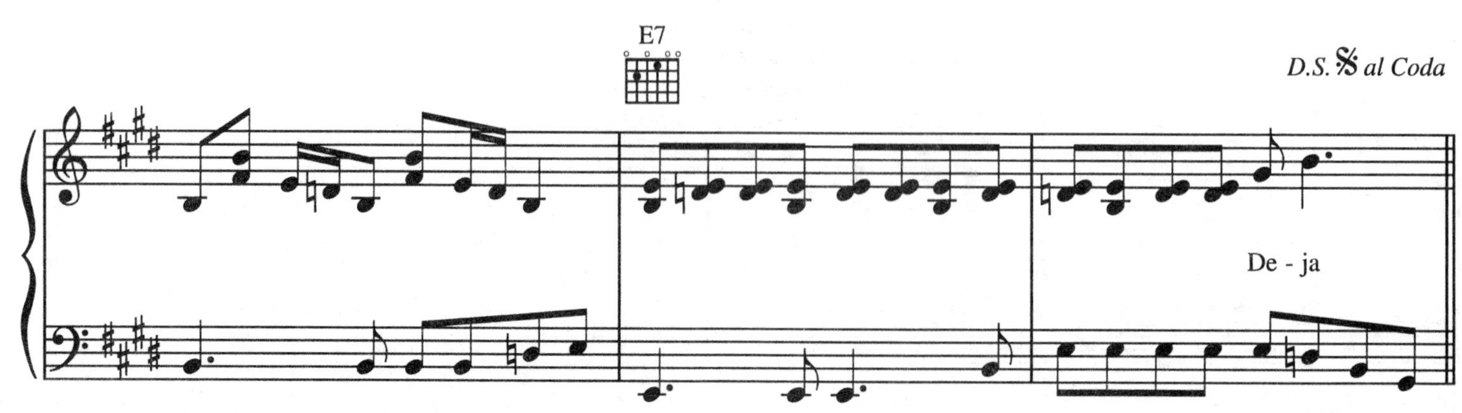
E7
D.S. 𝄋 al Coda
De - ja

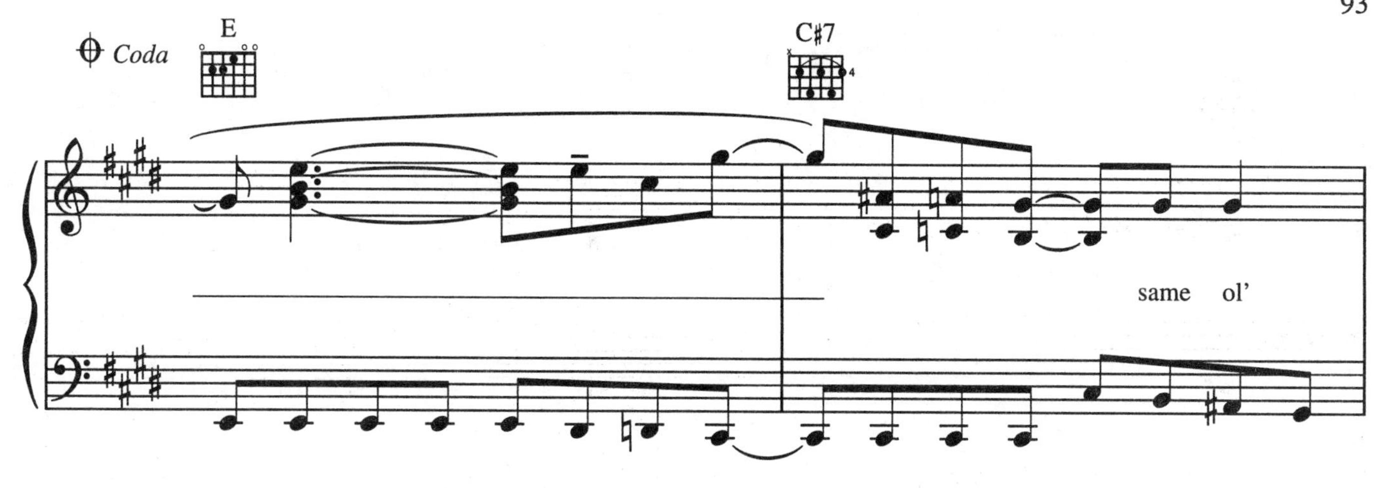

Verse 2:
Now, it started in the second grade,
With little blondie what's her name.
Yeah, I toted all her books
And gave her long and gooshy looks,
But all she wanted was my brother Ray.
That first time nearly done me in,
But I've been there a hundred times since then.
(To Chorus:)

BETWEEN THE TWO OF THEM

Words and Music by
MICKEY CATES

C D C/G G D/F♯

times got bad, the hope would chase a - way the sad.
out just fine, he re - tired in 'eight - y-nine

Em Am D

And hope was some-times all they had be-tween the two of
left with, oh, so lit - tle time be-tween the two of

1. G C(9)/G 2. G C(9)/G

them. them.

G(9)/B E7sus *Verse:* A

3. To-day I braved the

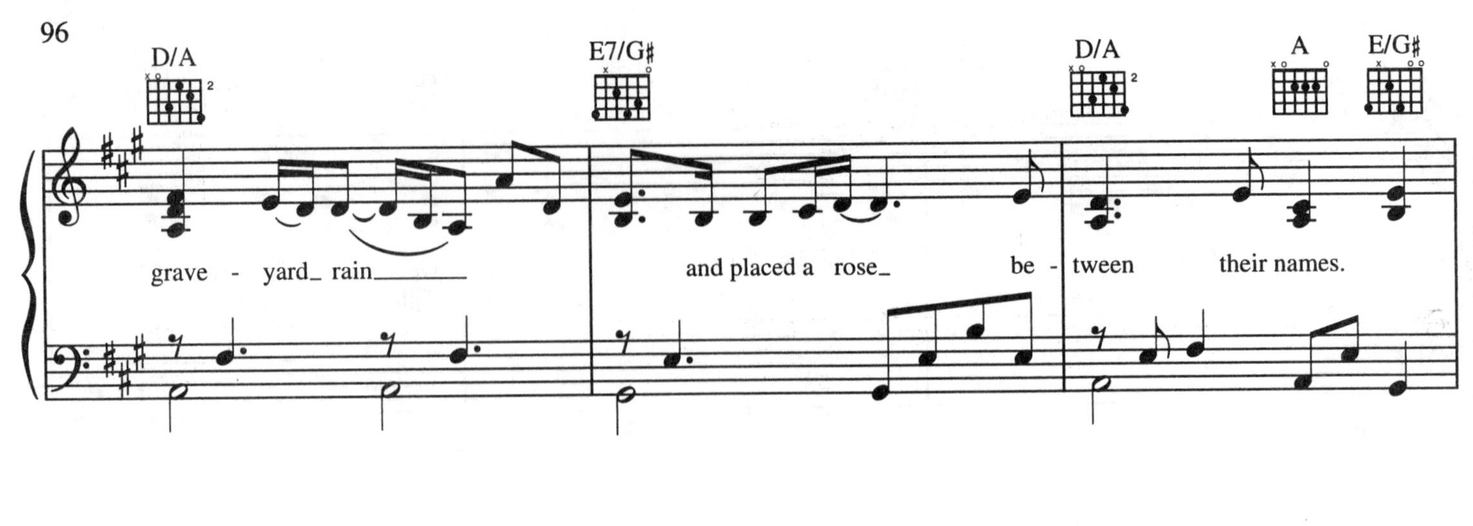
D/A
E7/G♯
D/A
A
E/G♯
grave - yard_ rain_____
and placed a rose_
be - tween
their names.

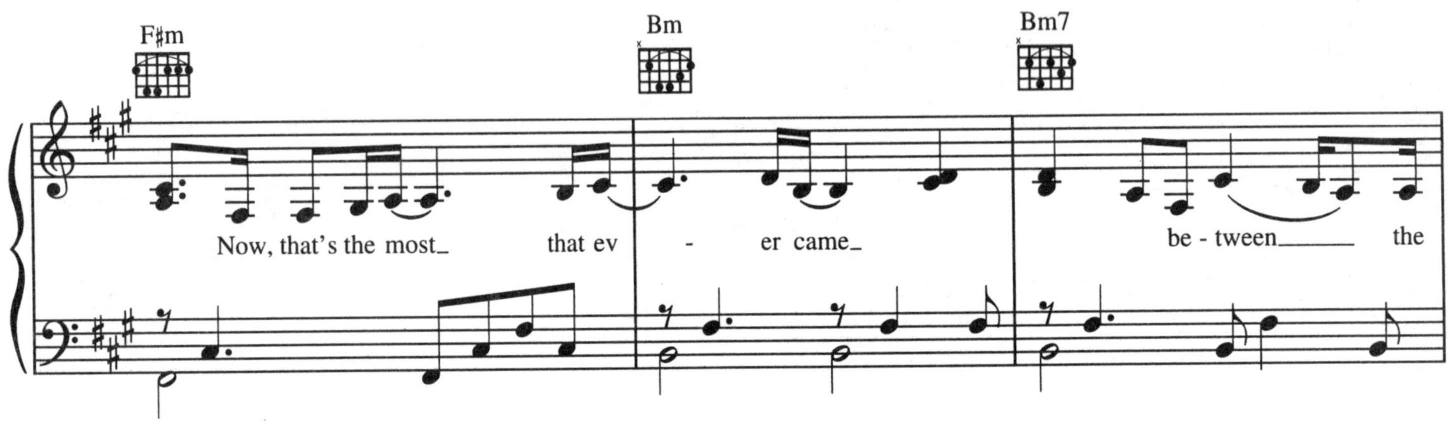
F♯m
Bm
Bm7
Now, that's the most_
that ev
- er came_
be - tween_____
the

E
E7/G♯
A
D
two of them.
And oh, I
miss
them___
both
so__ much,

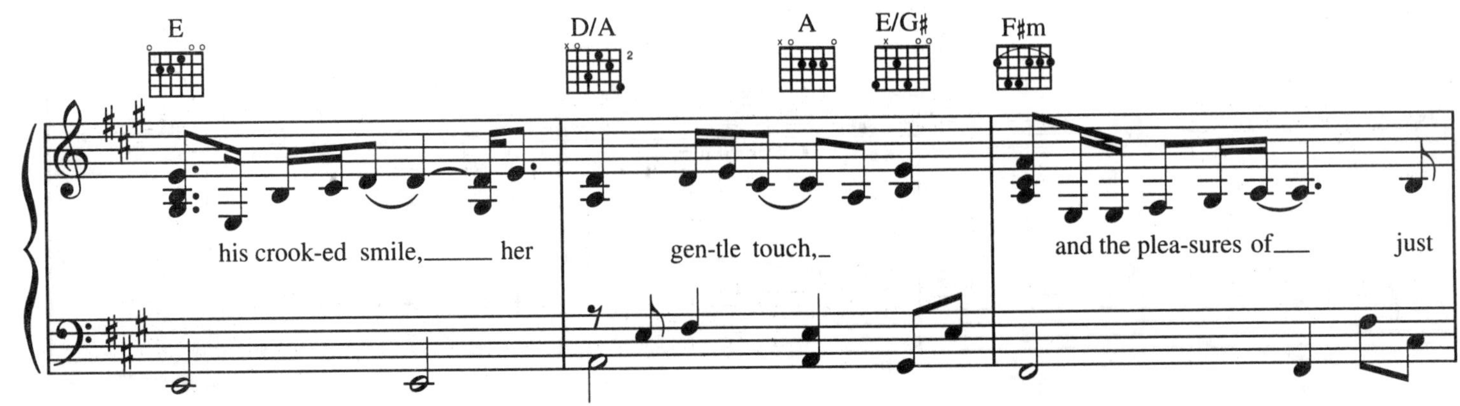
E
D/A
A
E/G♯
F♯m
his crook-ed smile,_____ her
gen-tle touch,_
and the plea-sures of___
just

Bm
E
A
Bm
C♯m
grow - ing up
be-tween the two of
them.
Oh, I miss them both
D
D/F♯
E
D/A
A
E/G♯
so much,
his crook-ed smile,
her
gen-tle touch,
F♯m
Bm
E
N.C.
and the plea-sures of
just
grow - ing up
be-tween the two of them.
molto rit.
A
D/A
Esus
E
A
a tempo
dim. e rit.
p

EUGENE YOU GENIUS

Moderate beat ♩ = 120

Words and Music by
LONNIE WILSON and BILLY LAWSON

B♭7
mf

Verses 1 & 2:
B♭7
1. Saw you come through them
2. See additional lyrics

swing-ing doors, had 'em hang-ing on ya, could-n't hold one more.

N.C.
You walked by with a sil - ly grin, they were kiss - ing all o - ver your
Chorus:
B♭7
chin - ny chin chin. Eu - gene, you gen - ius,
E♭7
what book did you read that made you so smart,
B♭7
you could steal a heart an - y - time that you please? Eu - gene,
F7
To Coda
tacet
you gen - ius, could you teach

1.
B♭7
me?
2.
B♭7
2. It's more me? Is it some-
Bridge:
E♭7
B♭7
- thing that you tell 'em, love letters that you mail 'em? Your se-cret's safe with me.
E♭7
To get those kind of glanc-es do you have to take class-es for a
F7
B♭7
Mas-ter Ro-me-o de-gree? Eu-gene, you gen-

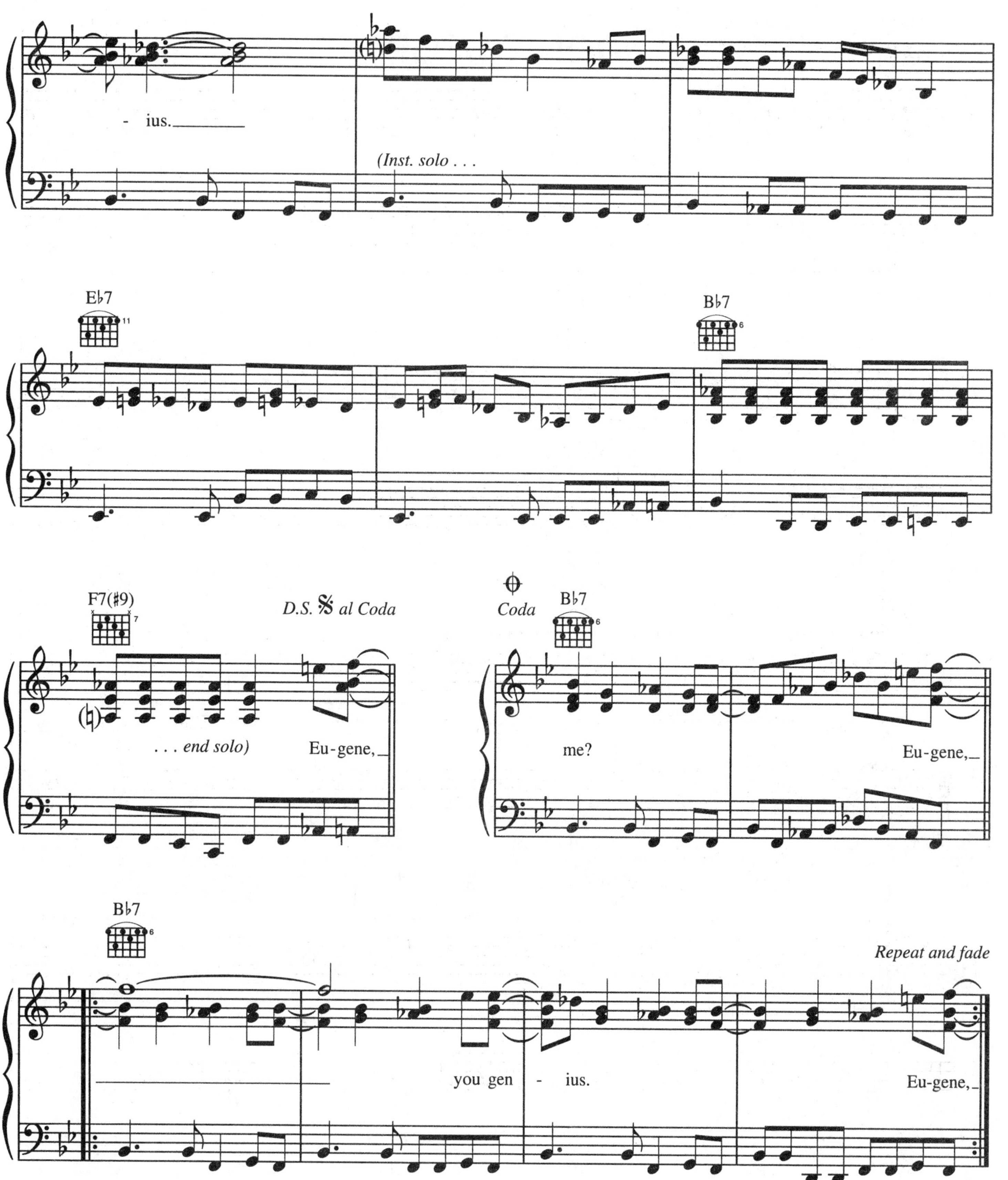

Verse 2:
It's more than the way you comb your hair,
That's making all the pretty girls stop and stare.
Tell me Eugene, I just gotta know,
Can I go down and buy it at the grocery store?
(To Chorus:)

DON'T STOP

Words and Music by
TOM SHAPIRO and CHICK RAINS

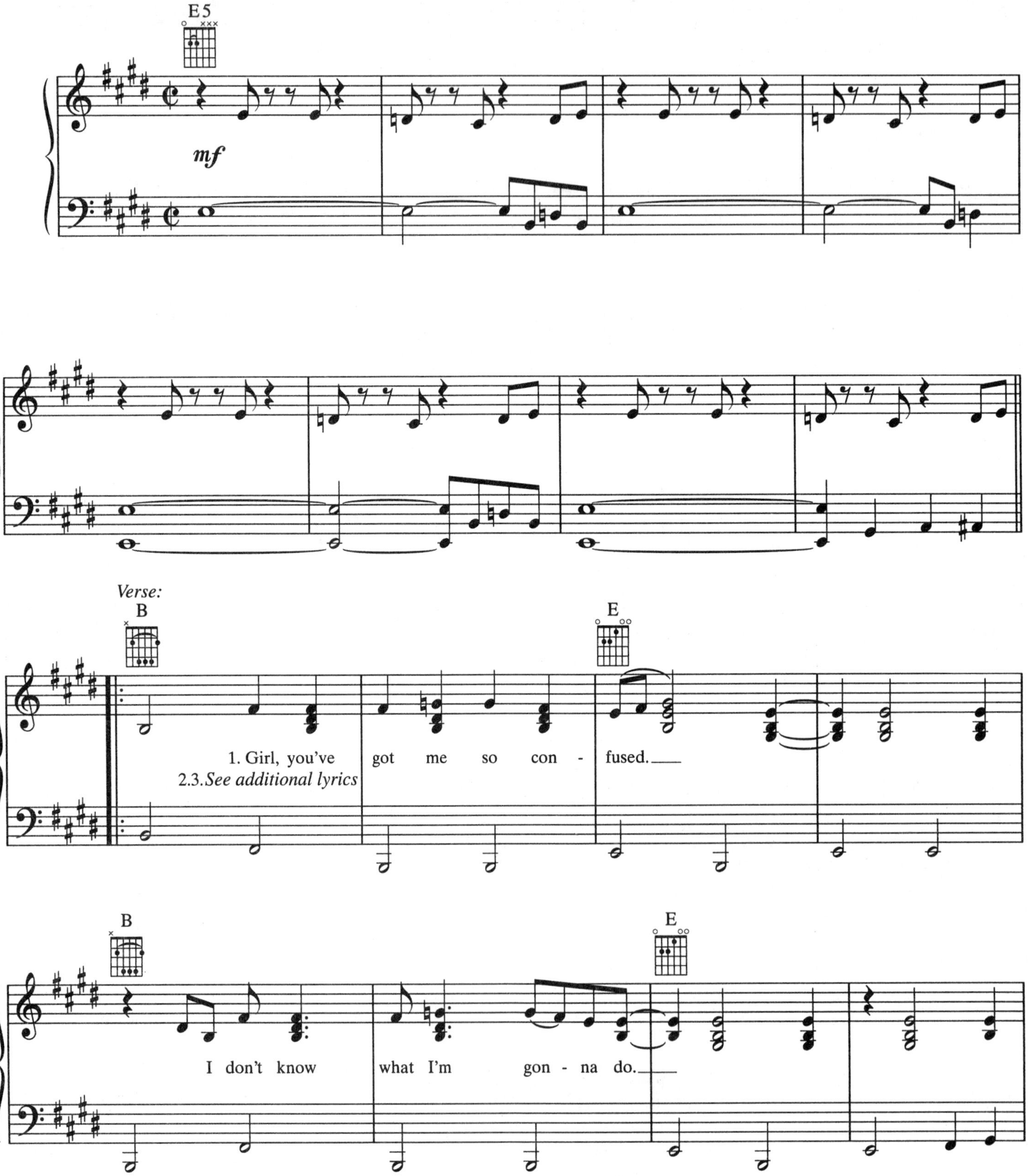

Verse:

B — E

1. Girl, you've got me so con - fused.___
2.3. *See additional lyrics*

B — E

I don't know what I'm gon - na do.___

A
C
D
Part of me says, "Take it slow." And part of me says, "Let it go!" Now,
Chorus:
E
don't stop.
Don't stop. Don't
1.
B7
E5
stop do-in' what you're do-in' to me!
2.
B7
stop do-in' what you're do-in' to me!

Verse 2:
I think we're movin' way too fast.
We need to take it slow and make it last.
But I can't keep holdin' back
If you keep doin' things like that.
(To Chorus:)

Verse 3:
You start a spark of love, no doubt,
But I've watched the flames of love go out.
Burnin' love takes a toll
And I don't wanna lose control.
(To Chorus:)

GIVE ME ONE MORE SHOT

Words and Music by
RANDY OWEN, TEDDY GENTRY
and RONNIE ROGERS

Give Me One More Shot - 5 - 1

Am7
Bm7
Dsus
E♭sus
this old car I drive, well, you'd pro - bab - ly won - der and e -
D
E♭
C
D♭
D
E♭
G
A♭
- ven pon - der why I e - ven want to stay a - live. Well, give me one more shot,
Chorus:
G
A♭
C(9)
D♭(9)
I'll give it all I got. Let me
Dsus
E♭sus
D
E♭
G
A♭
o - pen my eyes to a new sun - rise, I pray.

Dsus / E♭sus — G / A♭ — C(9) / D♭(9)

Give me one more chance, I'll learn to dance the dance.

Am7 / B♭m7 — Dsus / E♭sus — D / E♭ — *To Coda* 𝄌 — 1. G / A♭

I'm sat-is - fied just be-ing a-live, give me one more day.

2. G / A♭

When I

Bridge:

Dm7 / E♭m7 — Cmaj7 / D♭maj7

look a - round there's lots of folks worse off than me.

A7sus
B♭7sus
A7
B♭7
So I just thank the good Lord,
Fmaj7
G♭maj7
Dsus
E♭sus
D.S. 𝄋 al Coda
and ask him please,
give me one more shot,
Coda
G
A♭
Am7
B♭m7
Dsus
E♭sus
D
E♭
I'm sat-is-fied just be-ing a-live,
give me one more day.
G
A♭
Give me one more shot,

Verse 2:
I could complain about taxes, or the weather that we're having.
Go on and on about things that are wrong from New York to L. A.
But it's just not my nature to sit around feeling sad,
We're only here for a little while, so why not smile.
Living ain't all that bad.
(To Chorus:)

FALL IN LOVE

Words and Music by KENNY CHESNEY
BUDDY BROCK and KIM WILLIAMS

D
Mar-ried" writ-ten on a blue Chev-ro-let. Don't
Chorus:
G
Em7
that make you wan-na fall in love? Don't that look like a
C
pic-ture of us? A match made in heav-en if there ev-er was, don't
D
G
that make you wan-na fall? That just makes me wan-na

Em7

give you my heart, ev - 'ry for - ev - er needs a place to start. Got -

C D

- ta be a sign from up a - bove. Don't that make you wan - na

G Em7

fall in love?

Verse 2:
Old folks sitting in a front porch swing
Still holding hands like they were sixteen.
Fifty good years, they're a lover's dream.
Darling, that could be you and me.
(To Chorus:)

FORGIVENESS

Words and Music by
BOB DiPIERO and VICTORIA SHAW

Am
F
G
oth - er tear - drop falls and spills o - ver till it hits the bot - tom line.
right there in our hands is a mes - sage in a bot - tle we should send.
C
G
Chorus:
C
Am
Em
cresc.
mf
For - give - ness, such a sim - ple word to say. But I've been
F
Dm7
G
C
wit - ness to how eas - y pride gets in the way. We're all in this, oh, and
Am
Em
F
Am
G
ev - 'ry day I pray for you, for me, for -

1.
2.
F/C
C
Csus2 sus4
C
Csus2 sus4
C
give - ness.
dim.
2. We
mp
Bridge:
B♭
F
B♭
F
That clock up - on the wall,
it's tick - ing for us all.
B♭
G
A
On - ly our hearts can call a
truce.
Oh, for -
Chorus:
D
Bm
F♯m
G
give - ness, such a
sim - ple word to say.
But I've been
wit - ness to how eas - y

Em7
A
D
Bm
F♯m
pride gets in the way. We're all in this, oh, and ev - 'ry day I pray for you,
G
Bm
A
D
for me, for - give - ness. For you,
G
Bm
A
N.C.
for me, for - give - ness.
mp
G/D
D
Dsus2 sus4
D
G/D
D
A7sus
D(9)
rit. e dim.
p

GO REST HIGH ON THAT MOUNTAIN

Words and Music by
VINCE GILL

G D A7sus4 A7
to face the dev - il. You're no stran - ger to the
D D G D D/F♯
rain. Go rest high on that moun - tain. Son, your
G D G
work on earth is done. Go to heav - en a - shout -
D G D A 1. D
in', love for the Fa - ther and the Son. Oh, how we
3

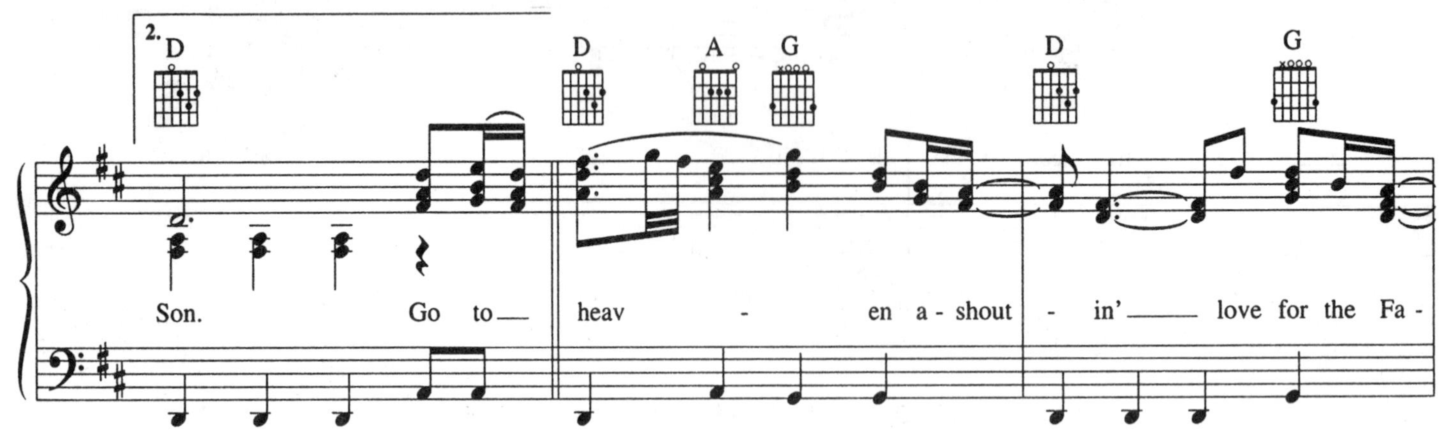

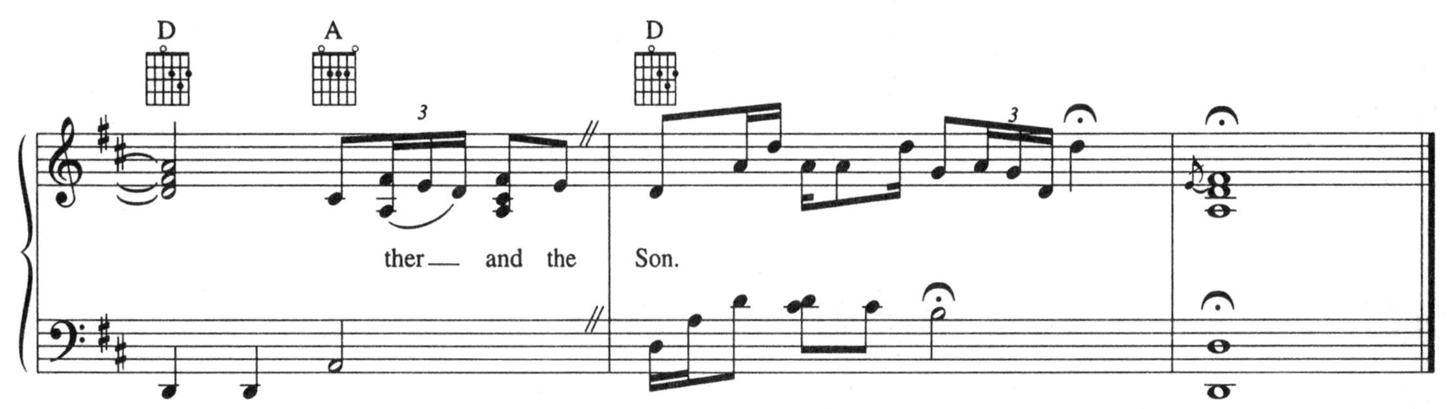

Additional lyrics

2. Oh, how we cried the day you left us,
We gathered 'round your grave to grieve.
I wish I could see the angels' faces
When they hear your sweet voice sing.
(To Chorus)

HERE I AM

Words and Music by
TONY ARATA

Moderately ♩ = 88
G
capo
1st fret
A♭
D
E♭
mf
G
A♭
D
E♭
Verses 1 & 2:
D
E♭
1. Don't do it, dar - lin,' don't you dare look in there.
2. See additional lyrics
G
A♭
You said you did - n't want to see me, but you've been

D
A
E♭
B♭
look - in' for me ev - ery - where.
And you
know that you're gon - na find
G
D
G
A
A♭
E♭
A♭
B♭
me if you
keep on drink-in' fast.
'Cause,
hon-ey, I'm right here wait-
Bm
G
D
Cm
A♭
E♭
- in' on you at the
bot-tom of your
glass.
And
Chorus:
G
A♭
here I am,
here I am,

D
G
D
E♭
A♭
E♭
in the bour - bon and the wat - er that
A
G
To Coda
A
B♭
A♭
B♭
burn you just like a brand,
here I am.
1.
2.
D
D
E♭
E♭
And hon - ey,
Bridge:
Em7
D/F♯
G
A
Fm7
E♭/G
A♭
B♭
I got o - ver you pass - in' me o - ver a long

Bm7
D/F♯
G
Cm7
E♭/G
A♭
time a - go. And my pride
Em7
D/F♯
G
A
F♯7/A♯
Fm7
E♭/G
A♭
B♭
G7/B
was strong - er when I was young - er now I'd
Bm
Bm/A
G
G(9)
D.S. 𝄋 al Coda
Cm
Cm/B♭
A♭
A♭(9)
rath - er have you to know, that
Coda
D
G
E♭
A♭
Mm, mm.

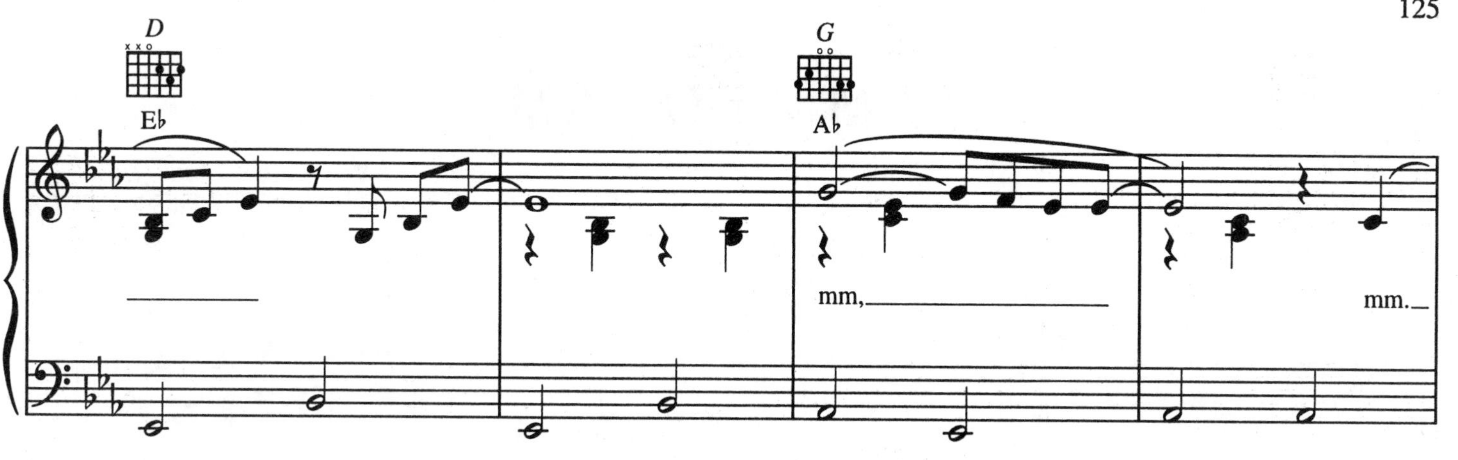

Verse 2:
It ain't workin' darlin', hard as you may try.
You keep hearin' the words you told me in everyone's goodbyes.
And you know that you're just one step from another one being gone.
I know I've seen 'em all unravel,
I've been watchin' it all along.

Chorus 2:
Here I am, here I am,
In every lie you're hearin'
That burn you just like a brand,
Here I am.
(To Bridge:)

Chorus 3:
Here I am, here I am,
I still carry a flame for you
Burnin' me like a brand,
Here I am.

I AM WHO I AM

Words and Music by
TOM SHAPIRO, CHRIS WATERS
and HOLLY DUNN
Rock ♩ = 120
E A(9) E
mf
A(9) E A(9) E
Verse:
A(9) B7sus E A(9) B
1. What - ev - er you want, I've been will-ing to try. But what -
chang-in' my - self from my hair to my shoes. Now, I'm
E A(9) B C♯m
ev - er I do, you're not sat - is - fied. Why don't you ad - mit that I'm
chang-in' my mind a - bout chang - in' for you. I'll nev - er be per - fect, but

A(9)
E/B
B
not what_ you need,_ so I can_ find some - one_ who'll love me_ for me?_
I'll be_ al - right_ now that_ I've start - ed_ to live my_ own life._
I
Chorus:
E
A(9)
E
A(9)
am who_ I am._ I am who_ I am._ You've
B
A/C♯
B/D♯
tried to_ re - make me_ a - gain and_ a - gain. You can bend but_ not break me,_ I'm
To Coda
1.
A/E
E
A(9)
B7sus
E
tak - in'_ a stand. You get what_ you see, ba - by._ I am who_ I am._
I'm all I_ can be, ba - by._

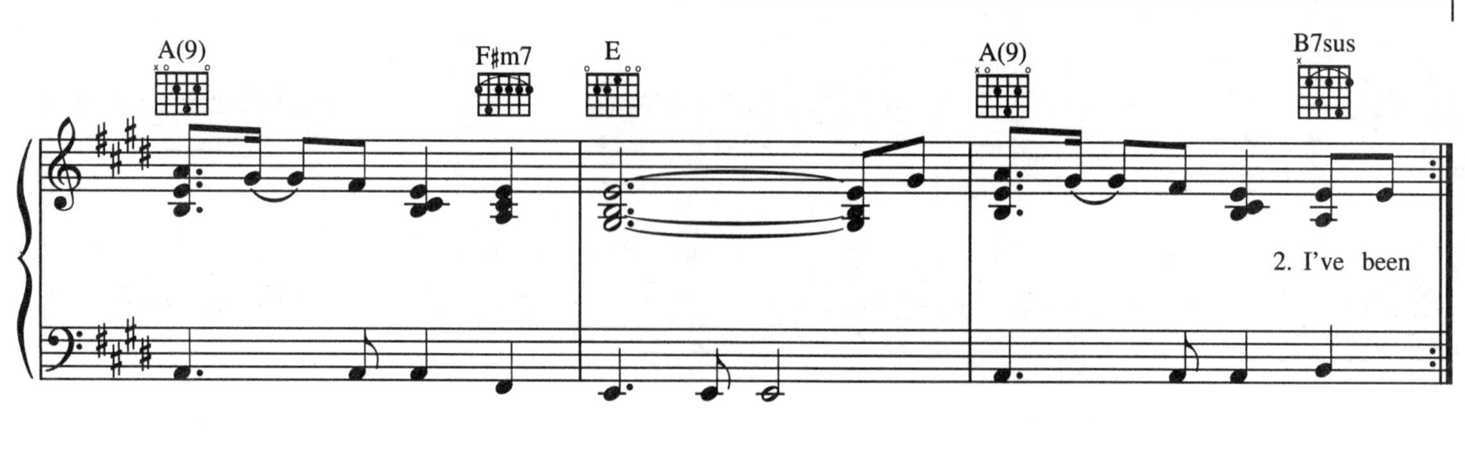
A(9)
F♯m7
E
A(9)
B7sus
2. I've been

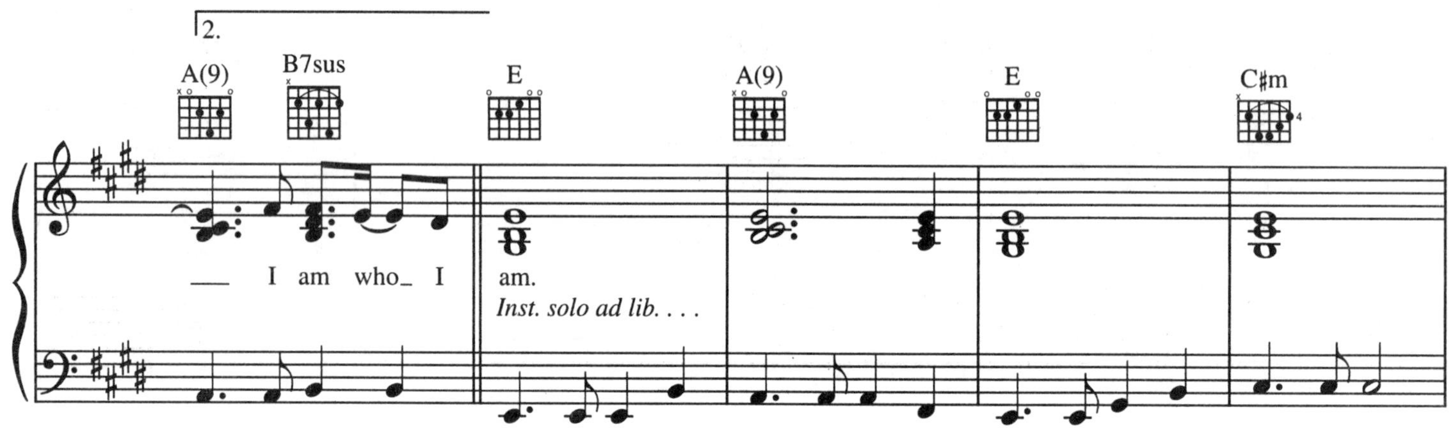
2.
A(9)
B7sus
E
A(9)
E
C♯m
I am who I am.
Inst. solo ad lib. . . .

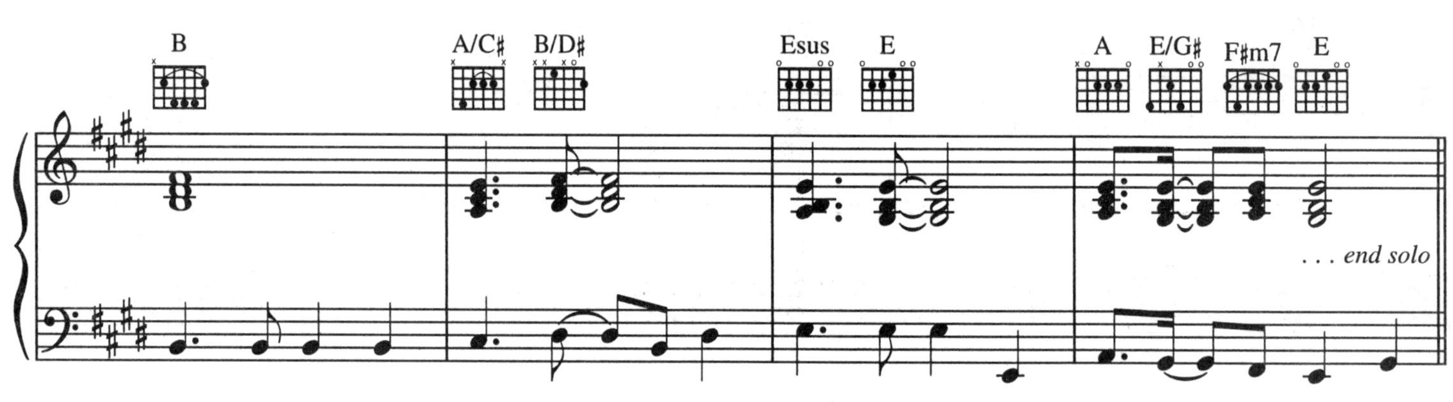
B
A/C♯
B/D♯
Esus
E
A
E/G♯
F♯m7
E
. . . end solo

Bridge:
F♯m7
D(9)
E
A(9)
No regrets, no apologies. I

F♯m7
E
D(9)
B
D.S. 𝄋 al Coda
can't be right for you if it's not right for me. I
𝄌 Coda
A(9)
B7sus
E
C♯m
A/C♯
B/D♯
I am who I am. I'm
E
A(9)
B7sus
E
all I can be, ba - by. I am who I am.
A(9)
F♯m7
E
A(9)
F♯m7
E
I am who I am.

I CAN LOVE YOU LIKE THAT

Words and Music by
STEVE DIAMOND, MARIBETH DERRY
and JENNIFER KIMBALL

G7sus
Em7
F
Ju - li - et.
it comes to you. You
All this time that you've been wait - ing,
dream of love that's ev - er - last - ing,
well
Em7
F
G7sus
you don't have to wait no more.
ba - by, o - pen up your eyes.
cresc.
mf
I can love you like that.
Chorus:
C
Em
F
I would make you my world, move heav - en and earth if you were my girl.
G7sus
C
Em7
I will give you my heart, be all that you need, show you you're ev -

F
B♭
- 'ry - thing that's pre-cious to me.
If you give me a chance,
G7sus
1.
C
F
G7sus
I can love you like that.
2. I
2.
C
Bridge:
Gm7
You want
ten-der - ness, I've got ten -
Dm7
C
- der - ness and I see through to the heart of you. If you

Gm7 Dm7 F

want a man___ who un - der - stands,___ you don't have to look ver - y far.___

Gsus G

___ I can love you. I,___ I can love you like that.___

Chorus:

C Em F

___ I would make you my world,___ move heav - en and earth___ if you were my girl.___

G7sus C Em7

___ I will give you my heart,___ be all that you need,___ show you you're ev -

Repeat ad lib. and fade

F G7sus

- 'ry - thing that's pre - cious to me.___ I can love you like that.___

I'LL NEVER FORGIVE MY HEART

Words and Music by DEAN DILLON,
RONNIE DUNN and JANINE DUNN

Moderately slow country swing ♩ = 84

D
B
E
I fell for it.
Now she's say - in' she's
found some-one new;
G
A
how could I have
been such a
fool?
Oh,
...end solo)
Chorus:
G
D
close the door turn out the
lights,
draw the
cur-tain.
I'll get
E
G
A
D A
o - ver her in
time,
gon-na take some
hurt-in'.
Oh, I

G
D
B
tell my-self I told you so as I fall a-part. I can't blame love.
E
G
A
1.
D
But I'll nev-er for-give my heart.
2.
D
C
B
E
G
A
heart. Oh, I can't blame love. But I'll nev-er for-give my
molto rit.
D
G
A7
D
heart.
a tempo
poco rit.

I SEE IT NOW

Words and Music by PAUL NELSON,
LARRY BOONE and WOODY LEE

F
C
B♭
You sure look good since your new love came in your life.
Gm7
C7sus
You know I did-n't see that fire in you he's found.
B♭
Csus
C
Oh, but I can see it now.
cresc.
Oh,
Chorus:
F
Dm7
B♭
C
I nev-er saw that look in your eyes. And
mf
F
Dm7
B♭
A
I nev-er had you hold me that tight. And

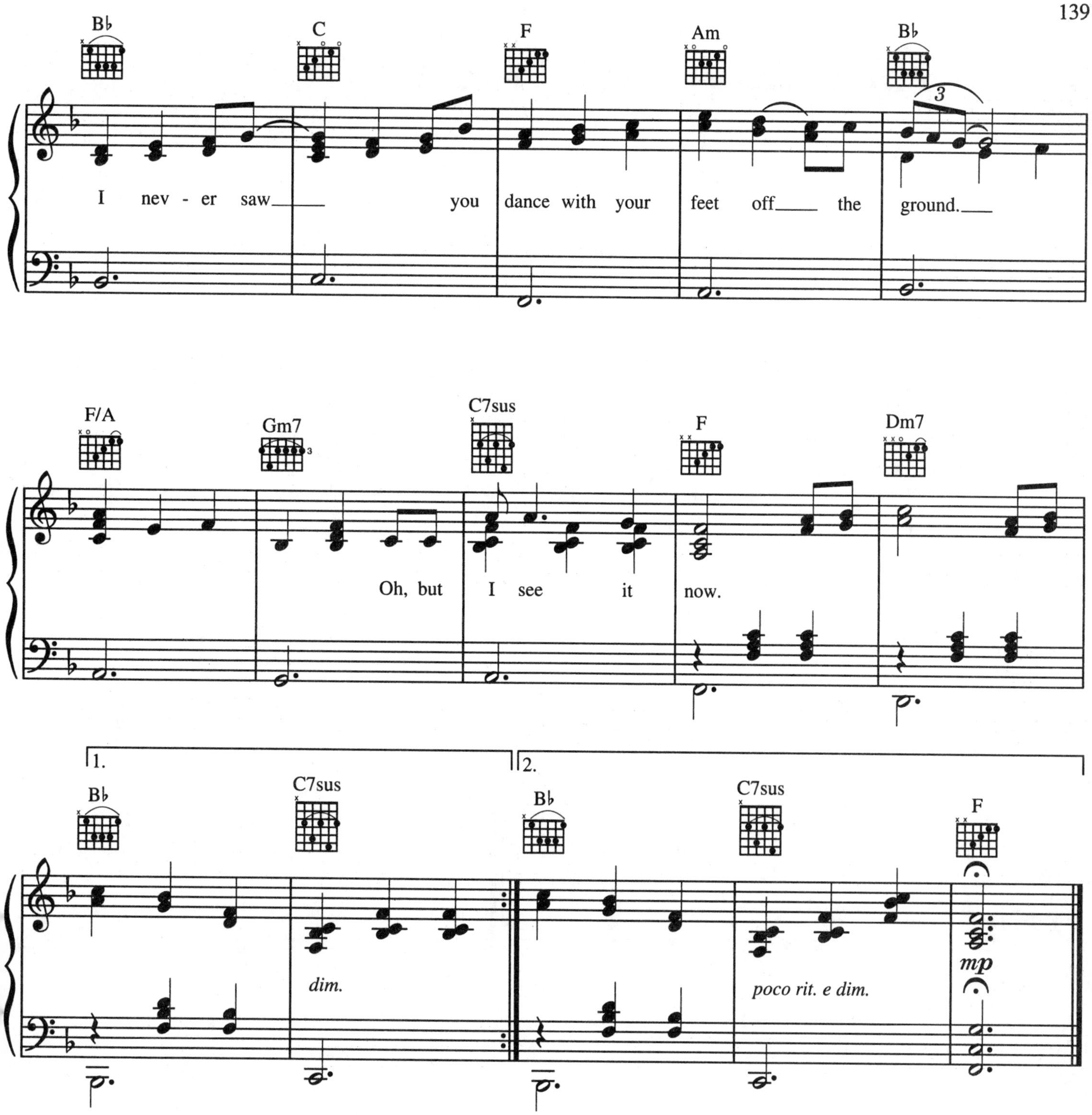

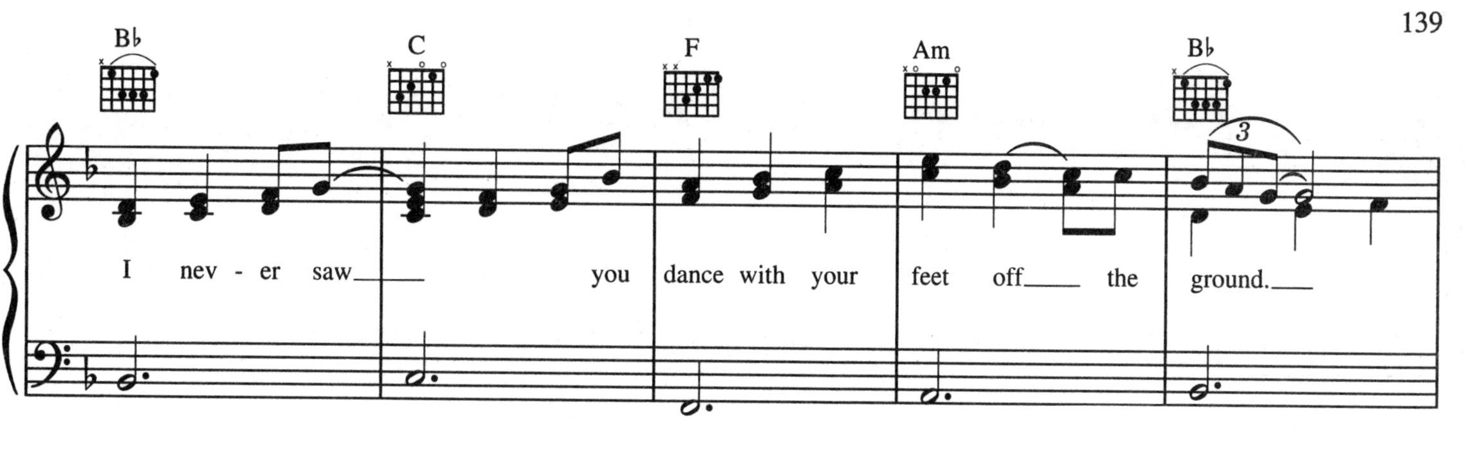

B♭
C
F
Am
B♭
I nev - er saw you dance with your feet off the ground.
3
F/A
Gm7
C7sus
F
Dm7
Oh, but I see it now.
1.
2.
B♭
C7sus
B♭
C7sus
F
dim.
poco rit. e dim.
mp

Verse 2:
Holding him, you never looked more beautiful.
Letting go has been so hard on me.
And sitting here it's clear to see what he means to you.
The way you look at him it ain't no mystery;
He's all I couldn't be.
(To Chorus:)

I'M IN LOVE WITH A CAPITAL "U"

Words and Music by
CRAIG WISEMAN and
PAUL NELSON

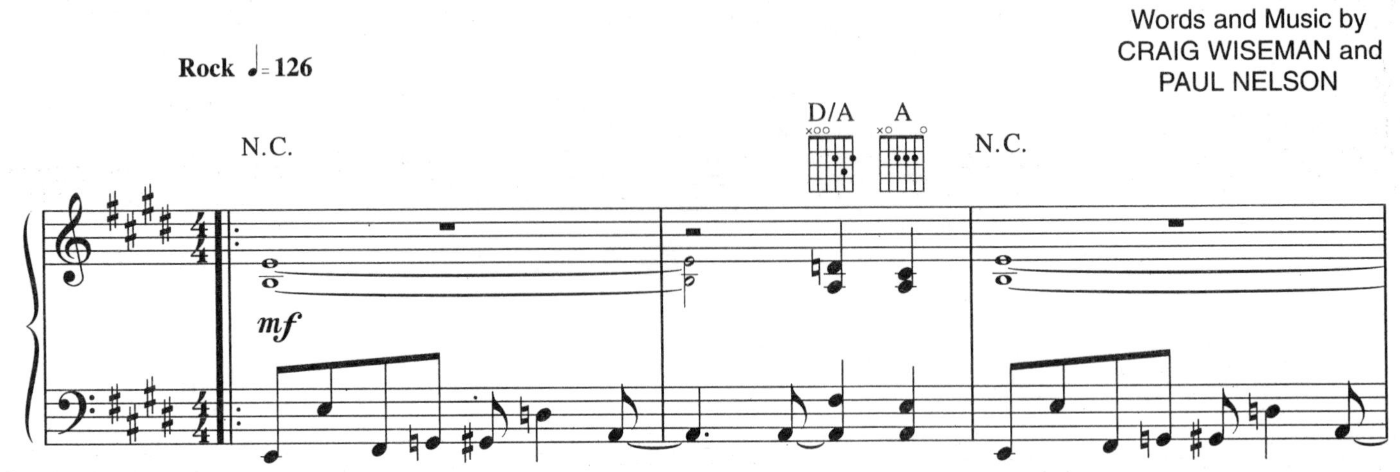

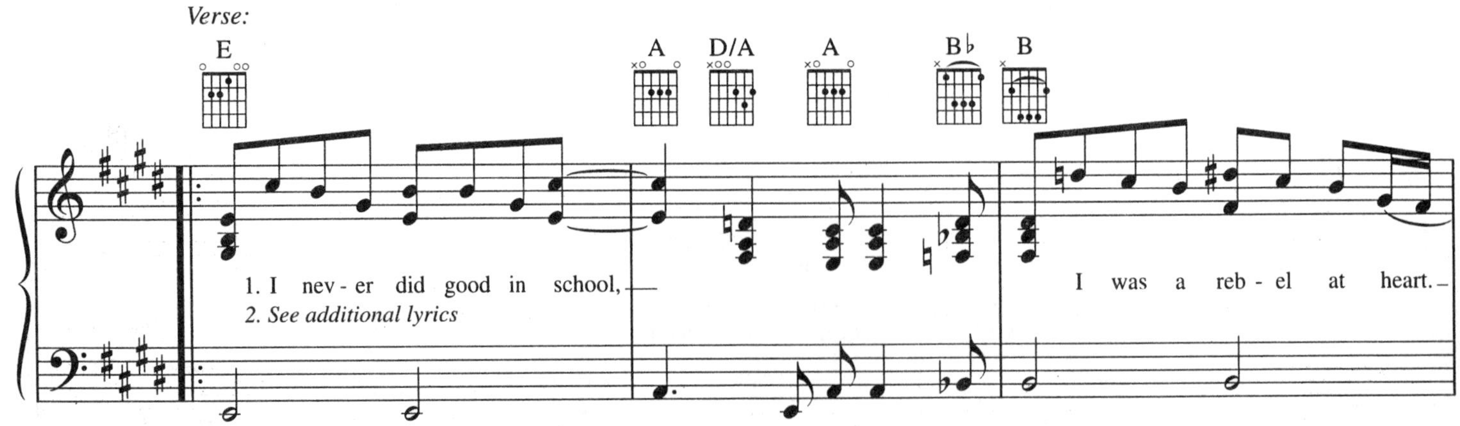

E
A
While ev - 'ry - bod - y was making the grade, I was
B
N.C.
E
get - ting up to no good down to an art. But then you came a - long,
A
D/A
A
B♭
B
E
and ba - by, there I went. Dar -
A
B
E
ling, with a kiss, all of that Eng - lish fi - n'ly start - ed mak - ing sense.

Chorus:
E7
A
D/A
A
You got me feel-ing so G - U - D. It's more
E7
A
D/A
A
E
E7/G♯
bet-ter than I thought it would be. Girl, you taught me things that I
A
B♭dim7
B
1.
E
nev-er learned in school. I'm in love with a cap-i-tal "U".
E
A
D/A
A
E
A
D/A
A

Verse 2:
I always hated math,
It never did add up.
Every time the teacher said "pi r square",
All that I could think about was going to lunch.
Science and history,
They only wore me out.
But darlin', since we've met, I finally found a subject
I know a little something about.
(To Chorus:)

I'M NOT STRONG ENOUGH TO SAY NO

Words and Music by
ROBERT JOHN "MUTT" LANGE

D♭

fens - es go___ down, | feel-ings get strong - er, | looks get long - er. The

G♭(9) | A♭

clos - er you come,_ the | weak-er I get.__ If it | ain't hap-pened now,_ just ain't_

N.C.

Chorus:

G♭(9)

___ hap-pened yet.___ So | please, please,_ please | go,___ I'm not

A♭ | D♭ | G♭(9)

strong_ e - nough___ to say | no.__________ | Please, please,_ don't | stay, I'm not

A♭ | D♭ | B♭m

man_ e - nough_ to walk a - | way.__________ | Please, please_ pass | by,___ I can't re -

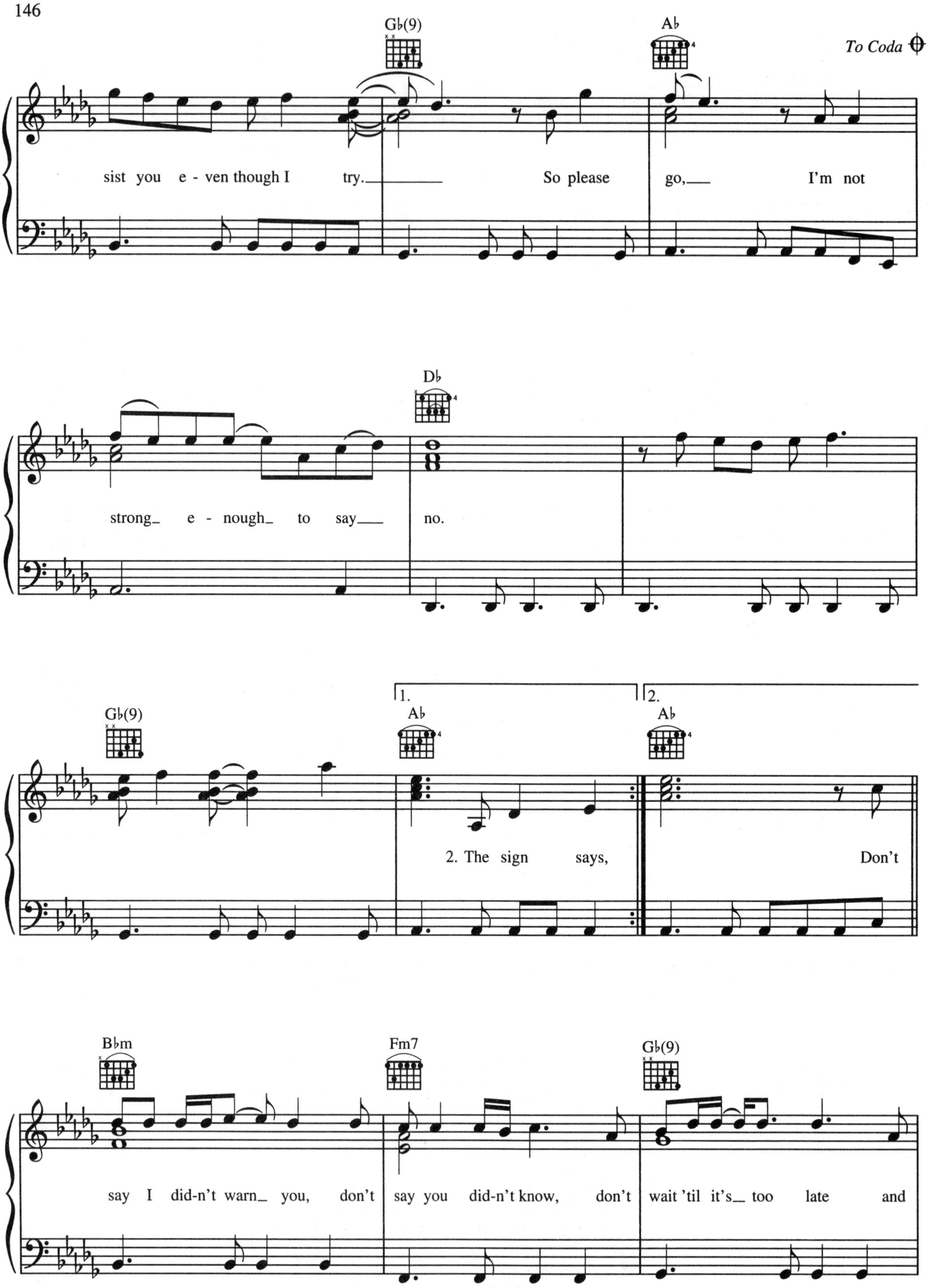

G♭(9) A♭ *To Coda* 𝄌

sist you e - ven though I try.___ So please go,___ I'm not

D♭

strong_ e - nough_ to say___ no.

G♭(9)
1.
A♭
2.
A♭
2. The sign says,
Don't

B♭m
Fm7
G♭(9)
say I did-n't warn_ you, don't say you did-n't know, don't wait 'til it's_ too late and

Verse 2:
The sign says, "Slow Down - Slippery Ice,"
You've got dangerous curves, don't think twice.
It says, "Not For Sale", you're spoken for,
Just take your heart and walk out the door.
(To Chorus:)

IF I AIN'T GOT YOU

Words and Music by
CRAIG WISEMAN and TREY BRUCE

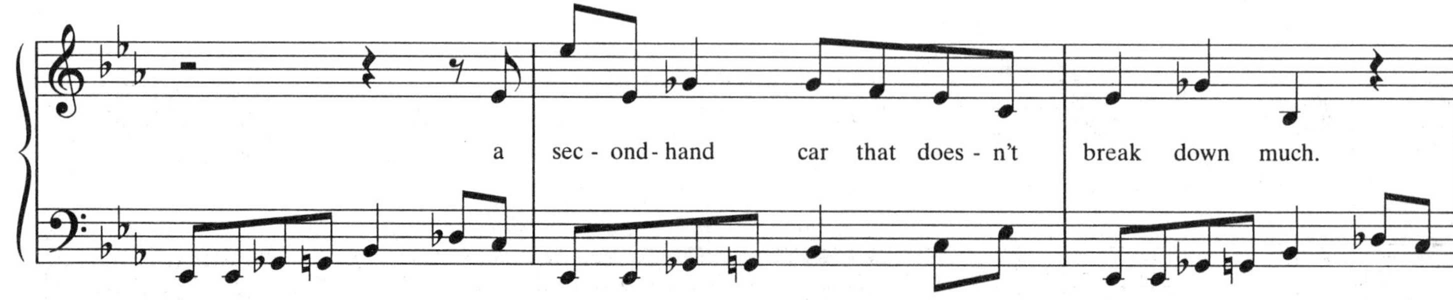

A♭7
I've got a two - tone hound dog
E♭7
wag-ging his tail, — Ed — Mc-Mahon prom - is - ing a mil - lion in the mail. Ought
A♭7
— to be e-nough to see a
1. D♭ A♭7 E♭7 N.C.
poor boy through, — but it don't — mean — noth-ing if I
G♭5 E♭7
ain't got — you.
2. I've got ev -

2.
D♭
A♭7
E♭7
N.C.
G♭5
lov - er's moon, — but it don't — mean — noth - ing if I ain't got —
E♭7
To Next Strain
3.
D♭
you.
If I ain't got you, —
whole life through, —
A♭7
E♭7
N.C.
but it don't — mean — noth - ing if I
G♭5
E♭7
Chorus:
A♭7
ain't got — you.
If I ain't got you, —

E♭7
ba - by, it's all in vain. If I ain't got you,
F 7
B♭7
it's like a hon - ey - moon with - out
1.
D.S. 𝄋
cham - pagne, a shin - y set of rails with - out a train. 3. Well, I've got
2.
E♭7
a train.
I've got a
B♭7
D♭
A♭7
dou - ble wide heart with room for two,

Verse 2:
I've got every eight track that Elvis ever made,
Crank it up loud and dance the night away.
I've got Chardonnay chillin' in the Frigidare,
A dozen ways of telling you how I care.
Just out the window there's a lover's moon,
But it don't mean a thing if I ain't got you.
(To Chorus:)

Verse 3:
Well, I've got a little dream about the rest of my life,
Find the perfect girl and make her my wife.
Start a little family and watch it grow,
Visit on Sundays after we get old.
Make enough love to last a whole life through,
But it don't mean nothing if I ain't got you.
(To Chorus:)

IF I COULD MAKE A LIVING

Words and Music by
ALAN JACKSON, KEITH STEGALL
and ROGER MURRAH

Moderate country two-beat ♩ = 72
F
mf
Chorus:
If
I could make a liv - ing out of
B♭
F
lov - ing you, I'd
be a mil - lion - aire in a
C
F
week or two. I'd be
do - ing what I love and lov - ing what I do if
I could make a liv - ing out of

C7
F
Verse:
B♭
lov - ing you.
1. Ear - ly ev - 'ry morn-ing when the
2. See additional lyrics.

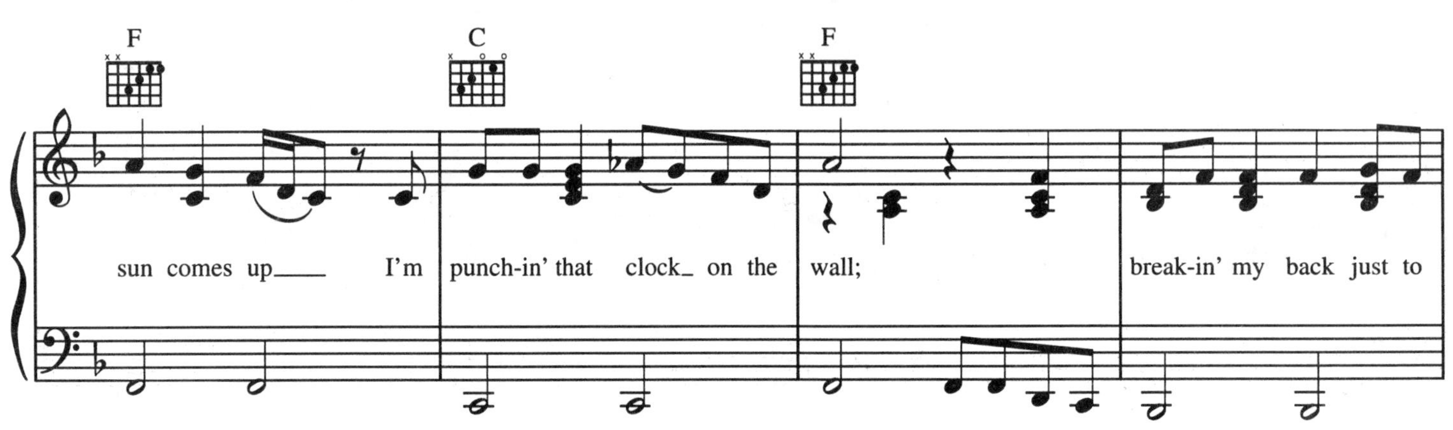
F
C
F
sun comes up I'm punch-in' that clock on the wall; break-in' my back just to

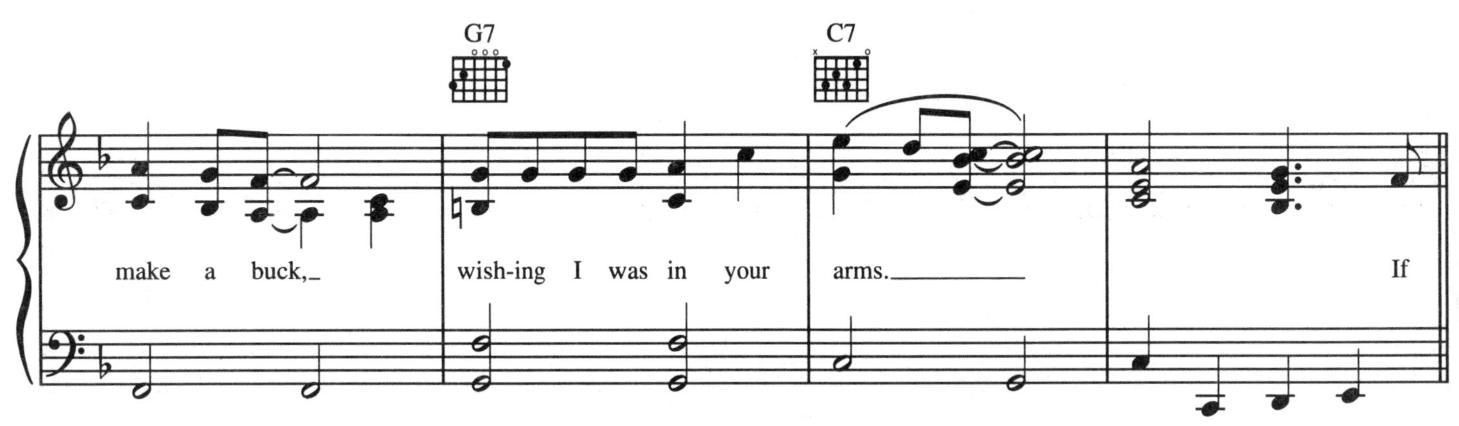
G7
C7
make a buck, wish-ing I was in your arms. If

Chorus:
F
B♭
F
I could make a liv - ing out of lov - ing you, I'd be a mil - lion - aire in a

C
F
B♭
F
week or two. I'd be doing what I love and lov - ing what I do if
C7
F
B♭
F
I could make a liv - ing out of lov - ing you.
1.
C
F
2. I could
2.
C
F
B♭

Chorus:
F
C
D
G
C
G
If
I could make a liv-ing out of
lov - ing you,
I'd

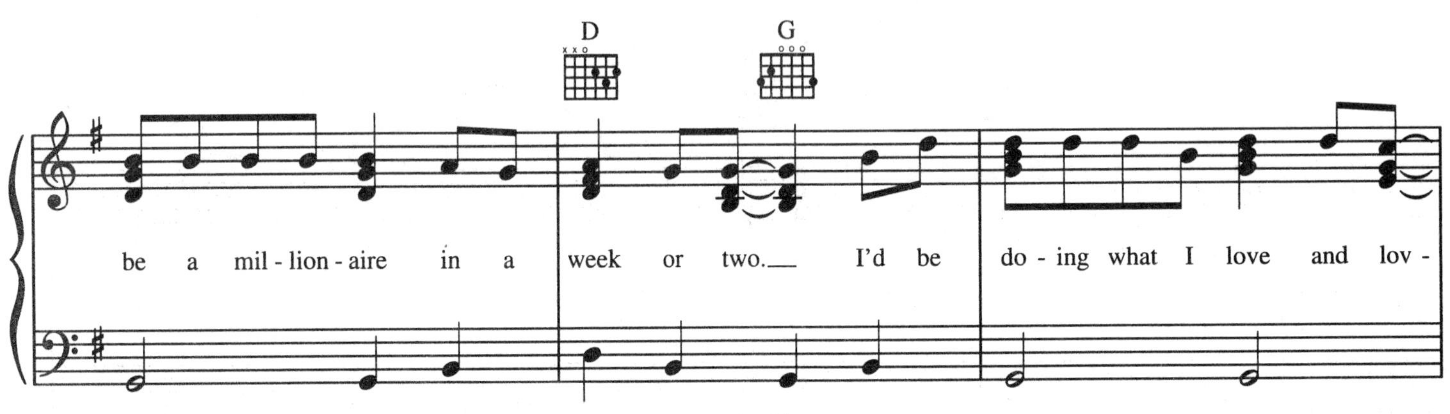
D
G
be a mil-lion-aire in a
week or two.
I'd be
do - ing what I love and lov -

C
G
D7
G
- ing what I do
if
I could make a liv-ing out of
lov - ing
you.
If

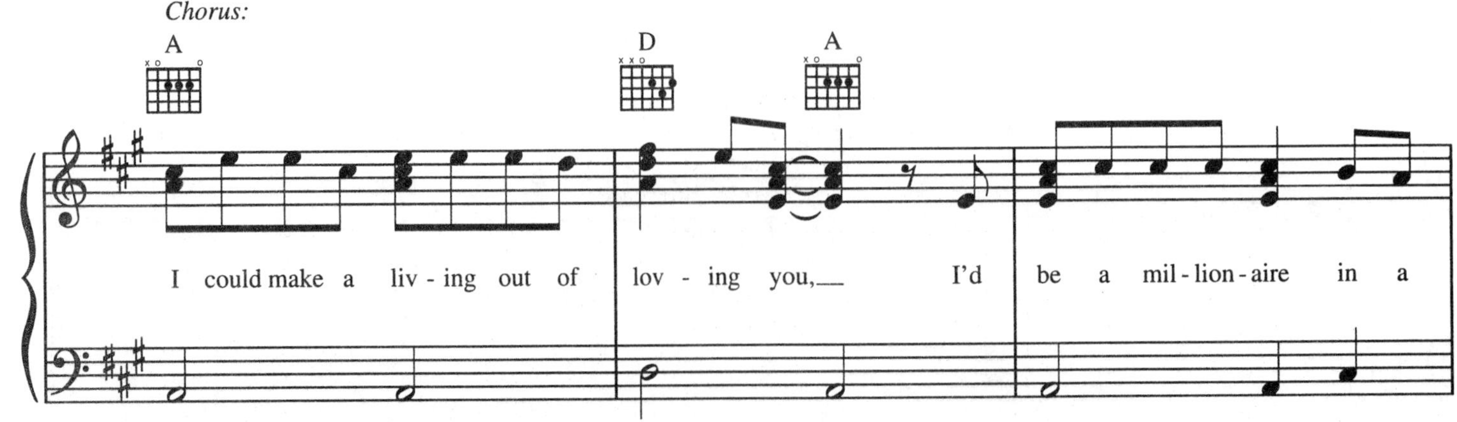
Chorus:
A
D
A
I could make a liv-ing out of
lov - ing you,
I'd
be a mil-lion-aire in a

E
A
D
A
week or two. I'd be do - ing what I love and lov - ing what I do if

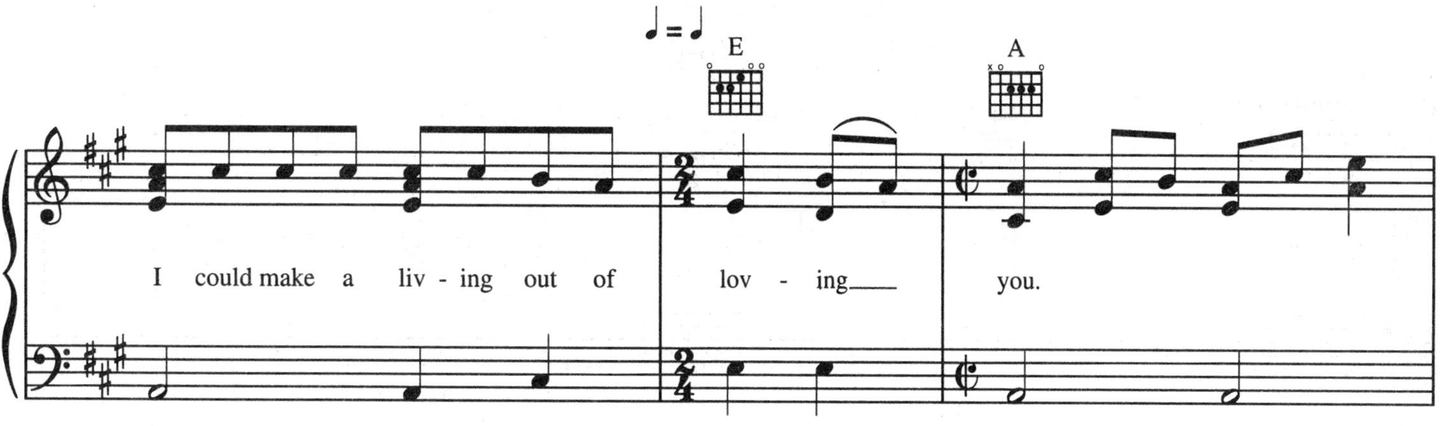
E
A
I could make a liv - ing out of lov - ing you.

D
A
E
A

Verse 2:
I could work all day and feel right at home
Loving that 8 to 5,
And never have to leave you here alone
When I'm working over-time.
(To Chorus:)

I DIDN'T KNOW MY OWN STRENGTH

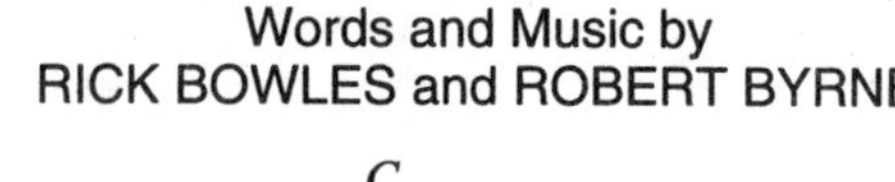

Capo 1st Fret: G Em C

Moderately ♩ = 152

Concert: A♭ Fm D♭

mf

D G Em C D

E♭ A♭ Fm D♭ E♭ *

1. I've been

Verse:

Em D

Fm E♭

liv - in' with a heart___ on the___ mend,___ won - d'rin'

2. *See additional lyrics*

F C

G♭ D♭

how will I ev - er be strong.___ I

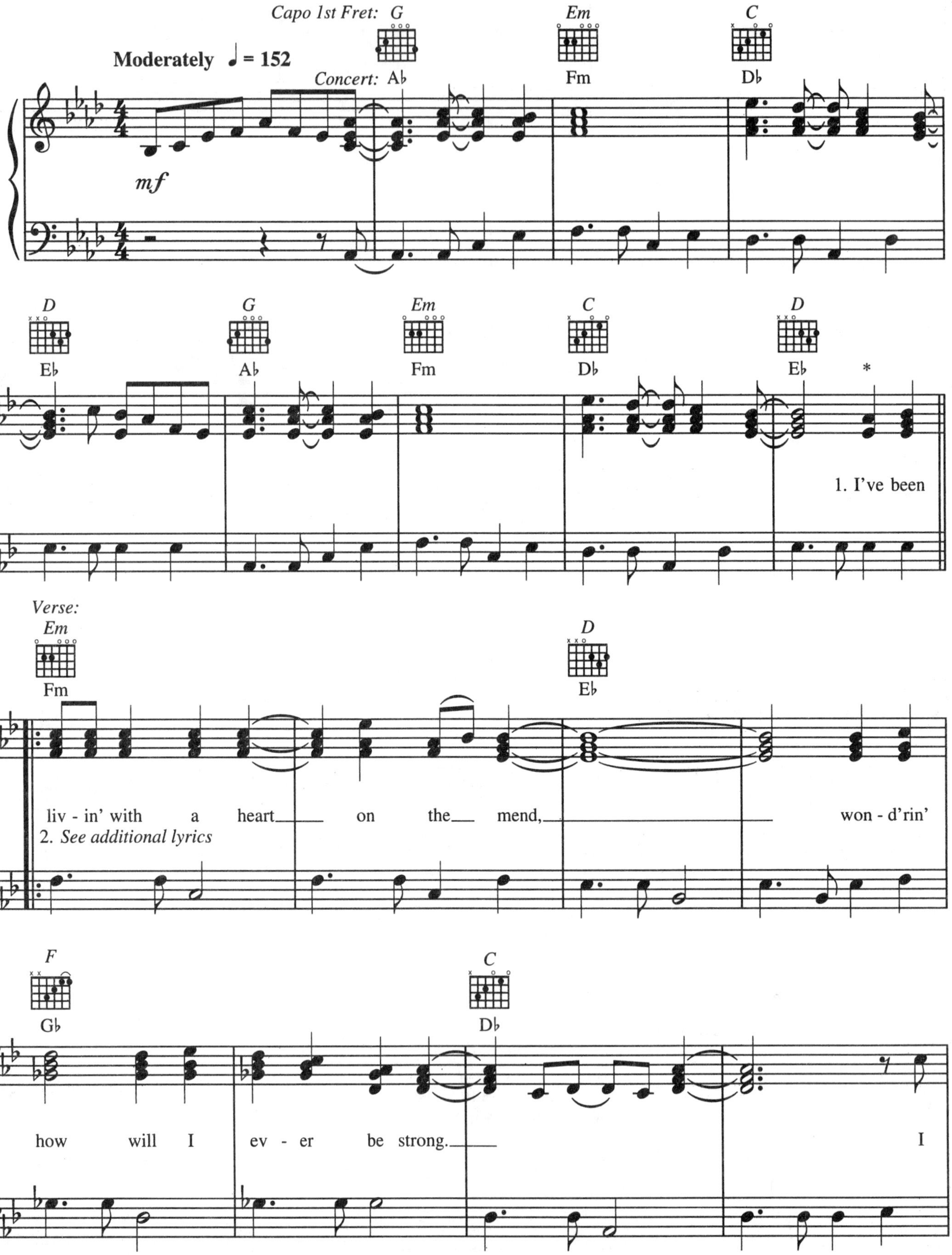

*Vocal sung one octave lower.

Em Fm D E♭

know I'll live to love a - gain,

F G♭ C D♭

I just leaned on you too long. It's

Am7 B♭m7 G/B A♭/C C D♭ D E♭

been an up - hill fight, but I'm gon - na be al - right.
3. *See additional lyrics*

Chorus:

G A♭ Em Fm C D♭ D E♭

I did-n't know my own strength till I had to

Bm
Em
C
D
Cm
Fm
D♭
E♭
pick my-self up and car-ry on with-out your love.
G
Em
C
D
A♭
Fm
D♭
E♭
I'm get-tin' back on my feet. It's
Bm
Em
Am7
G/B
Cm
Fm
B♭m7
A♭/C
been a long, hard fall, but I'll make it af - ter all. No, I
To Coda
C
D
G
Em
D♭
E♭
A♭
Fm
did-n't know my own strength.
(Second time, Guitar solo ad lib....

Verse 2:
I've had oceans of tears to get through
And the weight of the world on my mind.
There've been mountains of memories to move
And I've been beating back the blows to my pride.
But till the times got tough,
I never knew what I was made of.
(To Chorus:)

Verse 3:
Then the times got tough
And I knew what I was made of.
(To Chorus:)

I DON'T BELIEVE IN GOODBYE

Words and Music by BRYAN WHITE,
SCOTT EMERICK and MARK MILLER

Moderately ♩ = 122
F
B♭
mf
F
B♭
Verse:
Dm
F
1. I keep roll - in' it o - ver and o - ver,
2. See additional lyrics
Gm
B♭
C
all the things I want to say.
Dm
C
F
B♭
I'll nev-er quit, give up, or for-get you.

Gm
F/A
E♭
C
Csus
C
My love will stand in the way. And I
Chorus:
F/B♭
F
don't be - lieve in good - bye.
F/B♭
C
Csus
C
And I be-lieve it takes time
Gm
B♭
Gm
to build some - thing strong. It won't take long
B♭
Dm
C
To Coda
for you to be - lieve in me, just look in my

B♭
1.
F
eyes.
I don't be - lieve in good - bye.
B♭
F
B♭
2.
Dm
E♭
I don't be - lieve in good - bye.
F
Dm

Verse 2:
Where love goes we must follow,
And let our hearts lead the way.
We'll be the last of the true believers,
First in love and last to stay.
(To Chorus:)

I GOT IT HONEST

Words and Music by
AARON TIPPIN, BRUCE BURCH
and MARCUS F. JOHNSON

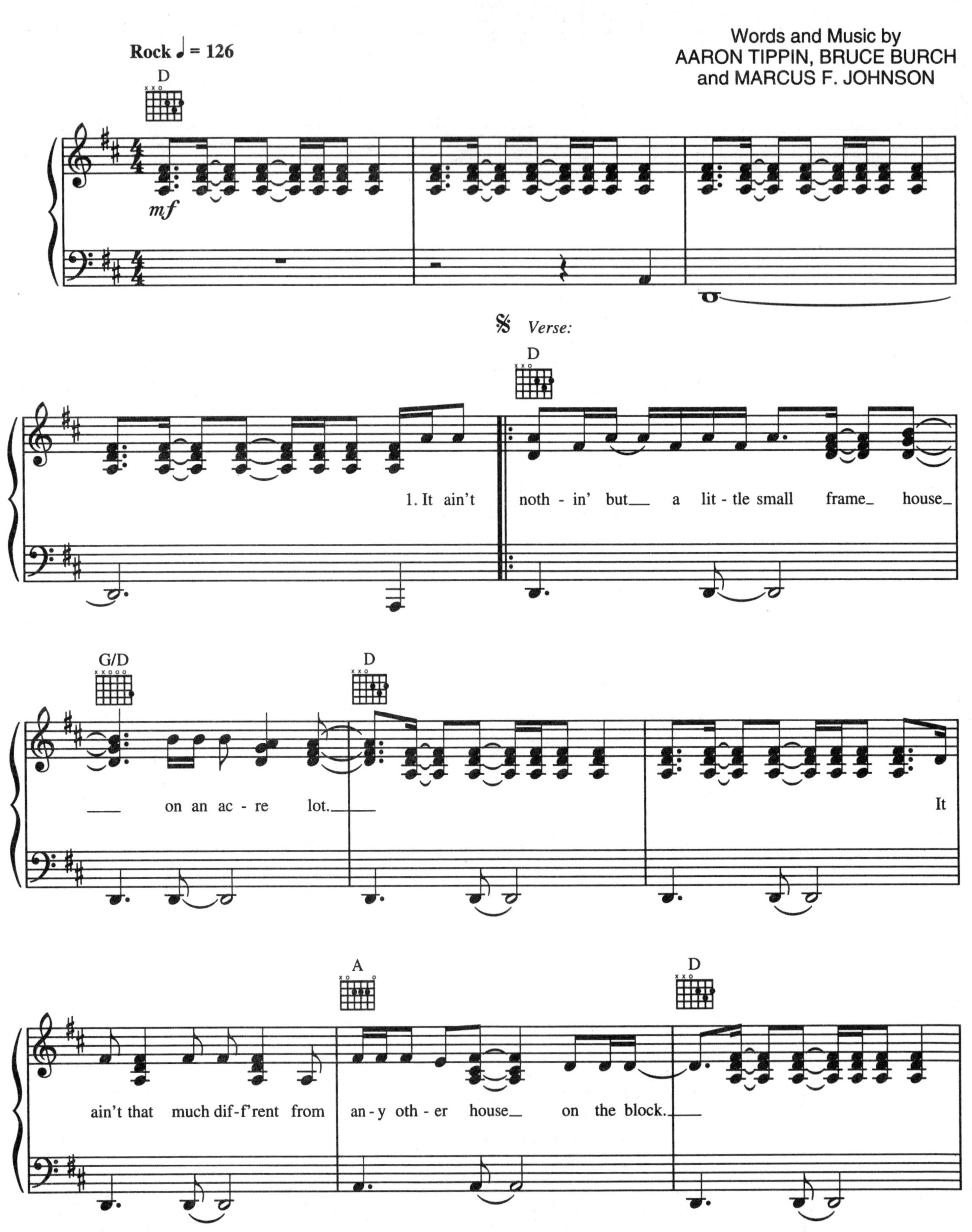

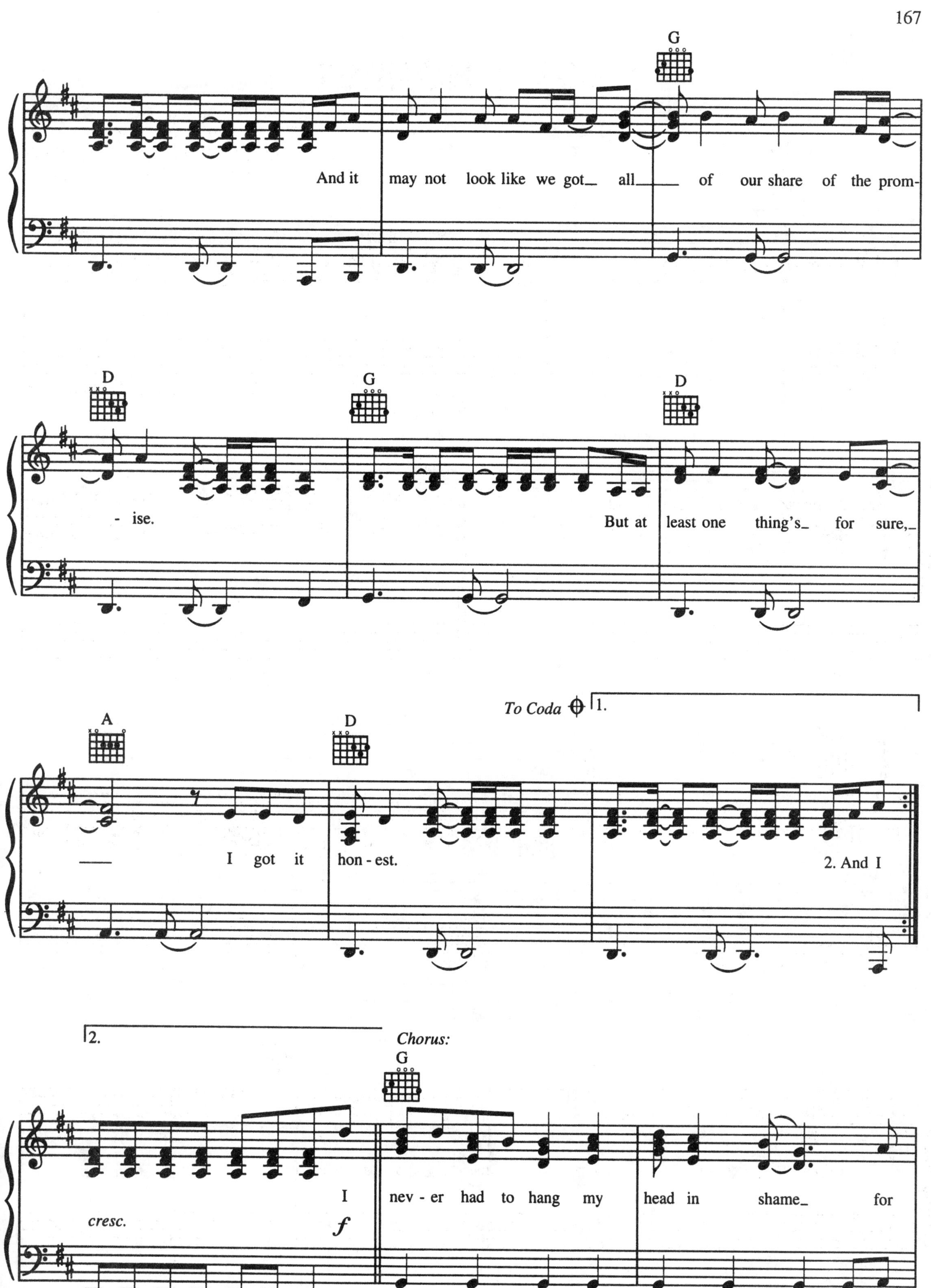
G
And it
may not look like we got all of our share of the prom-
D
G
D
- ise.
But at
least one thing's for sure,
A
D
To Coda
1.
I got it
hon - est.
2. And I
2.
Chorus:
G
I
cresc.
f
nev - er had to hang my
head in shame for

D
G
put - tin' a price - tag on my name.
Nev - er turned my back on what
E
A
I be - lieved or let my heart be ruled by greed.
D
G
'Cause bud-dy, if I did - n't earn it, I don't
D
Dsus
G
D
want it.
That way, I can al - ways say
A
D
D.S. 𝄋 al Coda
I got it hon - est.
dim.
3. Now,

Coda
E
Verse:
4. Now, when I die, I may not leave
A/E
E
my kids a for - tune,
but I
B
E
hope they know that my life stood for the things that were im - por - tant.
A
I'll hand down the same old stur - dy val - ues of my dad - dy and my
E
A
E
ma - ma.
It made me ev - 'ry ounce of what I

B
E
am, I got it hon - est.
I
cresc.
f
Chorus:
A
E
nev - er had to hang my head in shame_ for put - tin' a price - tag on_
A
___ my name._ Nev - er turned my back on what I be - lieved_ or
F♯
B
let my heart_ be ruled_____ by greed.___ 'Cause
E
A
E
broth-er, if I___ did - n't earn___ it, I don't want it.

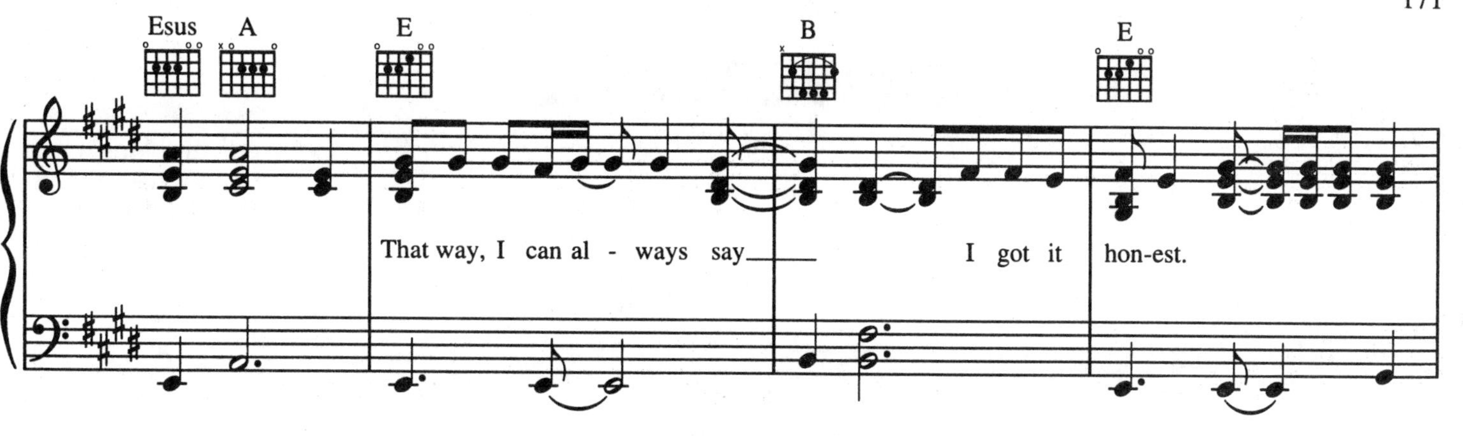

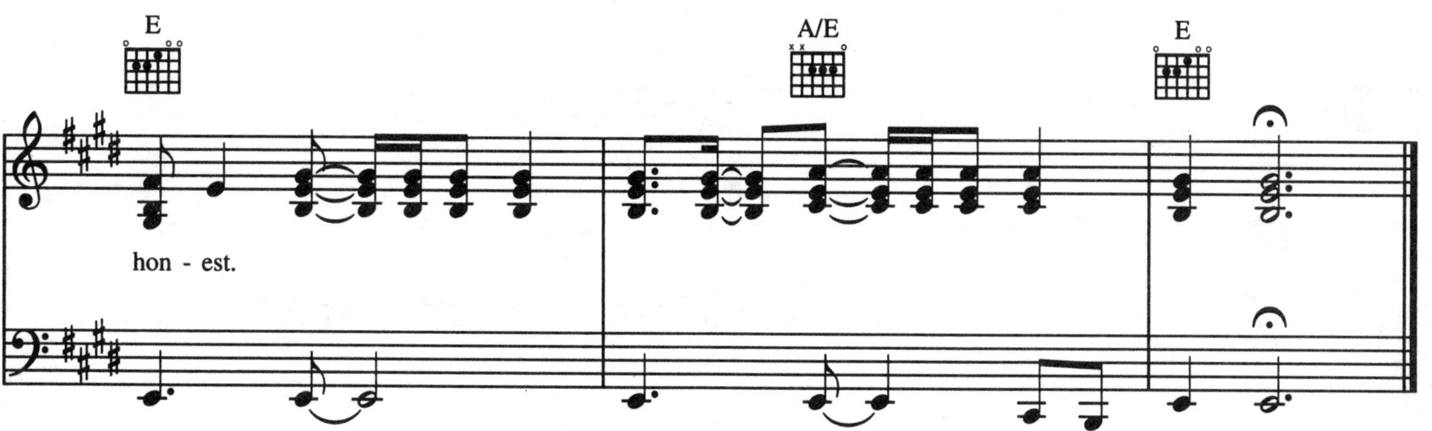

Verse 2:
Now, I roll out of the sack every mornin', head on down to the mill.
I give 'em all I got for eight, 'cause that's the deal.
If you check out my paycheck, well, you may find there ain't that much on it.
But every single penny I'm paid, I got it honest.
(To Chorus:)

Verse 3:
Now, you ain't lookin' at some dude that was born with a silver spoon in his mouth.
And I might seem like some kind of lowlife to that high-falutin' crowd,
But I'm plain spoken, straight talkin', and damn proud of what I have accomplished.
And some folks 'preciate that, some don't, but I got it honest.
(To Chorus:)

IF I WERE YOU

Words and Music by
CHRIS FARREN and
JOHN HOBBS

Dm7 G7sus G7

ba - by, who knows? 2. So, you're ask - ing

Verse:

F G7sus G7 C

me what do we do, cuz time moves so
close, I'll kiss a - way your fears. I won't prom - ise the

F G Am Asus4/2 Am

fast and the chanc - es seem so few. Is it too
moon, but I prom - ise to be here. And what if to -

F G C G/B Asus4/2 Am

much to think that we could have it all? Who knows?
geth - er it gets bet - ter ev - 'ry day? Who knows?

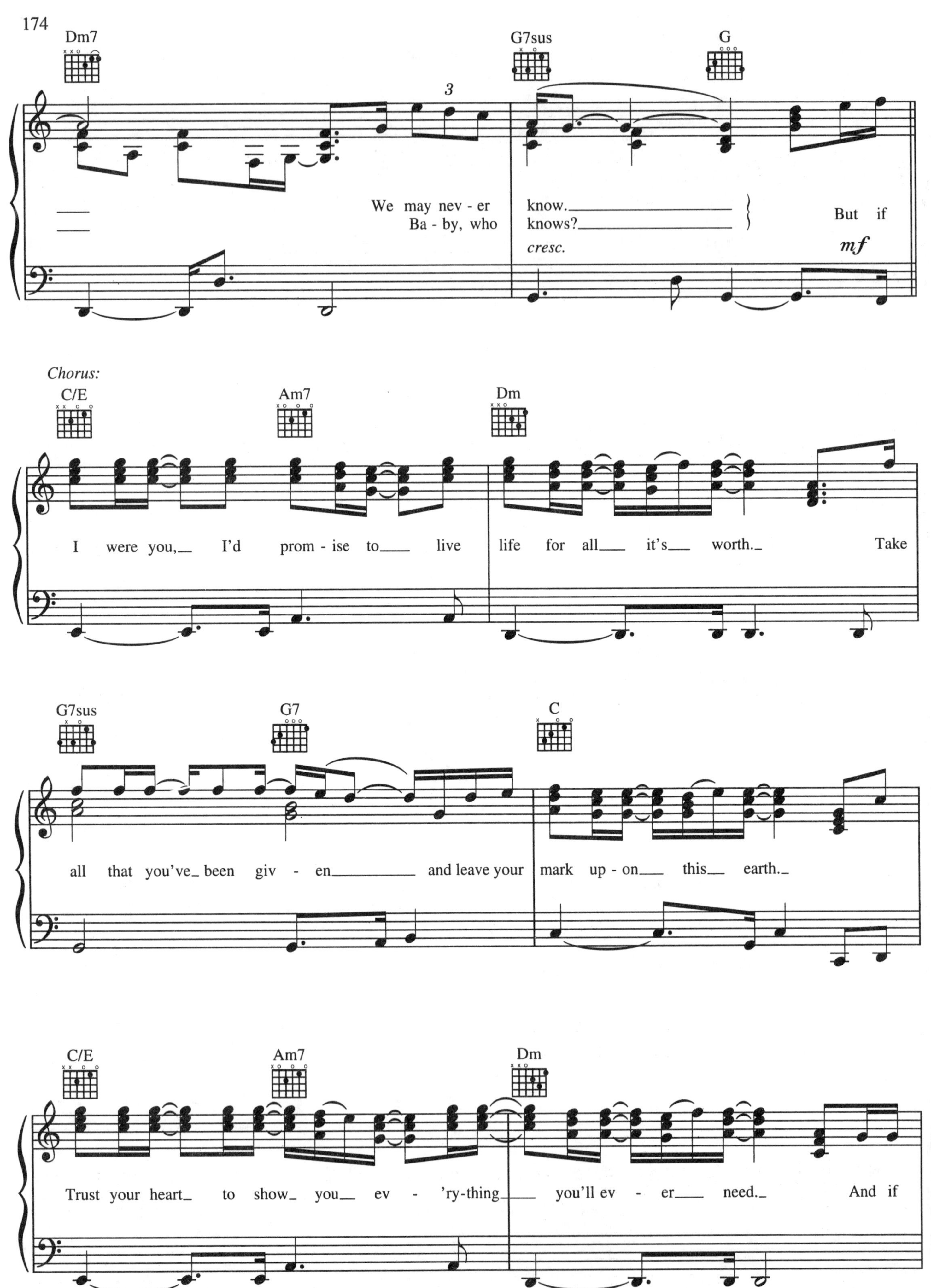
Dm7
G7sus
G
3
We may nev - er
Ba - by, who
know.
knows?
But if
cresc.
mf
Chorus:
C/E
Am7
Dm
I were you, I'd prom - ise to live life for all it's worth. Take
G7sus
G7
C
all that you've been giv - en and leave your mark up - on this earth.
C/E
Am7
Dm
Trust your heart to show you ev - 'ry-thing you'll ev - er need. And if

1.
C/G
G7sus
G7
C(9)
F(9)
I were you, I'd fall in love with me.
dim.
C(9)
F(9)
2.
C/G
G7sus
G
3. So, hold me
mp
I were you, I'd fall in love with me.
F
Gsus
G
F/A
G/B
F
Am/G
G
F/A
G
G/F
But if
Chorus:
C/E
Am7
Dm
I were you, I'd prom - ise to live
life for all it's worth. Take

G7sus
G7
C
all that you've been giv - en and leave your mark up - on this earth.
C/E
Am7
Dm
Trust your heart to show you ev - 'ry-thing you'll ev - er need. And if
C/G
G7sus
G
Am
Am/G
F♯m7(♭5)
I were you, I'd fall in love with me. If
C/G
G7sus
G7
C(9)
F(9)
I were you, I'd fall in love with me.
dim.
C(9)
F(9)
C(9)
mp
rit. e dim.
p

A LITTLE BIT OF YOU

Words and Music by
CRAIG WISEMAN and TREY BRUCE

D N.C. Am/G 𝄋 *Chorus:* G Am/E

what's a lit - tle gam - ble when there's one sure bet?
Is it an - y won - der that I nev - er give up? } When I'm fad - ing at the fin - ish, and doubt -

Em7 C6 C(9) C6 D Am/G

ed and di - min - ished and feel - ing for a min - ute that I can't en - dure, — no mat -

G Am/E Em7 C6 C(9) G

ter what the prob - lem, — you — know how to solve 'em. Ain't noth - in' that a lit - tle bit of

D G Em7 C(9) 1. D7 G

you can't cure. — There ain't noth - in' that a lit - tle bit of you can't cure. —

C(9) G D G C(9) G D G

2.
D.S. 𝄋
3.
D7
G
D/F♯
Em7
C (9)
N.C.
D
you can't cure.___ When I'm fad -
you can't cure.___ There ain't noth -
in',
there ain't noth - in' that a lit - tle bit of
you can't cure.___ There ain't noth - in',
there ain't noth-
in' that a lit - tle bit of
you can't___ cure.___

I WANNA GO TOO FAR

Words and Music by
KENT ROBBINS and
LAYNG MARTINE, JR.

G
F/A
G/B
mon - ey for a rain - y day,
but now I've had e - nough of play - in' it safe.
boat, I need to speak my mind,
just this once, let it all un - wind.
Chorus:
C
F(9)
Gsus
G
Gsus
I wan - na go too far, I wan - na go too fast.
G
C
F(9)
Some - bod - y draw the line so I can blow right
Gsus
G
F
past.
I wan - na spend too much.
G
C
C/E
C/F
F
I wan - na stay too late.
I'm gon - na roar too loud,
I'm gon - na be that way.

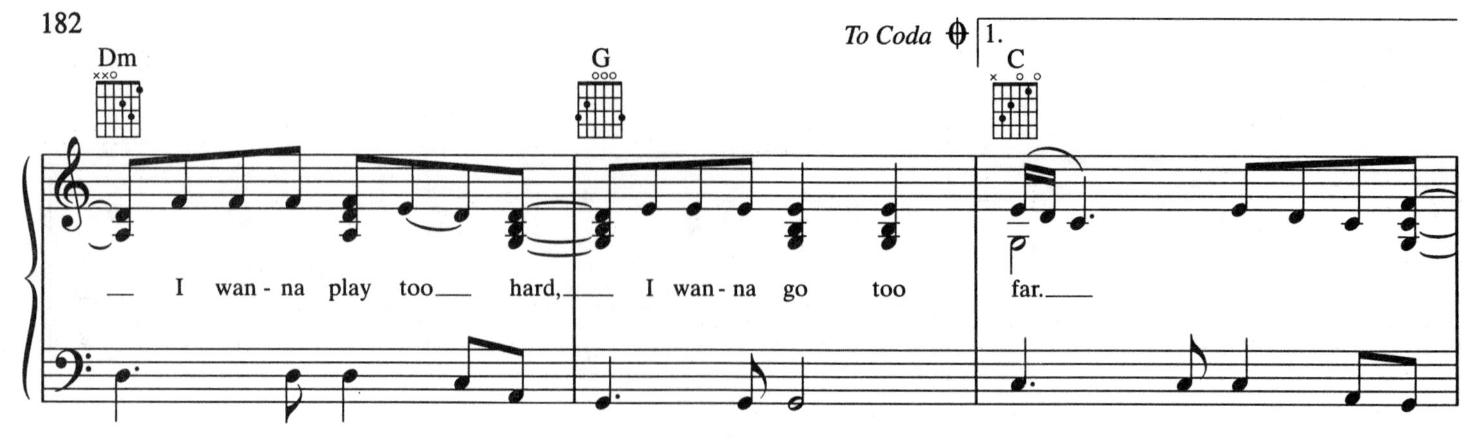
To Coda
1.
Dm
G
C
I wan - na play too hard, I wan - na go too far.

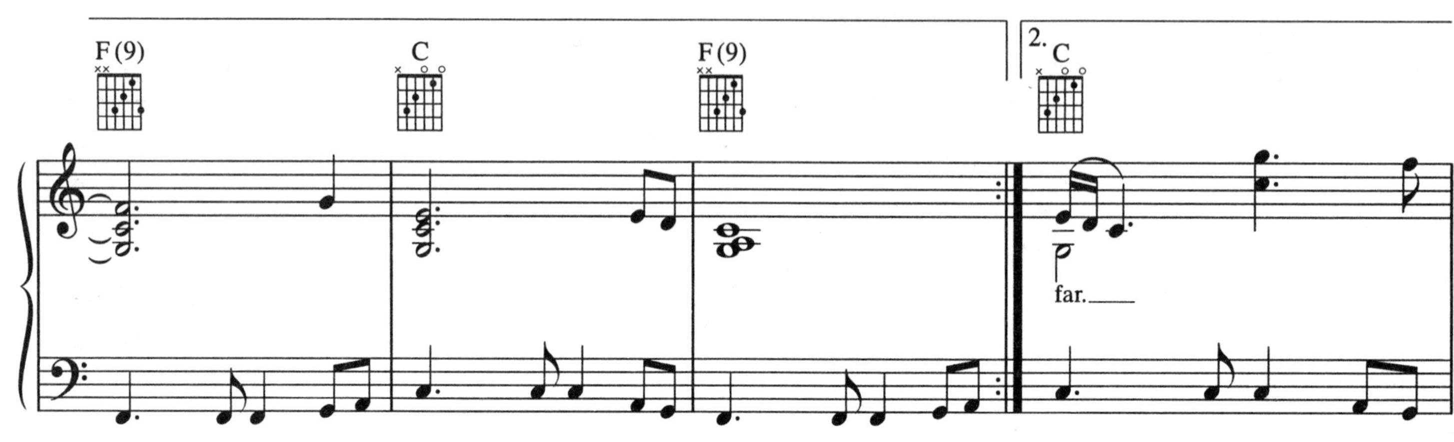
F(9)
C
F(9)
2.
C
far.

Bridge:
G
F(9)
I've got - ta set this spir - it free, it's hid - ing here in - side.

C
Am7
G
Am7
I feel like a bird in a cage, it's

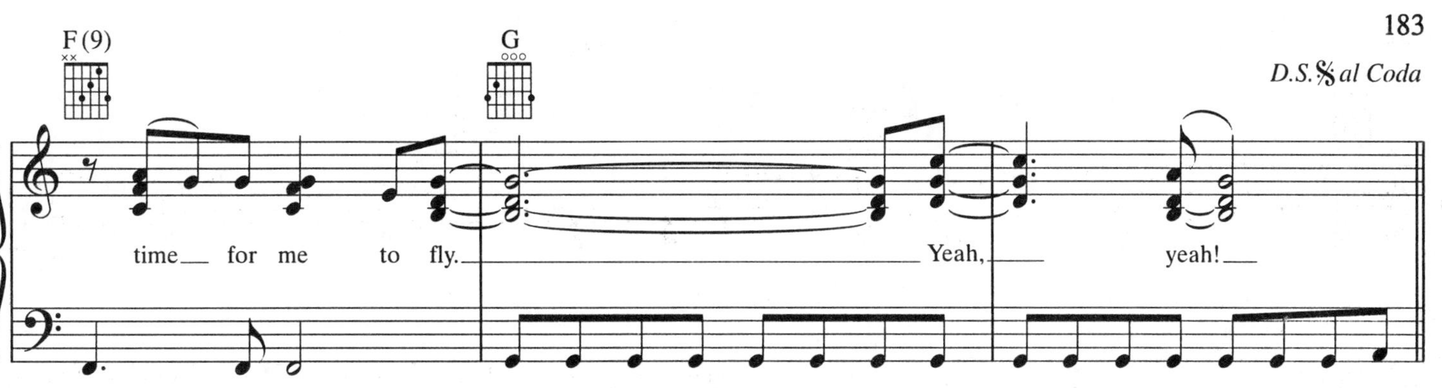
F(9)
G
D.S. 𝄋 al Coda
time for me to fly. Yeah, yeah!

Coda
C
F(9)
C
far. I wan-na go too far.

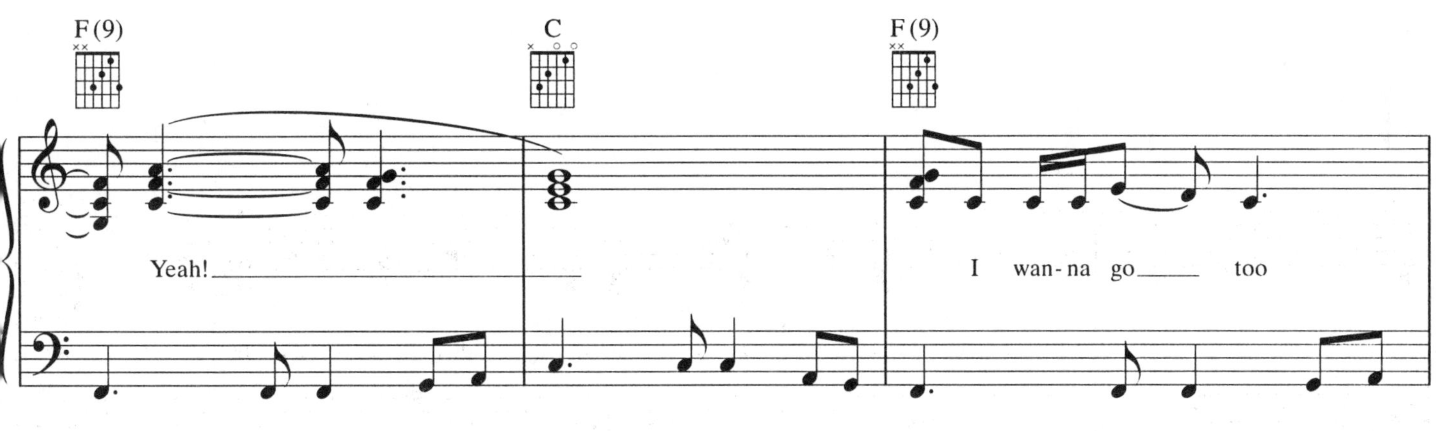
F(9)
C
F(9)
Yeah! I wan-na go too

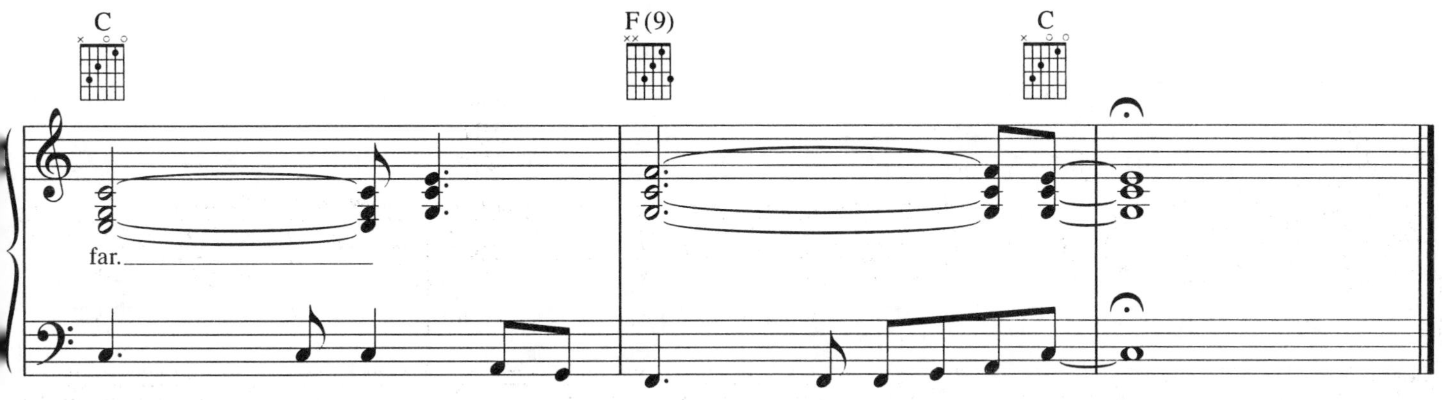
C
F(9)
C
far.

I WANT MY GOODBYE BACK

Words and Music by
PAT BUNCH, DOUG JOHNSON
and DAVE BERG

Moderately bright country rock ♩= 160
F5
G5
C/G
G7
C/G
F5
G5
C/G
1.
G7
C/G
F5
f
2.3.
G7
C/G
Verse:
G
1. I didn't mean to break your win - dow, I was
2. See additional lyrics
mf
C
G
try - in' to wake you up.
When I saw you out
D
G
last night, it hit me like a truck.
I tried to call all day

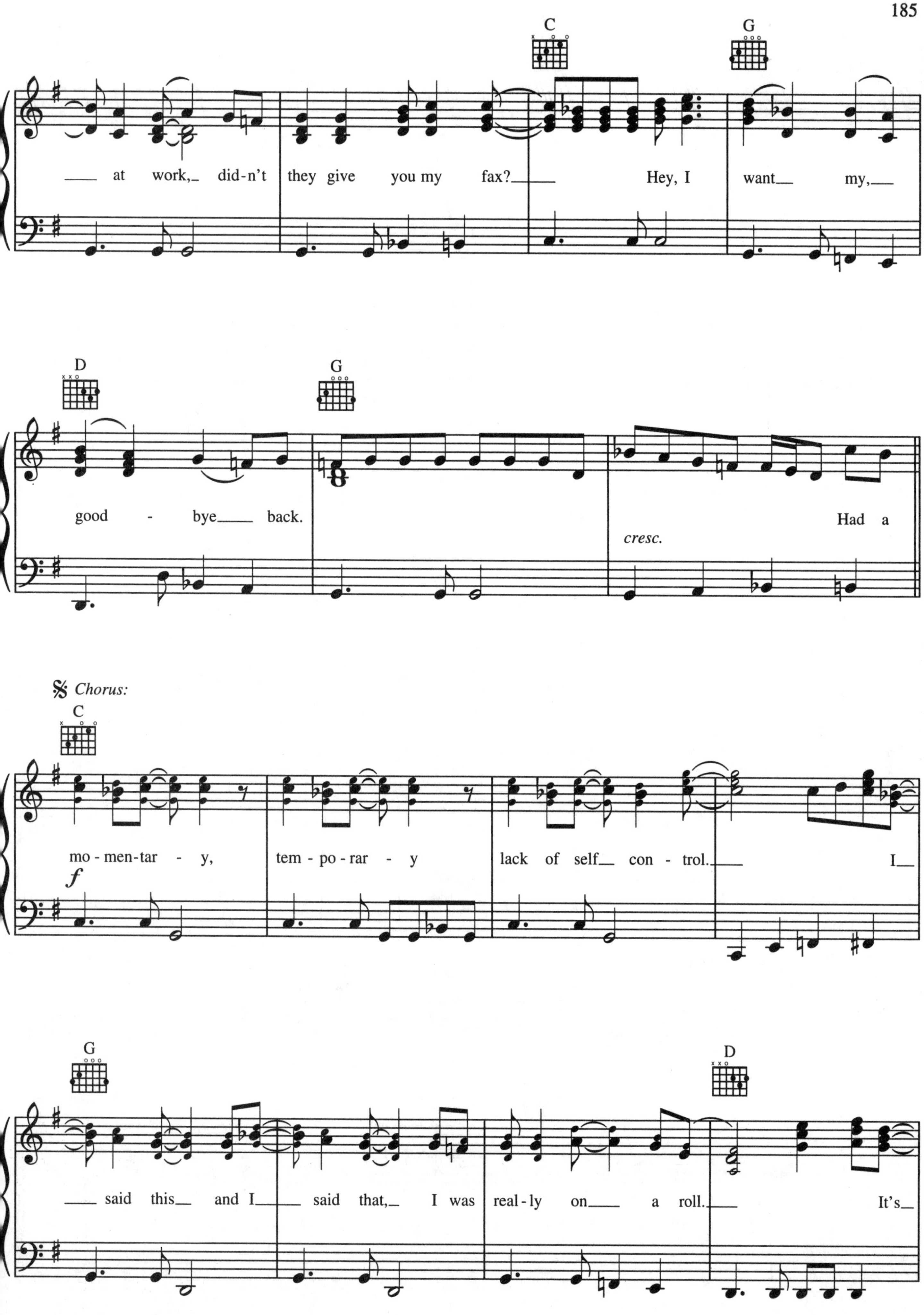

C G

___ at work,_ did-n't they give you my fax?___ Hey, I want__ my,___

D G

good - bye___ back. Had a

cresc.

G
been down hill ev - er since my good sense jumped the track
To Coda
1.
2.
C
G
D
F5
D
and I want my good - bye back.
good - bye back.
Bridge:
G
B♭
Well, I might have been in - sen - si - tive, I have learned a lot.
C
I know what I can't live with-out, and I know what I ain't got.
D
D.S. 𝄋 al Coda
Had a

Verse 2:
My doctor says I'm better now
But I still feel the pain.
I showed him your picture,
He said: "Man, you are insane."
He asked me for your number
And now his left eye is black,
And I want my goodbye back.
(To Chorus:)

IF THE WORLD HAD A FRONT PORCH

Words and Music by
TRACY LAWRENCE, PAUL NELSON
and KENNY BEARD

G
Am
and how to pray.
It was where we made our own
Em
F
C
ice cream those sultry summer nights,
where the
Dm
Em
1.
F
bull - dog had her pup - pies and us brothers had our fights.
G
2.3.
F
G
2. There were
pray I had the gift.
If the world
Chorus:
C
F
G
had a front porch like we did back then.

Am
F
C
we'd still have our prob - lems
G
Am
but we'd all be friends.
Treat - ing your
Em
F
C
neigh - bor like he's your next of kin
F
C
Am
G/A
would - n't be gone with the wind
Am
F
C
if the world had a front porch like

1.
G
C
F
we did back then.
D.S. 𝄋
2.
G
C
we did back then.
Am
Em
F
Treat - ing your neigh - bor like he's your next of kin
C
F
C
would - n't be gone with the wind
Am
G/A
Am
F
if the world had a front

Verse 2:
There were many nights I'd sit right there
And look out at the stars
To the sound of a distant whippoorwill
Or the hum of a passing car.
It was where I first got up the nerve
To steal me my first kiss.
And it was where I learned to play guitar
And pray I had the gift.
(To Chorus:)

Verse 3:
Purple hulls and pintos,
I've shelled more than my share
As lightning bugs and crickets
Danced in the evening air.
And like a beacon, that old yellow bulb,
It always led me home.
Somehow, Mama always knew
Just when to leave it on.
(To Chorus:)

IN BETWEEN DANCES

Words and Music by
CRAIG BICKHARDT

B♭
E♭
B♭/D
feet.
The
floor's
get - ting
crowd
- ed,
but
sway.
I've
had my
mo
- ments
when
Cm
E♭/B♭
F
I
don't
wan - na
take
part.
I
I
could get
lost
in
the
sound.
But
E♭
B♭/D
Cm
E♭/B♭
bet
you can
guess
it's
got
some - thing to
do
with
my
when
the song
end
- ed,
the
one
in my
arms
let
me
F
Cm7
F
F7
heart.
down.
cresc.
mf
I could
sure
use
your
com -
Chorus:
B♭
E♭
F
F7
pa - ny,
now,
but
don't
be
mis - tak -

B♭
E♭
F
F7
ing my smile. I'm on - ly in
E♭
B♭/D
E♭
F
F7sus
be - tween danc - es, sit - ting it out for a
B♭
Cm7
Fsus
1.
F
while.
dim.
2. The
mp
2.
F
Bridge:
Gm
Have you been in my
E♭
B♭
shoes? I search your eyes for signs.

Gm C7

Will you remain, re - mem - ber my

E♭ F

name af - ter it's clos - ing time?

cresc.

Fsus F B♭

mf

I could sure use your com - pa - ny now.

E♭ F F7 B♭

but don't be mis - tak - ing my

E♭ F F7 E♭

smile. I'm on - ly in be - tween

B♭/D
E♭
F
Gm
dance - es,
sit - ting it
out for a
while.
Em7(♭5)
N.C.
I'm on - ly
E♭
B♭/D
E♭
F
N.C.
in be - tween
danc - es,
sit - ting it
out
for a
B♭
Cm7
Fsus
F
while.
B♭
Cm7
Fsus
F
B♭
rit. e dim.
mp

I LIKE THE SOUND OF THAT

Words and Music by
STEVE SESKIN and
ANDRÉ PESSIS

Em
C
I'm tired of play - in' in love's play - ground,
Am
D
Chorus:
G
so when you talk a - bout set - tl - in' down, I like the sound of that,
f
C
it's mu - sic to my heart.
You say you're
Am
D
G
meant to be for - ev - er lov - in' me, I like the sound of that.
I like the sound of that.
It's like a

C
Am
dream come true, to know that rain or shine, I can
D
G
To Coda
1.
Am
G/B
call you mine, I like the sound of that.
2. We'll
2.
C
Am
D
G
Bridge:
Am
When you whis-per my name soft-ly

Verse 2:
We'll build a house out in the country,
A place to call our very own.
With a little sweat and a lot of lovin'
We'll turn it into a home.
And every mornin' when I open my eyes
I'll see the woman who changed my life.
(To Chorus:)

IF YOU'VE GOT LOVE

Words and Music by
STEVE SESKIN and MARK SANDERS

G C Dsus D
noth - in' quite like life if you've got love.
you've got love, you've got what it takes.
If you've got
cresc.
Chorus:
C G C G
love you can move a moun - tain a lit - tle bit fur - ther down the line. You can do it
f
Am G/B C Dsus D G/B
all at once, or one rock at a time. You can turn an
C G C D
or - di - nar - y pic - ture in - to a price - less work of art. That's what you can do
Am G/B 1. C D G C D7sus
if you've got love in your heart.
dim.
mf

D.S. 𝄋
2.
G
C
D
C
D
2. Now there's
love in your
G
C2
D
G
C2
D
heart. (Instrumental solo ad lib. . . .
G
C2
D
G
C
D
. . . end solo)
If you've got
Chorus:
G
C
G
love you can move a moun - tain
fur - ther down the line.
C
D
Am
G/B
C
Dsus
You can do it all at once, or
one rock at a time.

D
G/B
C
G
C
You can turn an ordinary picture into a priceless work of art.
D
Am
G/B
C
D
That's what you can do if you've got love in your
G
C
D
Am
G/B
C
heart.
That's what you can do if you've got love
G
C2
D7sus
G
C
D
in your heart.
If you've got
Repeat ad lib. and fade
G
C
D
G
C
D
love.
(lead vocal ad lib.)
If you've got

LEAD ON

Words and Music by
DEAN DILLON and TEDDY GENTRY

D♭
ing thru, — but
— once, too, — but
girl, from — the looks — of you, — I,
I act - ed like — a fool. — Oh,
E♭
A♭(9)
I could — see — me set - tlin' down." —
what I'd give — to be — back in — her arms." —
Chorus:
Fm7
B♭7sus
B♭7
Then, she smiled — and said, — "The in - vi - ta - tion's o -
E♭
Fm7
pen, — 'cause you look — just like — what I've —

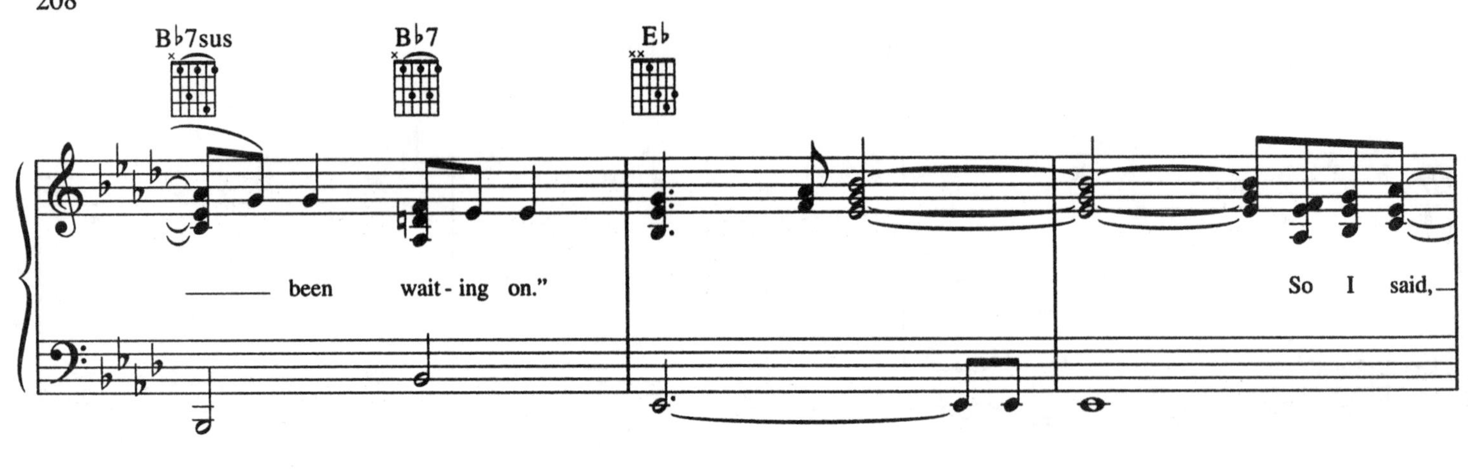

B♭7sus
B♭7
E♭
been wait - ing on."
So I said,

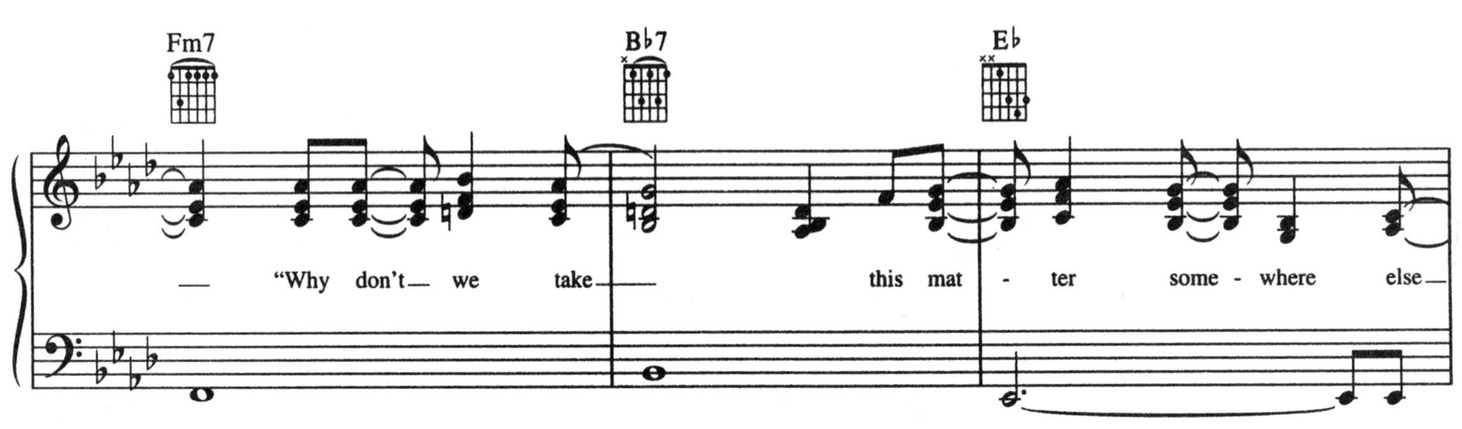

Fm7
B♭7
E♭
"Why don't we take this mat - ter some - where else

A♭(9)
D♭
and get to know this feel - ing that's so strong?
and pick up right where ev - 'ry thing went wrong?

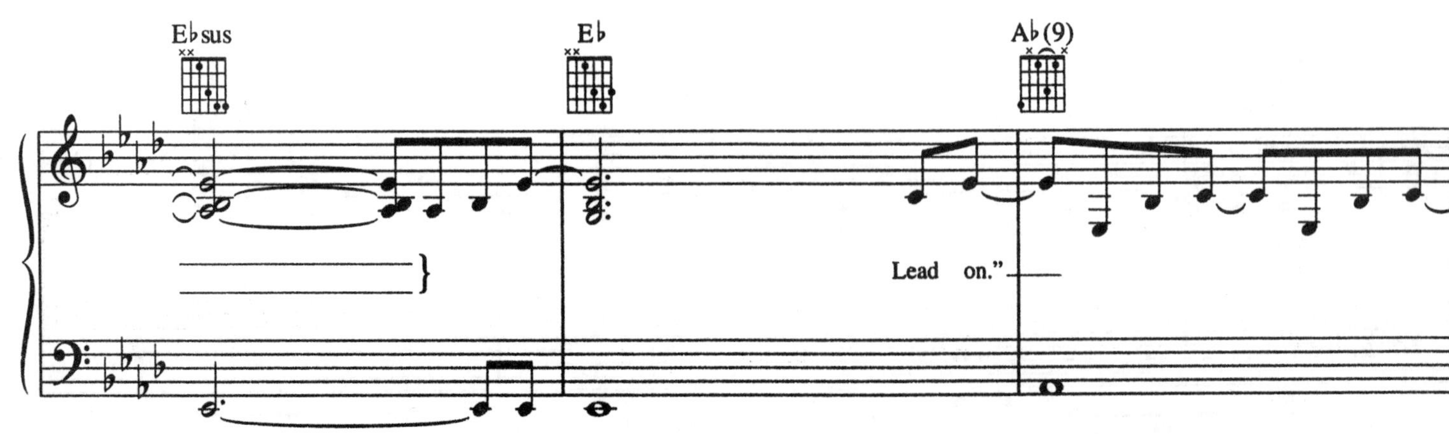

E♭sus
E♭
A♭(9)
Lead on."

1.
2.
D♭
E♭
N.C.
A♭(9)
She said, "I don't re - call see - ing you a - round here.
You must be new to this town."
rit.
a tempo
rit. e dim.
p

THE LIKES OF ME

Words and Music by
RICK BOWLES and LARRY BOONE

G
D5
A
D5
say-ing you gave_ your love___ and got tak - en,
and once a - gain___ your___ heart is break - ing.__
C(9)
G
A
You're think-in' lone - ly's your_ des - ti - ny.___
But
F2
G
D5
you ain't ev - er been_ loved by the likes of me.___
I'd like to be_
Chorus:
G
D5
A
___ at your beck and call,___ I'd like to stay a - round for the long haul.__
D5
G
D5
A
___ Start-ing to - night,___ I'd like to make___ sweet_ mem - o - ries.___

To Coda
F2
G
1.
D5
You ain't ev - er been loved by the likes of me.
F2
G5
2.
D5
D.S. al Coda
I'd like to be
Coda
F2
G
D5
You ain't ev - er been loved by the likes of me.
F2
G
I said, you ain't ev - er been loved by the likes of me.

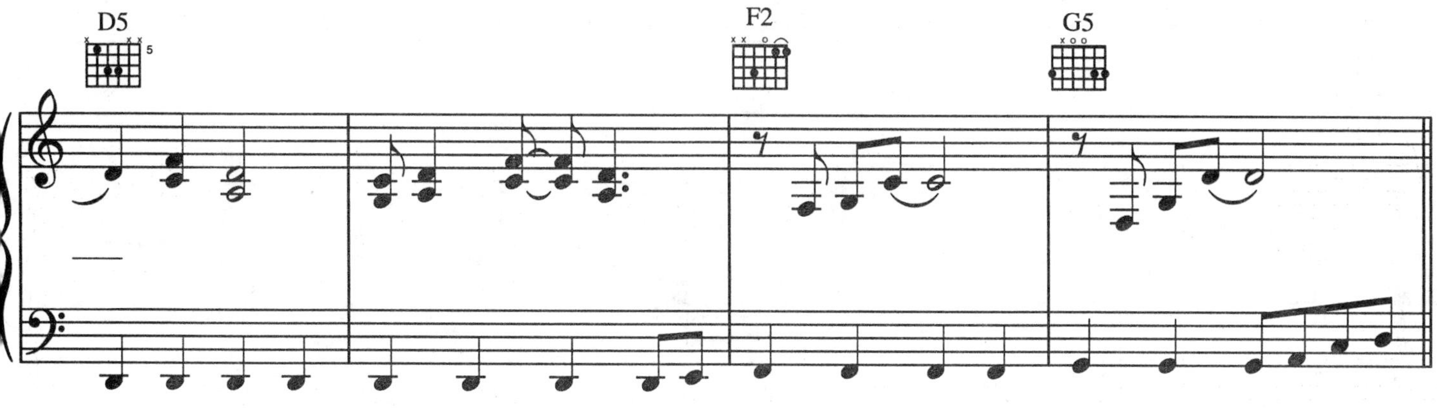

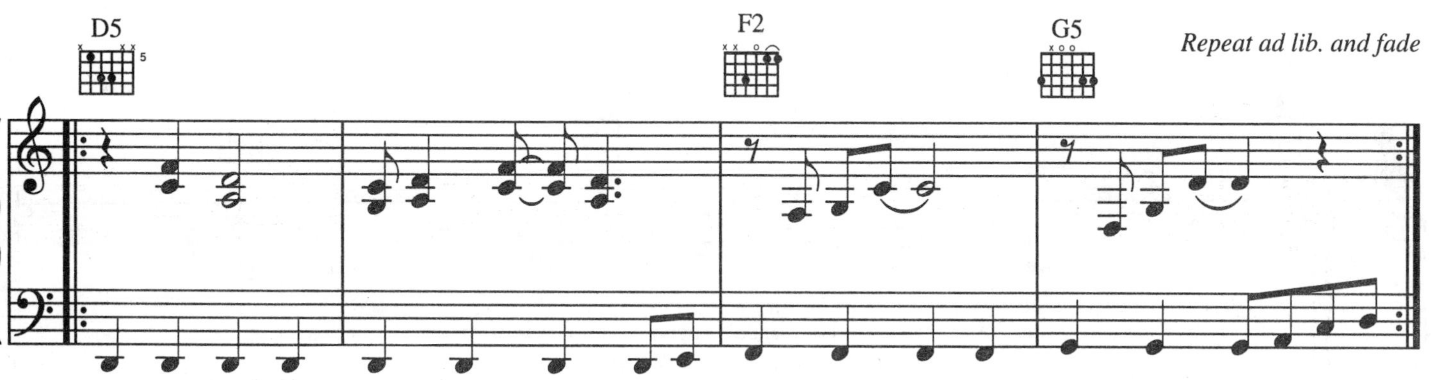

Verse 2:
If you need a helpin' hand to start over,
Baby, I can give you more than a shoulder.
You say you're having trouble believin'
That I won't be loving and leaving.
I say you've been hurt needlessly,
It's high time you were loved by the likes of me.
(To Chorus:)

JENNY COME BACK

Words and Music by
TIA SILLERS and JOHN TIRRO

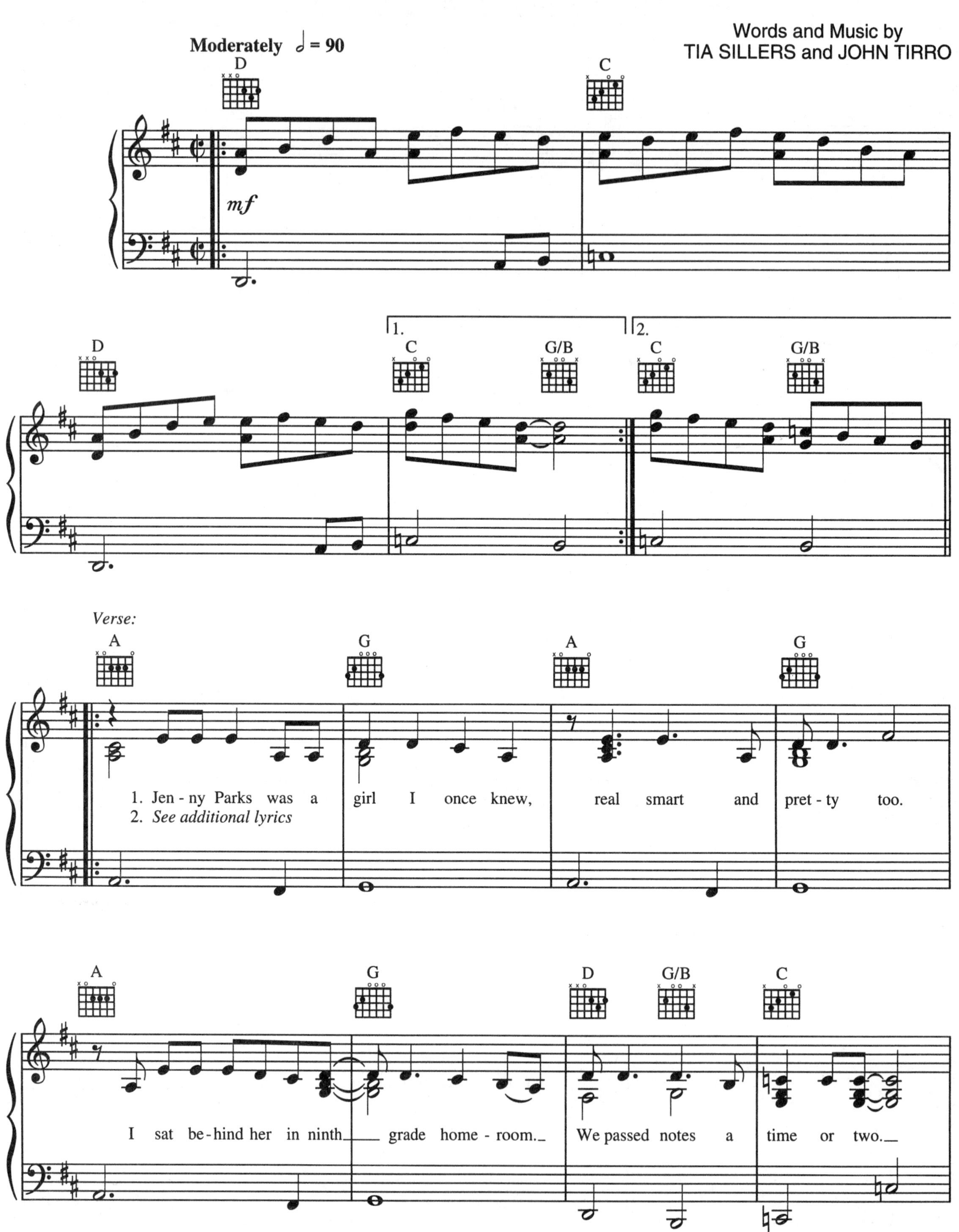
Moderately ♩ = 90
D
C
mf
D
1.
C
G/B
2.
C
G/B
Verse:
A
G
A
G
1. Jen - ny Parks was a girl I once knew, real smart and pret - ty too.
2. See additional lyrics
A
G
D
G/B
C
I sat be - hind her in ninth grade home - room. We passed notes a time or two.

A
G
A
G
'Round a - bout our fif - teenth sum-mer she hung out with the sen - ior guys.
A
G
D
G/B
C
They seemed to like the emp - ty air - heads, clouds rolled in a-round her eyes.
Chorus:
D
G
A
Oh Jen - ny, you could have been an - y-thing.
D
G
A
Why'd you think you had to change? Were you
D
G
D
A/C#
Bm7
play-ing the part, play - ing by the rules, why'd you de-cide to play the fool?

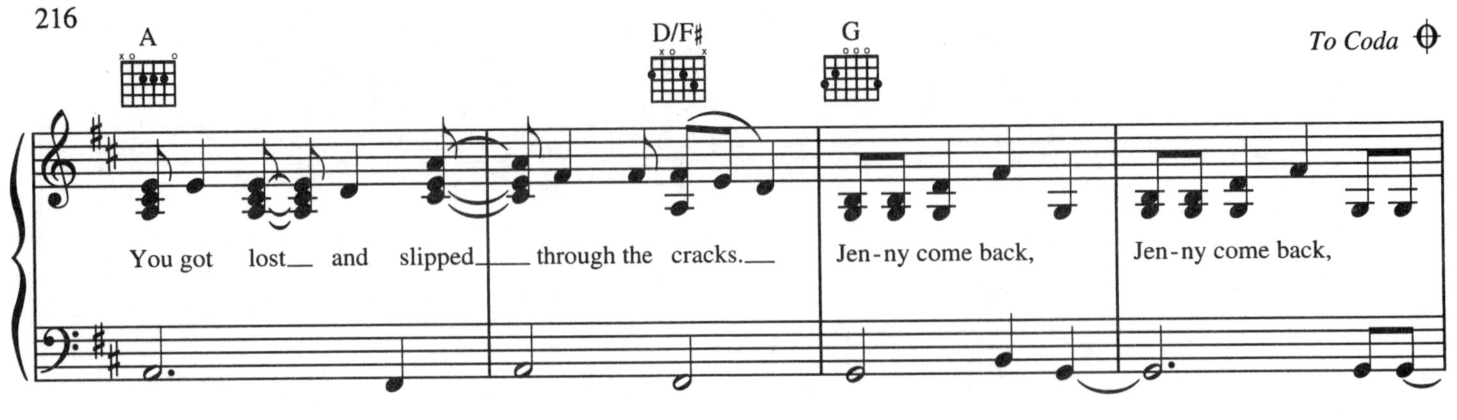
A
D/F♯
G
To Coda
You got lost and slipped through the cracks.
Jen-ny come back,
Jen-ny come back,

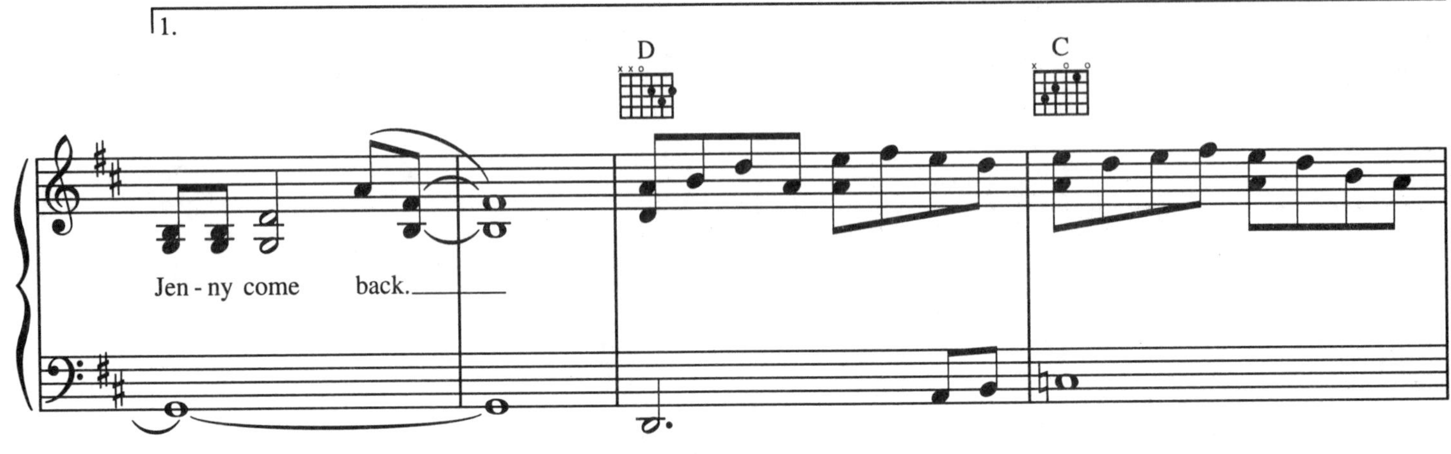
1.
D
C
Jen-ny come back.

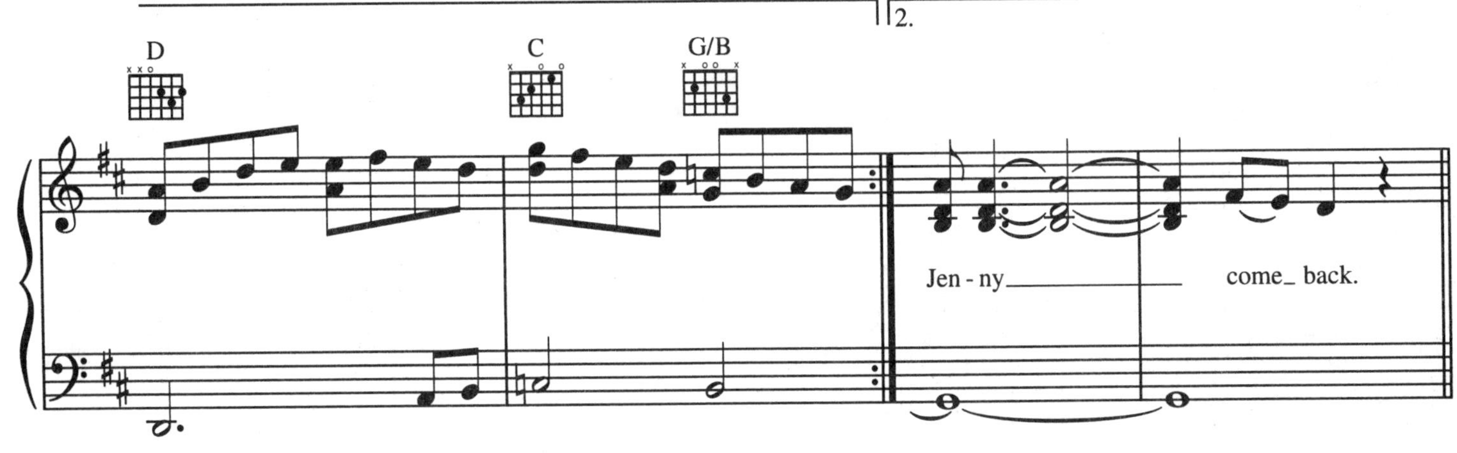
D
C
G/B
2.
Jen-ny come back.

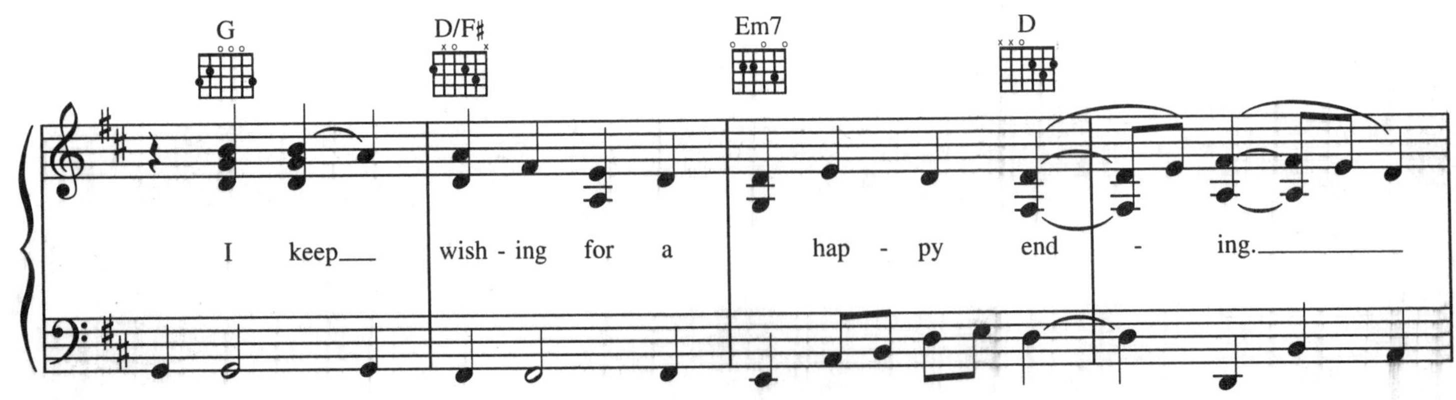
G
D/F♯
Em7
D
I keep wish-ing for a hap-py end-ing.

G
D/F♯
Bm
A
But I can't make that choice for you, no.
G
D/F♯
Em7
D
We lost touch long a - go now, Jen - ny. Oh,
C
G
3
what in the world are you gon - na do?
A
G
A
Was that you sell - ing tick - ets at the mov - ies down - town the
G
A
G
oth - er day? I said your name but you looked right through me,

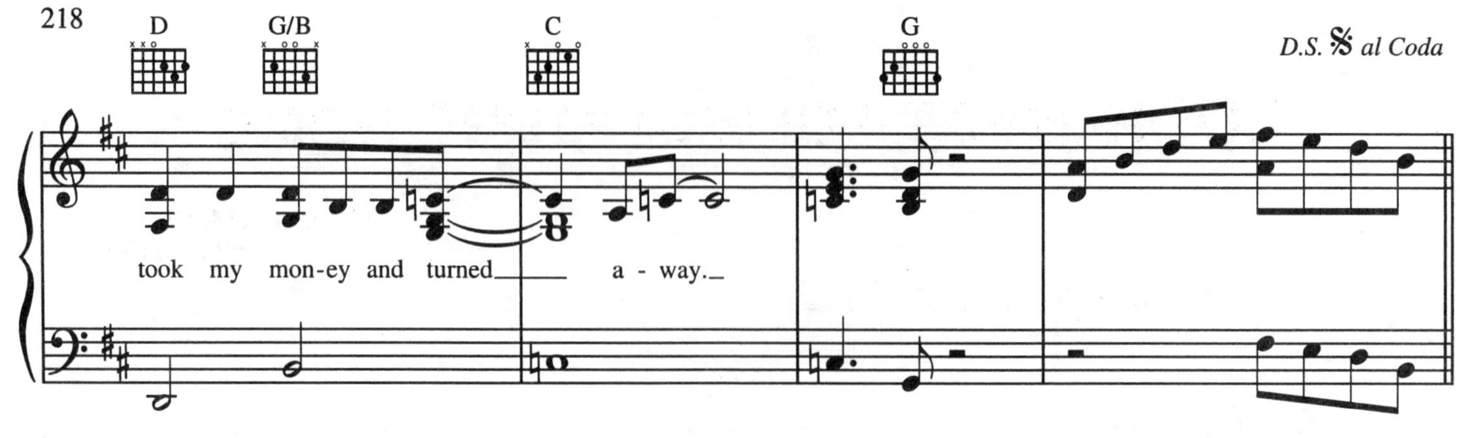

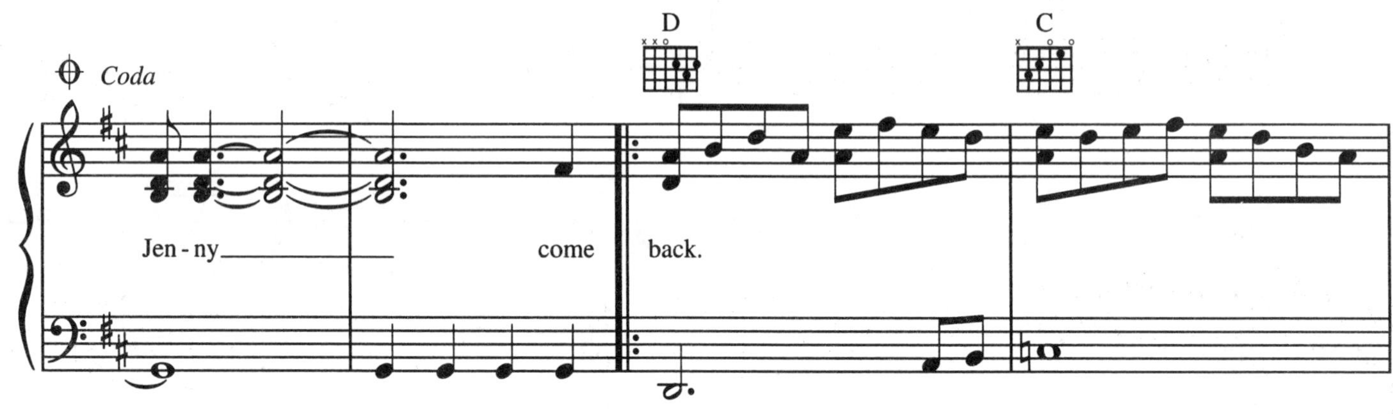

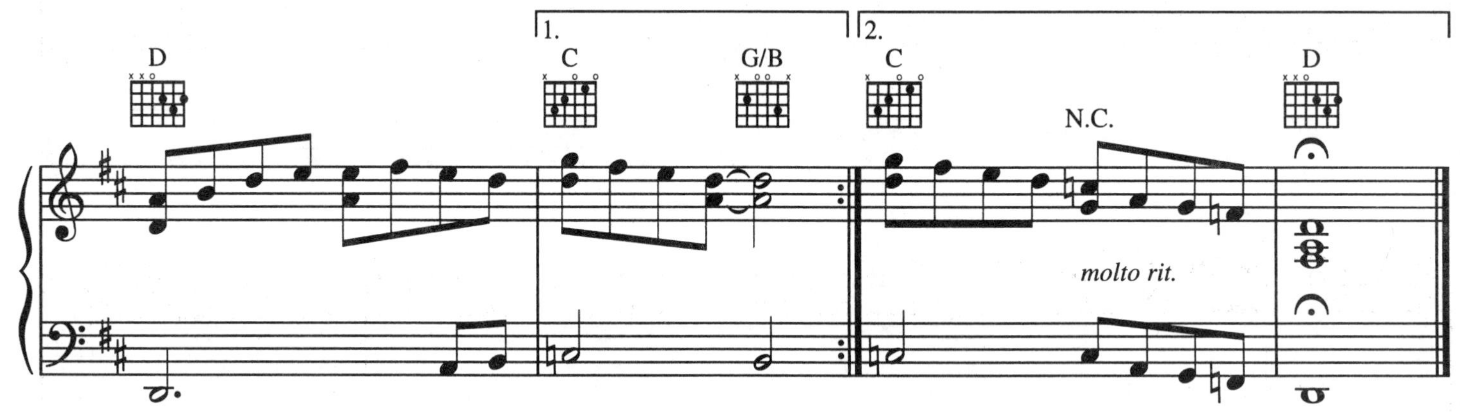

Verse 2:
Jenny fell for the star linebacker
With the free ride to L.S.U.
He said, "Come on" and nothing else mattered.
Sweet sixteen, she dropped out of school.
Made his bed through four years of college,
Waiting on a diamond he couldn't afford.
He called it quits 'cause he'd gotten knowledge
And she never did and he got bored.
(To Chorus:)

LOOK WHAT FOLLOWED ME HOME

Words and Music by
TOMMY POLK and DAVID BALL

Look What Followed Me Home - 3 - 1

E
on a mid - night ride down a dark and lone - ly back road and
E7
A
N.C.
left it there to die.
Look what fol - lowed me home!
Chorus:
A
D
A
I thought I was a - lone
3
but your mem-o - ry
is com - ing back to me.
E
Bm7
E7
A
I thought I'd left it be - hind

Verse 2:
Well, I walked down to the river at the break of dawn
With a picture of you, darling, up underneath my arm.
I said, "The heartache's over, today is your last day."
And I thanked that muddy river as it carried you away.
(To Chorus:)

LITTLE HOUSES

Words and Music by
MICKEY CATES and SKIP EWING

Moderately slow ♩ = 76

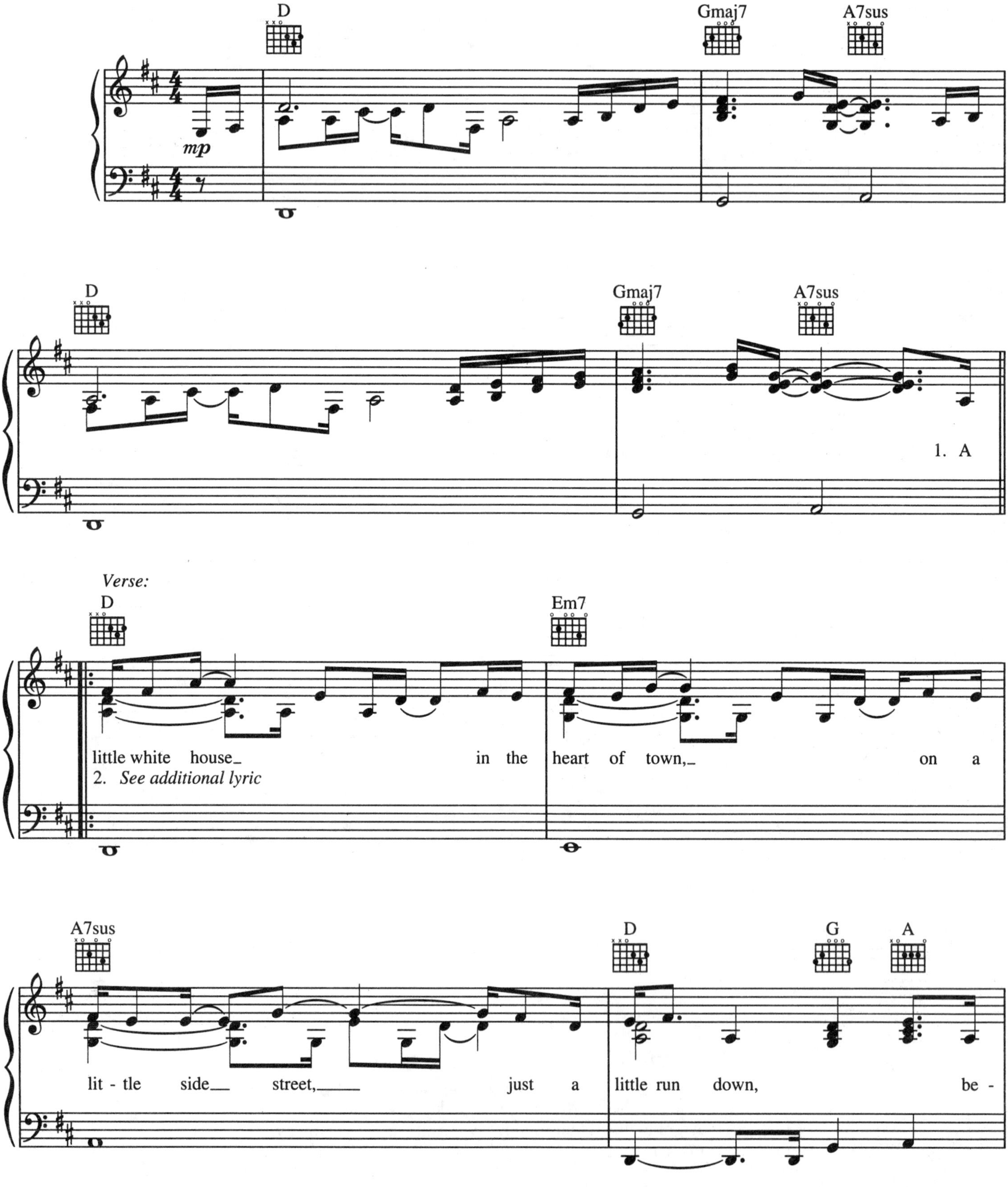

D
Gmaj7
A7sus
mp
D
Gmaj7
A7sus
1. A
Verse:
D
Em7
little white house_ in the heart of town,_ on a
2. See additional lyric
A7sus
D
G
A
lit - tle side__ street,____ just a little run down, be -

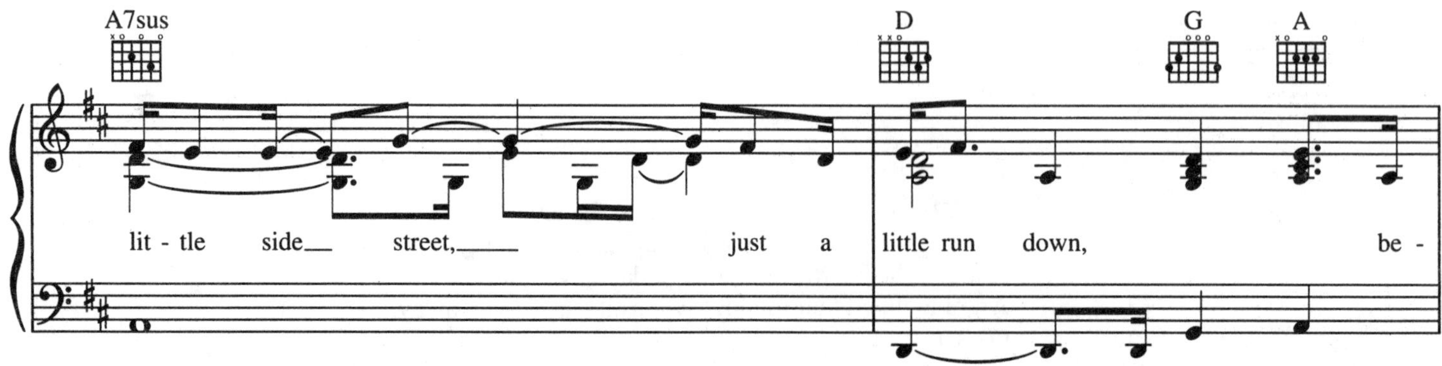

D
Em7
came a home_ for Bill and Sue,___ two
A7sus
A7
D
new - ly - weds_ who did the best_ that they could do.___
cresc.
Gmaj7
G6
F#m7
D/F#
Em7
mf
And when they'd brush each oth-er pass-ing in the hall,_ Sue would smile_ and say,_ "This
1.
A7sus
To Next Strain
2.
A7sus
place is real-ly small,_ but you know . . . place is real-ly, real-ly small.__ But you know . . .
Chorus:
D
love grows best_ in___ lit - tle hous - es,__ with few-er walls to sep - a - rate,___ where_ you

G A

eat and sleep so close_ to-geth-er, you can't help_ but com-mu - ni - cate._ Oh, and

D D/F♯ G

if we had_ more room_ be - tween_ us, think of all_ we'd miss._ Love_

Em7 A7sus *To Coda* 𝄌 1. D Gmaj7 A7sus

grows best in hous-es just_ like this." 2. Be-

dim. ***mp***

2. D *Bridge:* G D

this." That lit-tle white frame house still keeps_ them warm,_

Em7 A7sus

though it's been thir - ty - two_ years since the kids_ were born._

Verse 2:
Before too long, Sue and Bill
Were making plans for Jack and Jill.
Oh, happy day when the news came in;
But what to do? They found out Sue was having twins.
And when they could not pass each other in the hall,
Well, Sue would smile and say, "This place is really, really small.
But you know . . .
(To Chorus:)

LIVIN' ON LOVE

Words and Music by
ALAN JACKSON

Moderately

A E A

mf

D A E A

E A E A

Two young- peo- ple with- out a thing say some vows and spread their
(See additional lyrics)

D A

wings. And set- tle down with just what they need liv- in' on love.

E
A
She don't
care
'bout what's in
E
A
D
style,
she just
likes
the way he
smiles.
It takes
A
E
A
more
than mar - ble and tile,
liv-in' on
love.
E
A
Liv - in' on
love,
buy-in' on time,
with-out some -

D
A
D
body-y, noth-in' ain't worth a dime.
Just like an old fash-ioned stor-y book
A
E7
rhyme, liv-in' on love.
It sounds
A
E
A
sim-ple, that's what you're think-in' but love can walk through fire with-out
D
A
E
To Coda
blink-in'. It does-n't take much when you get e-nough, liv-in' on love.

Additional Lyrics

2. Two old people without a thing
   Children gone but still they sing
   Side by side in that front porch swing
   Livin' on love.
   He can't see anymore,
   She can barely sweep the floor.
   Hand in hand they'll walk through that door
   Just livin' on love.
   (To Chorus)

MI VIDA LOCA
(MY CRAZY LIFE)

Words and Music by
PAM TILLIS and JESS LEARY

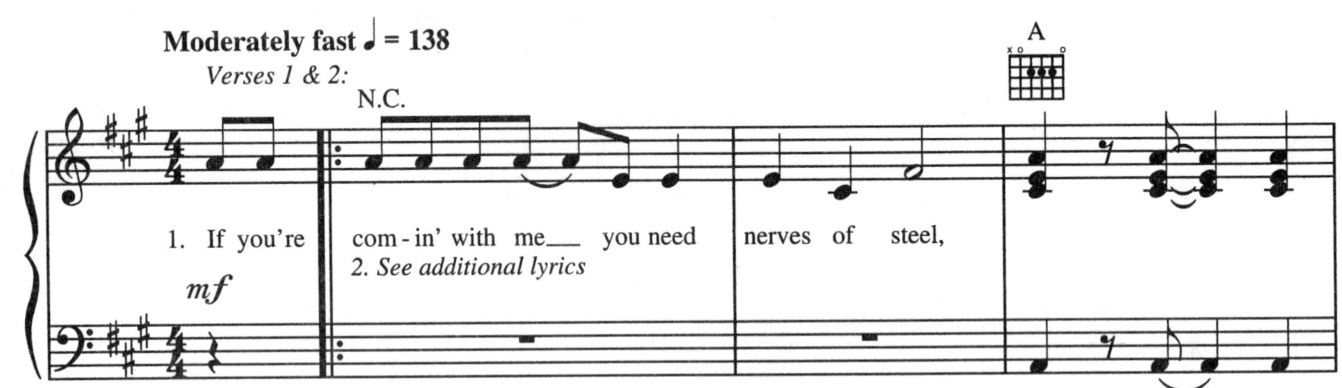

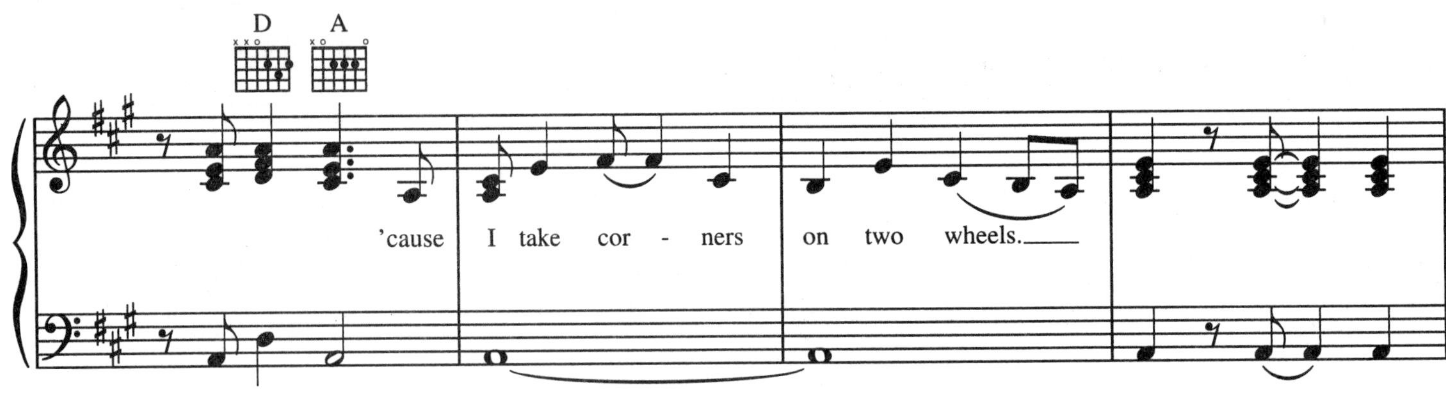

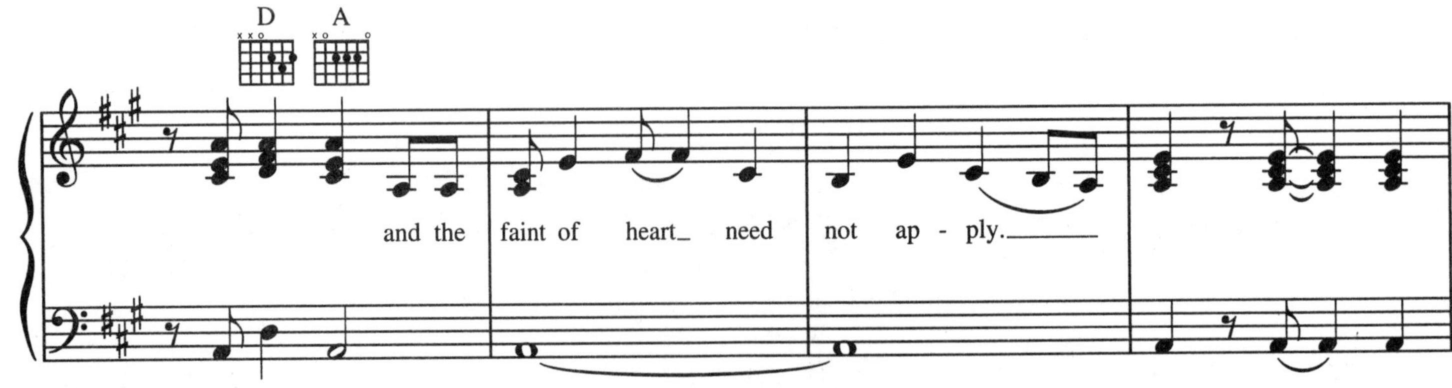

Chorus:

E A E7

Mi vi - da lo - ca, o - ver and o - ver. Des - tin - y turns on a dime.

A E7

I go where the wind blows, you can't tame a wild rose. Wel - come to my cra - zy life.

1. A

E7

2.
A
A
2. Sweet - life.
D
G

Bridge:
A
Here in the fire - light I see your tat - oo.
Mi vi - da lo - co, so you're cra - zy too?
B
Chorus:
B
F♯7
Mi vi - da lo - ca, o - ver and o - ver.
B
Des - tin - y turns on a dime. We'll

Verse 2:
Sweetheart, before this night is through,
I could fall in love with you.
Come dancin' on the edge with me,
Let my passion set you free.
(To Chorus:)

NO MAN'S LAND

Words and Music by
JOHN SCOTT SHERRILL
and STEVE SESKIN

Em7
F(9)
holding down a job. She'd rob Peter to pay Paul, but he's al-
Am
Em7
ready been robbed. She gets the food on the table, the clothes off the line. She'd
F
Fmaj7/G
G7
break down and cry, but she doesn't have time. She's got to
cresc.
Chorus:
Csus4/2
C
Em7
C/E
F
G
be strong; life goes on, though it's nothing like she had planned. She's gonna
mf
Csus4/2
C
Em7
C/E
F
F/G
To Coda
be O-K, gonna find a way, living in no man's land.

Verse 2:
Every now and then, late at night,
She thinks of how it would feel to hold someone tight.
There's a guy down at work; he keeps calling her up.
But she ain't ready for none of that stuff.
She's still sifting through the ashes of a love that's been and gone,
Looking for a clue, trying to find out what went wrong.
It ain't always easy, but she knows she's gotta try
Every time she looks into her babies' eyes.
(To Chorus:)

MY GIRL FRIDAY

Words and Music by
CURTIS WRIGHT and CARL JACKSON

D♭
E♭
A♭
she walks out the door.
I wish things could be dif -
D♭/A♭
- ferent, we did - n't have to say good - bye.
Some-one
E♭
else is in the pic - ture and we
1.
D♭
E♭
don't see eye to eye.
A♭
D♭/A♭
2. The
2.3.
D♭
E♭
face the lone - ly week.

Chorus:
A♭ B♭m7 A♭/C B♭m7 E♭ A♭ E♭/A♭
She's my girl Fri - day as far as I'm con-cerned.
A♭ B♭m7 E♭ A♭
I'm lost with-out her, don't know which way to turn.
Cm7 Fm7 B♭m7 E♭ A♭
Thurs-day takes for-ev - er and Mon-day comes too soon.
F7sus F7 B♭m7 E♭ D♭ E♭
To Coda
But at least she's my girl Fri - day 'til Sun-day af - ter - noon.

Verse 2:
The minute that she leaves here
She'll run straight to their arms.
Gotta find the strength to let her go
Even though it breaks my heart.
One last time I'll hold her tightly
And kiss her on the cheek.
As she rushes to the car,
I'm left to face the lonely week.
(To Chorus:)

Verse 3:
She stands up in the back seat
And softly waves goodbye.
I look away before I want to,
She don't need to see me cry.
I know that I'd go crazy
If it wasn't for the fact,
I'll always be her daddy
And they'll have to bring her back.
(To Chorus:)

NOT A MOMENT TOO SOON

Words and Music by
WAYNE PERRY and
JOE BARNHILL

G
All my wish - es were just way too much to
Em7
C
D
hope for. Lord, when I saw you I knew I'd seen the light.
(Double time) ♩ = 120
G
Chorus:
cresc.
And not a mo - ment too soon,
mf
Em7
with - out a min - ute to spare,
you touched my

C
D
heart,
when I did - n't have a
prayer.
G
In my dark - est
hour,
with my world filled with
Em7
C
gloom.
Your sweet love
saved
D
1.
(Half time) ♩ = 60
G
me not a mo - ment too
soon.
mp

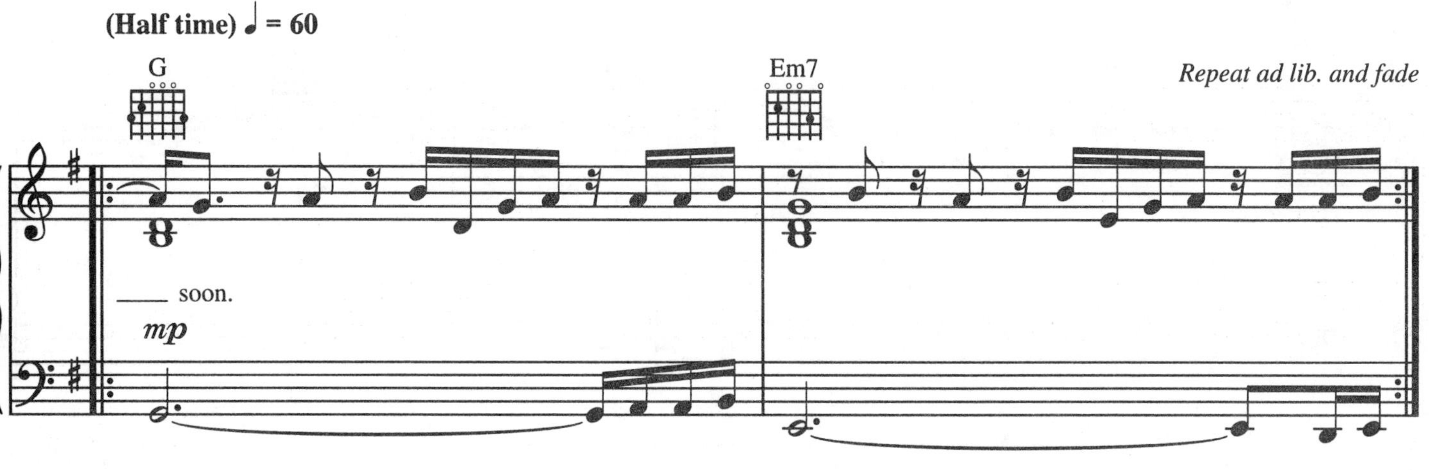

Verse 2:
I used to think that love would never find me,
And the one who cares was lost somewhere in time.
But when you found me I knew I'd found forever,
You rescued me just before I crossed the line.
(To Chorus:)

ONE EMOTION

Words and Music by
CLINT BLACK and HAYDEN NICHOLAS

D♭
A♭
Fm
pure and sim - ply, we be - long,
and what's come o - ver me are chills
B♭7
E♭
Chorus:
A♭
C7
of an - oth - er kind.
One e - mo - tion,
D♭
B♭m
A♭
Fm
B♭7
E♭
wrapped a - round me;
one e - mo - tion I can
hold on to.
A♭
C7
D♭
D♭m
Where-ev - er it's go - ing, it's ex -
act - ly where I want to be;
A♭
Fm
B♭7
E♭
one e - mo - tion's got a hold
of you and

Verse 2:
There's nothing left of the useless things I used to feel;
Only love now, as everything else just fades away.
It's all around us, though you might not see it, it's just as real
As the wild horses you would have to have to drag me away from...
(To Chorus:)

SHE CAN'T LOVE YOU

Words and Music by
CHRIS FARREN, JEFFREY STEELE
and RANDY SHARP

She Can't Love You - 5 - 1

D
A
B♭dim7
Bm
ten 'bout the prom - is - es we made.
So, be -
G
D
A7
fore it goes an - y fur - ther, I wan - na set the rec - ord straight.
𝄋 Chorus:
D
N.C.
D/G
G
D/G
G
mf
She can't love you.
She can't
D
Dsus
D
Bm
love you.
No mat - ter what she might say,
F♯m/A
G
A7
D/F♯
she's al - read - y giv - en her heart a - way. She can't

D/G G D/G G D

love___ you.__ There's no way that could be.

To Coda

Bm Em7 A7sus

How could she love you__ when she gave all of her love to__

D D/G G D

me?

dim.

mp

Verse:

D/G G D D/G G

2. From where you sit, it might look__

Em7 A7sus A7 D

like all the signs are there.___ You might e - ven tell__

D.S. 𝄋 al Coda
D/G
G
Em7
A7
D/F♯
— your - self —
you make a per - fect pair. —
But she can't
𝄌 Coda
A7sus
A7
D
G
N.C.
all of her love to — me.
I'm not
giv - ing it up!
G
N.C.
Em7
A
N.C.
Make no mis - take,
her love is not yours — to
take!
G
D
Dsus
D
(Instrumental solo...
...end solo)
No —
Bm
F♯m/A
G
mat - ter what she might say, —
she's
al - read - y giv - en her

A7
D/F♯
D/G
G
heart a - way. She can't
love you.
There's no way that could
D
Bm
Em7
be.
How could she
love you when she gave
A7sus
A7
D
Bm
all of her love to me?
How could she
Em7
A7sus
D
love you when she gave
all of her love to
me?
dim.
D/G
G
D
D/G
D/F♯
Em7
A7sus
D(9)
She can't
mp
love you.
rit. e dim.
p

NOT ON YOUR LOVE

Words and Music by
ANTHONY MARTIN, REESE WILSON
and TROY MARTIN

Bm7
D♯m7
Bm7/A
D♯m7/C♯
Em7
G♯m7
D/F♯
F♯/A♯
But ev - ery time we don't see eye to eye, you wor - ry I might say good-bye.
G
B
A7
C♯7
Chorus:
G
B
A7
C♯7
Not on your love, not in this life, could I ev - er leave.
F♯m7
A♯m7
Bm7
D♯m7
C
E
I would-n't think twice of let-ting you go. By now you should know
G/B
B/D♯
G
B
A7sus
C♯7sus
A7
C♯
G/B
B/D♯
A/C♯
C♯/E♯
I need you too much. Not on your love,

G
B
A7
C#7
F#m7
A#m7
— no way in this_ world,___ could I ev - er live___ with-out_ you, girl._
Bm7
D#m7
Em7
G#m7
D/F#
F#/A#
___ When times_ get tough___ I'm not giv - ing up,_
1.
G
B
A7
C#7
D
F#
Bm
D#m
— not on your love.
F#m7
A#m7
G
B
A7sus
C#7sus
A7
C#7
2.
G
B
A7
C#7
— not on your

Verse 2:
When we started out, we made a vow
Not to sleep 'til we settled the fight.
And there have been times we've seen the sunrise
But it always worked out alright.
Even in the darkest hour before dawn,
I never thought of moving on.
(To Chorus:)

THE RED STROKES

By
JAMES GARVER, LISA SANDERSON,
JENNY YATES and GARTH BROOKS

Moderately slow ♩ = 84
B♭
Gm7
E♭
F
mf
(with pedal)
Verse:
B♭
Gm
E♭
1. Moon-light on can-vas, mid-night and wine, two shad-ows start - ing to
mf
F7sus
F
B♭
soft - ly com - bine. The pic - ture they're paint - ing is one of the heart, and to
Gm
F7sus
F
those who have seen it, it's a true work of art. Oh, the
cresc.

*L.H. tacet 1st Verse on recording.

Chorus:
B♭
F
Gm
E♭maj7
red strokes,
(3rd time instr. solo . . .
pas-sions un - caged,
thun-der-ing mo - ments of
F7sus
F
B♭
F
Gm
ten-der-ness rage. Woah, the
red strokes,
tem-pered and strong,
1.
D.S.
F
E♭maj7
burn-ing the night like the
dawn.
decresc.
2.
E♭maj7
3.
E♭maj7
dawn.

Bridge:
F
Gm
F
Eb
Bb/D
...end solo)
Ah, but the blues will_ be blue and_ the jeal - ous - ies green, but when
Gm
Bb/F
F
F7sus
F
Fsus
F
love picks_ its shade, it de - mands to be seen.___ Oh,__ the
Chorus:
Bb
F
Gm
Ebmaj7
red strokes, pas-sions un - caged,_ thun-der - ing mo - ments of
F7sus
F
Bb
F
Gm
ten - der-ness rage.___ Woah,_ the red strokes, fear-less - ly drawn,_

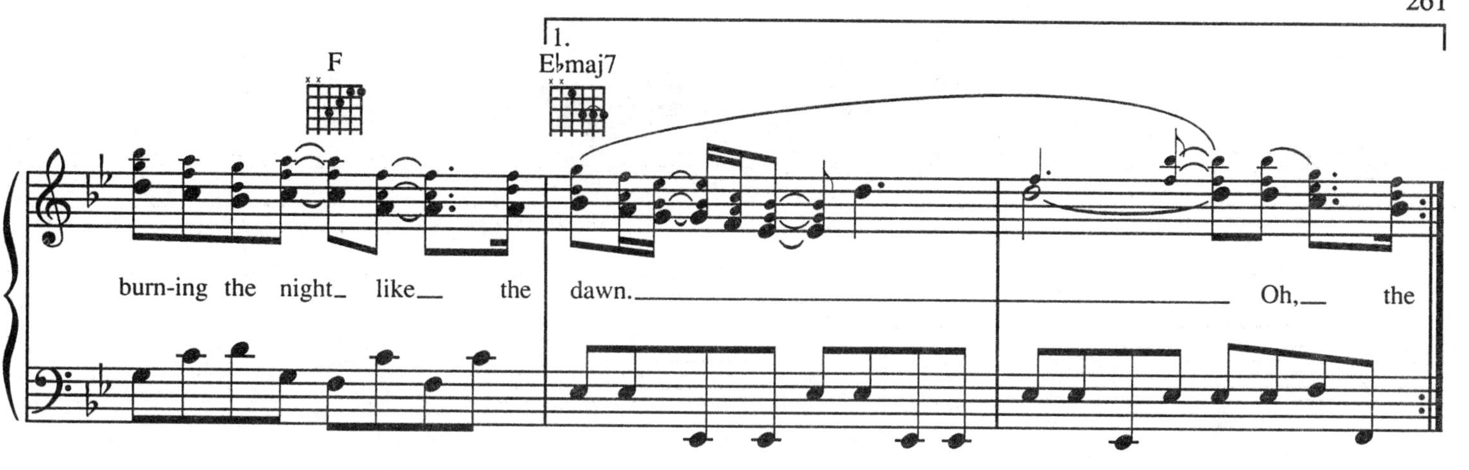
1.
F
E♭maj7
burn-ing the night like the dawn.
Oh, the

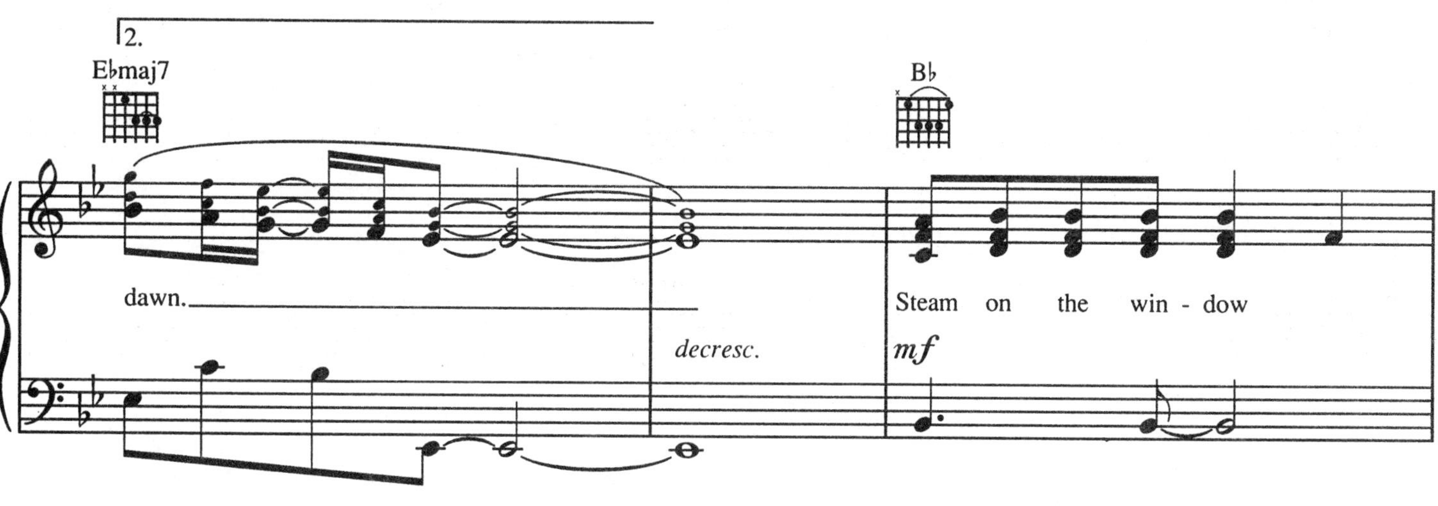
2.
E♭maj7
B♭
dawn.
Steam on the win - dow
decresc.
mf

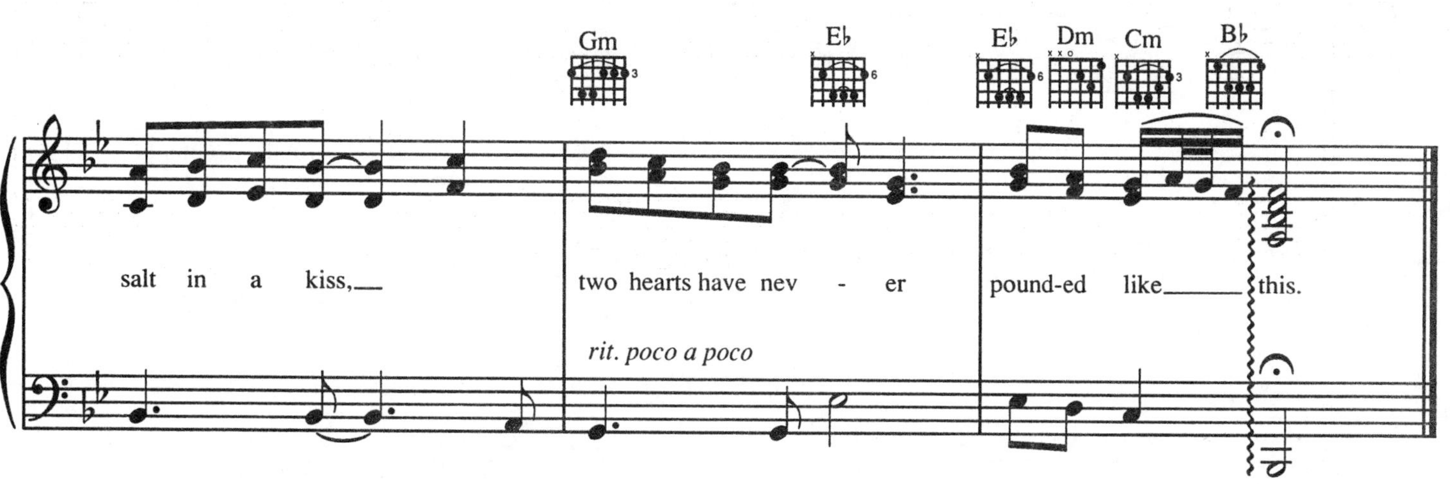
Gm
E♭
E♭
Dm
Cm
B♭
salt in a kiss,
two hearts have nev - er
pound-ed like this.
rit. poco a poco

Verse 2:
Steam on the window, Salt in a kiss:
Two hearts have never pounded like this.
Inspired by a vision
That they can't command,
Erasing the borders
With each brush of a hand.
(To Chorus:)

REFRIED DREAMS

Words and Music by
JIM FOSTER and MARK PETERSEN

C
D
G
And I kept on go - ing with -
So, full of your mem - 'ry but
out e - ven know - ing
feel - ing so emp - ty, I've
C
how much your love real - ly means.
run out of my self es - teem.
A
G
D7
Now, I'm messed up in Mex - i - co, liv - ing on re - fried
G
F
Chorus:
C
dreams.
I'm down here in Mex - i - co,

F/C
C
G
D
G
sick as a dog.
My head is pound - ing in this
bor - der - town fog.
C
G
Em
D
Down to my last dime and
com - ing a - part at the
seams,
C
D
G
D7
I'm
messed up in Mex - i - co,
liv - ing on re - fried
1.
G
D
G
dreams.

D
D.S. 𝄋
2.
G
2. This
dreams._
I'm
3.
G
C
G
dreams._
Oh,
I'm_
messed up in Mex - i - co,
D7
G
D
liv - ing on re - fried
dreams._
G
D
G

SAFE IN THE ARMS OF LOVE

Words and Music by
PAM ROSE, MARY ANN KENNEDY
and PAT BUNCH

Bm A D A(9)

so tired of liv - in'

D/G Bm D/G A(9)

sol - i - taire.

D D/G Bm A

Some - day I'm gon - na be safe in the arms of love.

1. D Bm A 2.3. D

Safe

Bm A G

in the arms of love.

cresc.

Chorus:
G
C
Em
C
f I want arms that know how to rock me, safe in the arms of love.
D
G
C
I wan - na fall and know that love has caught me
Em
D
G
Em
D
To Coda
safe in the arms of love, safe in the arms of love.
C
A
G
Bm
G
A

Verse 2:
Strip your heart and it starts to snow.
Love is a high-wire act, I know;
Someday I'll find a net below.
Someday I'm gonna be
Safe in the arms of love,
Safe in the arms of love.
(To Chorus:)

Verse 3:
I want a heart to be forever mine,
Want eyes to see me satisfied.
Gonna hang my heartache out to dry.
Someday I'm gonna be
Safe in the arms of love,
Safe in the arms of love.
(To Chorus:)

SHOULD'VE ASKED HER FASTER

Words and Music by
BOB DiPIERO, AL ANDERSON
and JOE KLEMIK

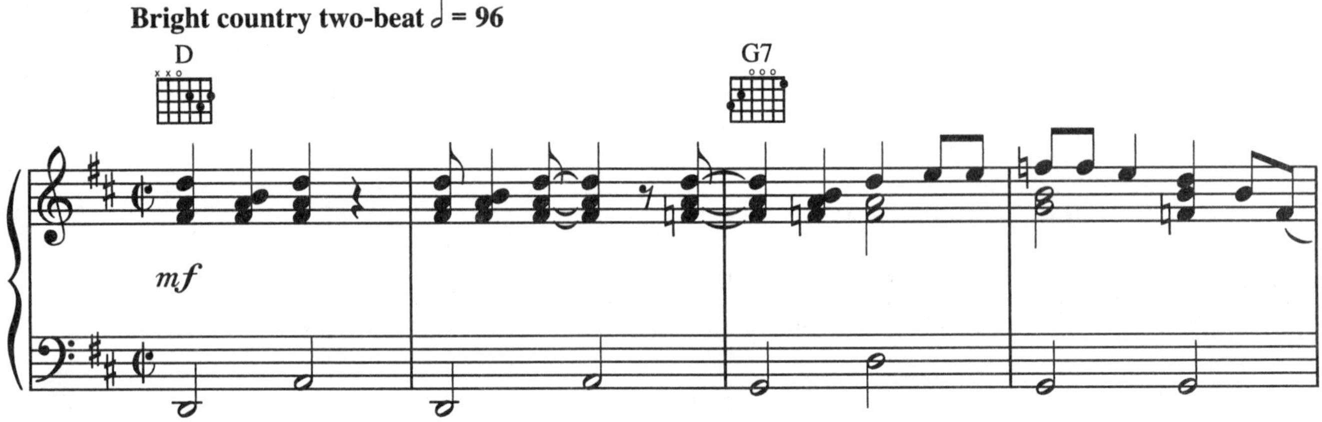

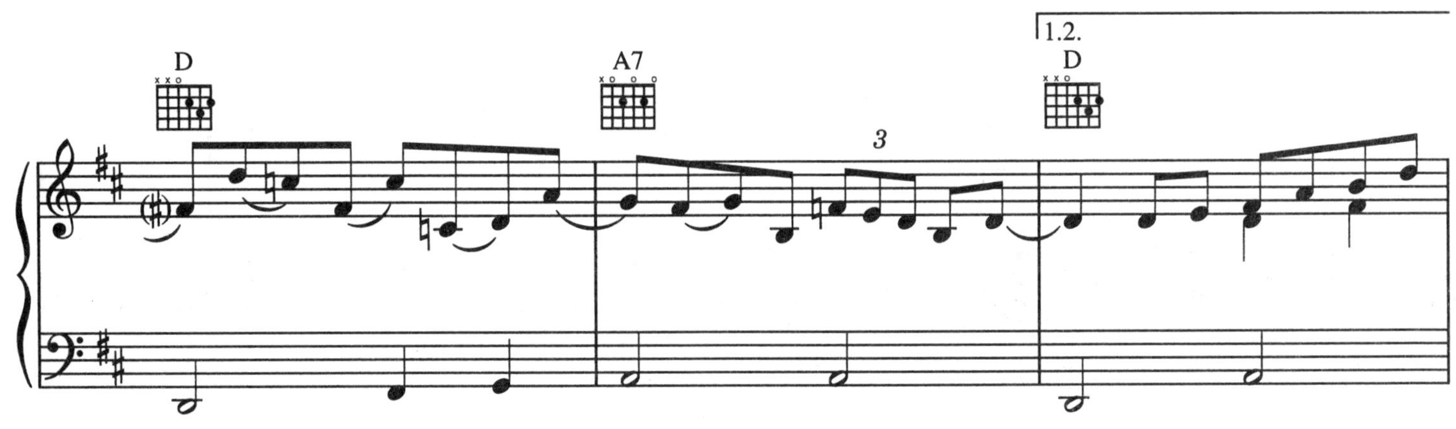

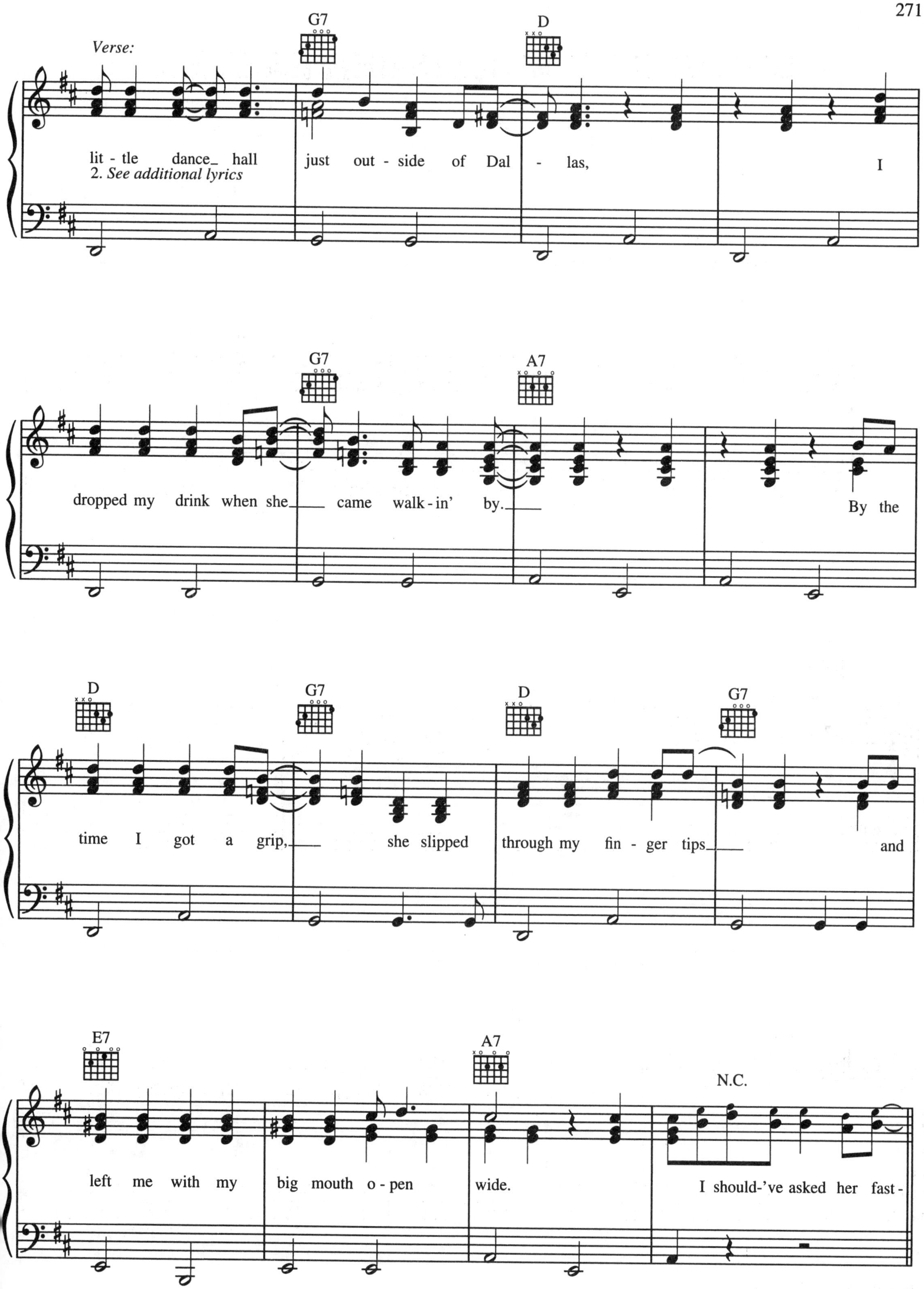

Verse:

G7 D

lit - tle dance_ hall just out - side of Dal - las, I

2. *See additional lyrics*

G7 A7

dropped my drink when she came walk - in' by. By the

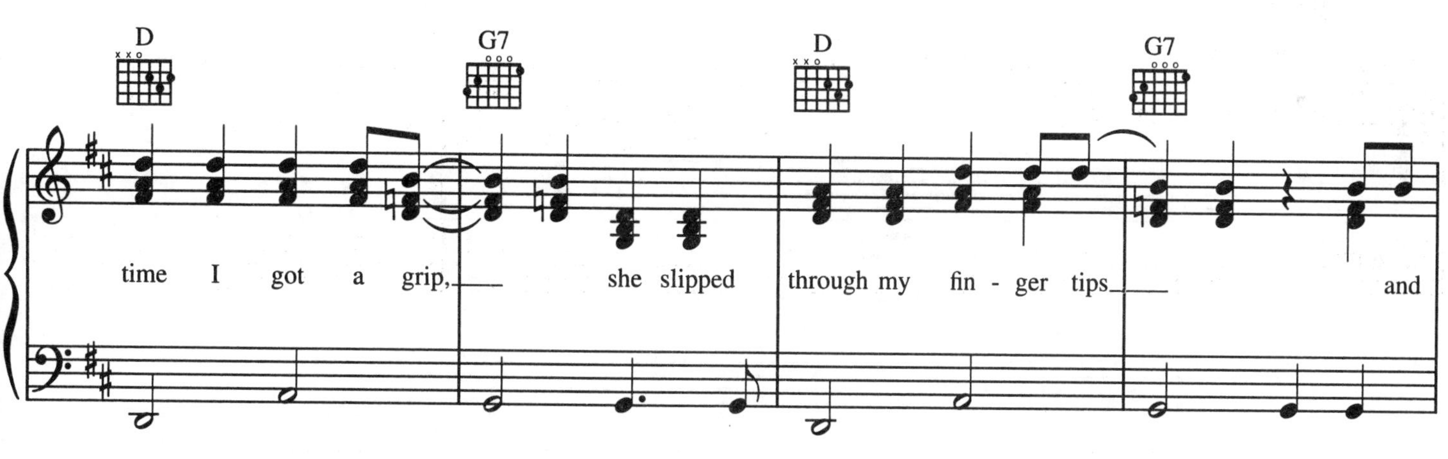

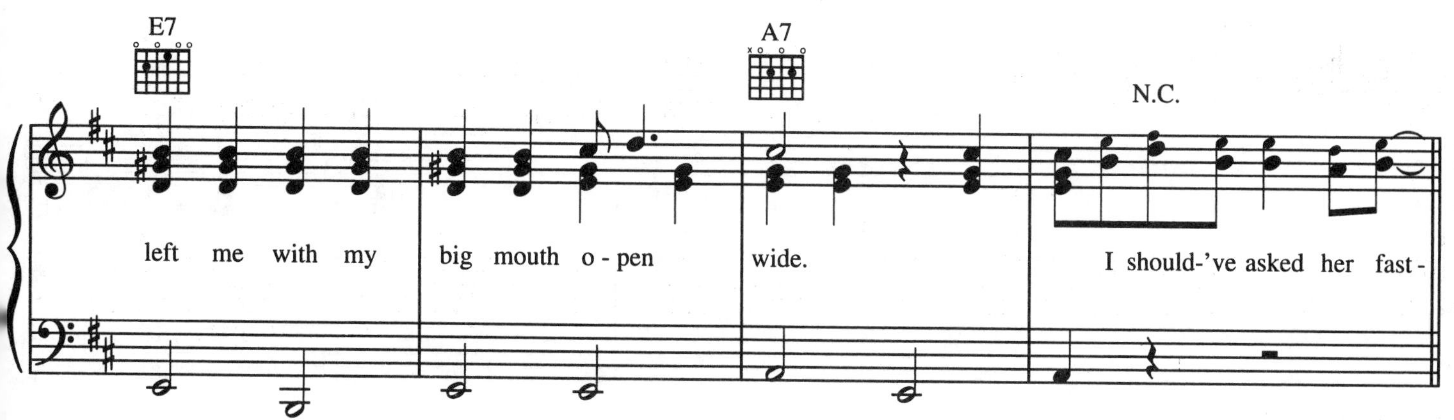

Chorus:
D
G
f
- er, but I wait-ed too long, in a red hot
A7
D
A7
min-ute like a flash she was gone. I did-n't get her num-
D
G
- ber, I nev-er got her name, a nat-u-ral dis-as-
1.
D.C.
A7
D
- ter, I should-'ve asked her fast - er.

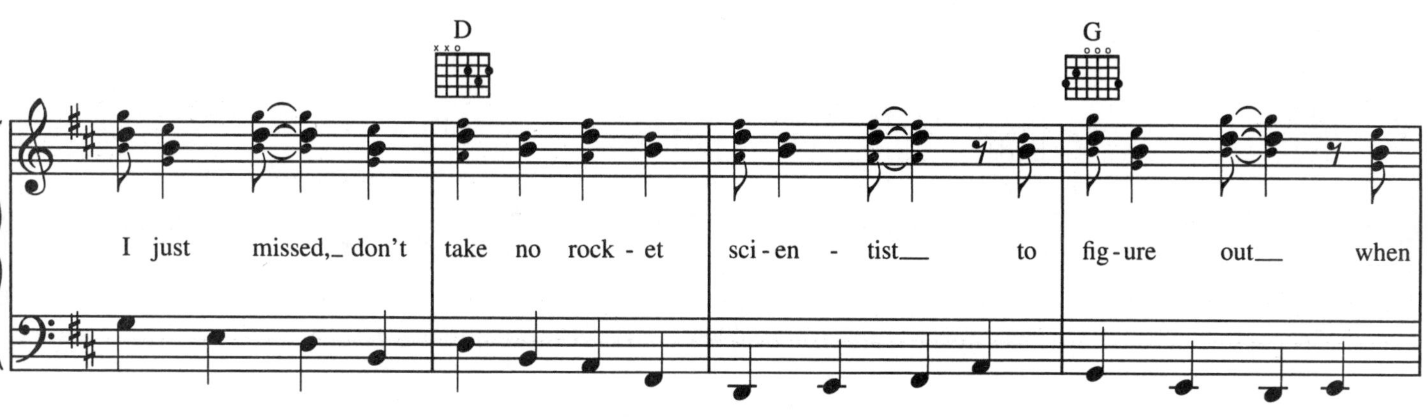

Verse 2:
She was talkin' to some cowboy in the corner,
My one last chance to ask her on the floor.
But just when I got the nerve,
I got what I deserve
As I watched him waltzin' her right out the door.
(To Chorus:)

SOMEONE ELSE'S STAR

Words and Music by
SKIP EWING and JIM WEATHERLY

G F♯m G A D Bm
A♭ Gm A♭ B♭ E♭ Cm
wish with all__ my__ might, for the love_ I'm__ dream-ing of and
Em A7 D A/D G/D
Fm B♭7 E♭ B♭/E♭ A♭/E♭
miss - ing in my____ life. 2.You'd
Verse:
D A/C♯ G D
E♭ B♭/D A♭ E♭
think that I___ could find___ a true love of my___ own. It
sit here in___ the dark___ and stare up at the___ sky, but
G A D Em A7sus A7
A♭ B♭ E♭ Fm B♭7sus B♭7
hap - pens all___ the time____ to peo-ple that I____ know. Their
I can't give_ my heart____ one good rea - son___ why.

D A/C♯ G F♯m
E♭ B♭/D A♭ Gm
wish-es all come true, so I've got to be-lieve
Ev-'ry-where I look, it's lov-ers that I see.
G A D Bm Em A7 D
A♭ B♭ E♭ Cm Fm B♭7 E♭
there's still some-one out there who is meant for on-ly me.
Seems like ev-'ry-one's in love with ev-'ry-one but me.
I
cresc.
mf
Chorus:
A D G A D
B♭ E♭ A♭ B♭ E♭
guess I must be wish-in' on some-one else-'s star. It
A D G A7sus A7
B♭ E♭ A♭ B♭7sus B♭7
seems like some-one else keeps get-tin' what I'm wish-in' for. Why

A
D
G
A
D
B♭
E♭
A♭
B♭
E♭
can't I be___ as luck - y as___ those
oth - er peo - ple are?___ I
Em7
D/F♯
G
G/A
Fm7
E♭/G
A♭
A♭/B♭
guess I must_ be_____ wish - in'
on some - one else - 's star.__
1.
D
A/C♯
G
D/A
A
D
A/C♯
E♭
B♭/D
A♭
E♭/B♭
B♭
E♭
B♭/D
dim.
2.
G
D/A
A7
D
A♭
E♭/B♭
B♭7
E♭
3. I
Why

A D G A D
B♭ E♭ A♭ B♭ E♭
can't I be as luck - y as those oth - er peo - ple are? Oh, I
Em7 D/F♯ G G/A
Fm7 E♭/G A♭ A♭/B♭
guess I must be wish - in' on some - one else - 's star.
D A/C♯ G D/A A
E♭ B♭/D A♭ E♭/B♭ B♭
dim.
D A/C♯ G D/A A7 D(9)
E♭ B♭/D A♭ E♭/B♭ B♭7 E♭(9)
mp
rit. e dim.
p

SOMETIMES SHE FORGETS

tells you she don't need a man, she's had all the com - fort she can stand, you
4. (Instrumental solo ad lib....
C
G
best be-lieve ev - ery word she says.
But
D
D7
G
don't give up 'cause some-times she for - gets.
...end solo)
Whoa, and
Bridge:
C
G
some-times she for - gets that not too long a - go she swore she
1.
2. D.S. 𝄋 al Coda
A
D
D7
D7
was-n't gon - na let her heart be bro-ken an - y - more. 3. So
more. 5. So

Verse 3:
So now she keeps it locked away,
And it grows colder every day,
And it won't warm to any man's caress.
That's what she says, but sometimes she forgets.

TEQUILA TALKIN'

Words and Music by
CHRIS WATERS and
BILL LaBOUNTY

E
A
D
to say I've been los - in' it since you left.
A
F♯m
E
D
Esus
E
Yeah, I may have said the words but they came from some - where else.
Chorus:
A
D
E
A
f
It was just the te - qui - la talk - in' when I told you I'm still
D
E
A
E/G♯
F♯m
not ov - er you.
I get a lit - tle sen -

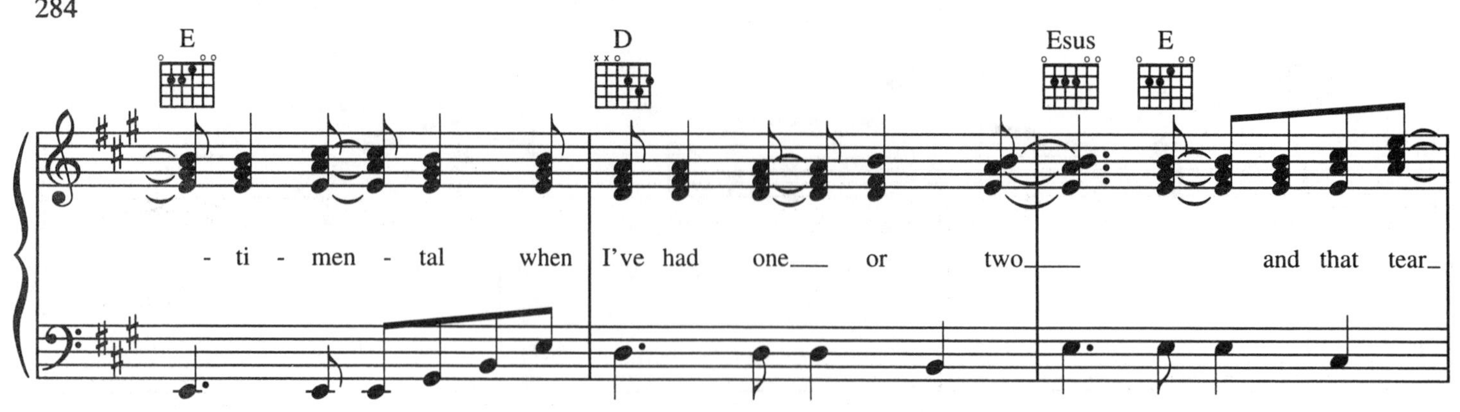
E
D
Esus
E
-ti - men - tal when I've had one__ or two__ and that tear__

D
E
A
__ in my eye__ was the salt__ and the lime__ not the mem - o - ry of__ you walk -

D
A
D
A
- in'. If I said I'm still in love with you,__ it was just__

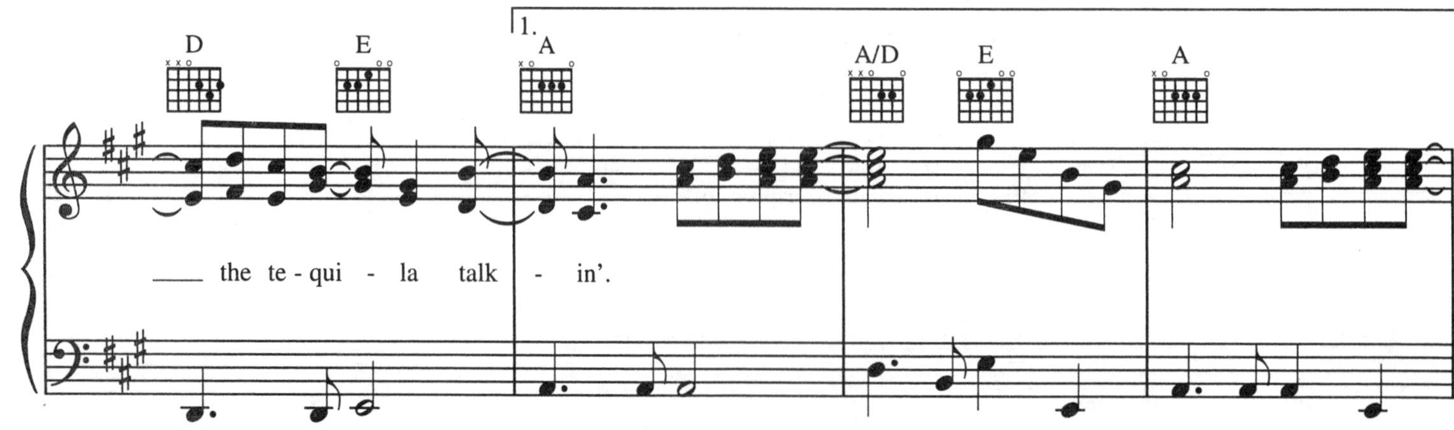
D
E
1.
A
A/D
E
A
__ the te - qui - la talk - in'.

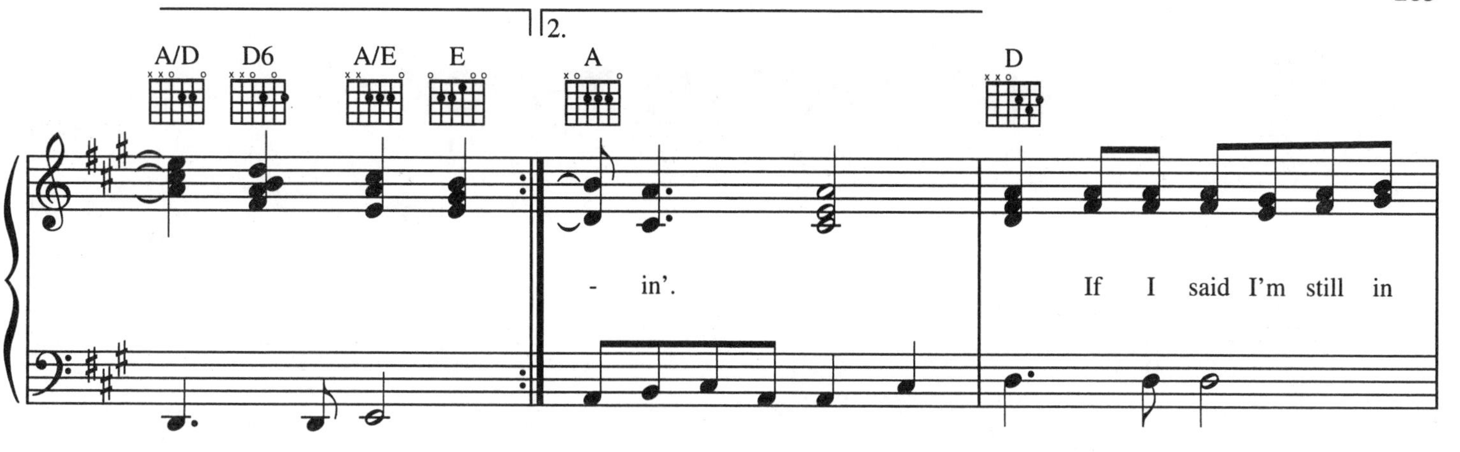

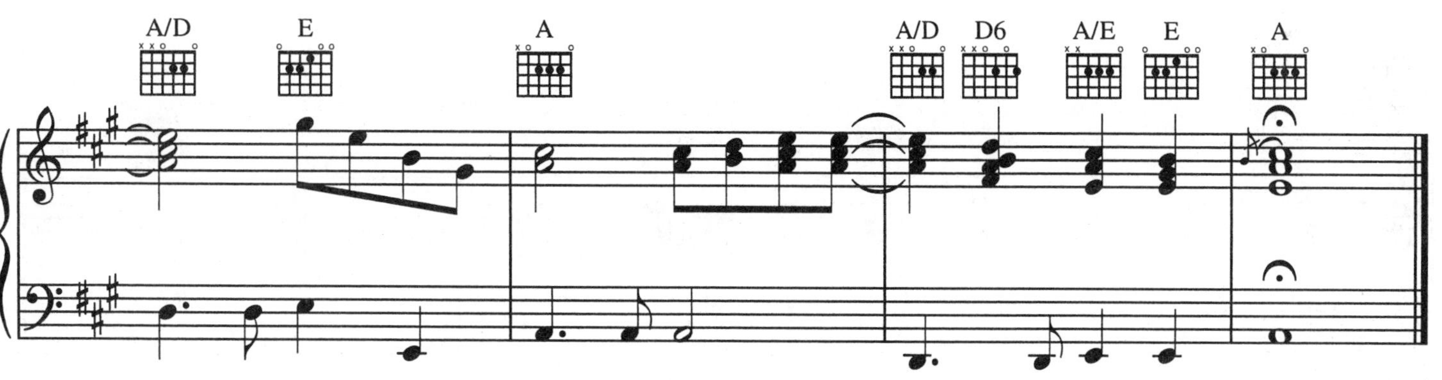

Verse 2:
I don't know what they put in Cuervo
That got me to say those things.
Usually I wouldn't care so much or make such a scene.
But seein' you there in that dress you were wearin'
Just drove me right out of my head,
So don't hold me responsible for anything I might have said.
(To Chorus:)

THAT AIN'T MY TRUCK

Words and Music by
TOM SHAPIRO, CHRIS WATERS
and RHETT AKINS

C
D
C(9)
So I wait - ed by the phone but she
D
Em
D
C
nev - er called me up, had to know what was go - in' on, so
C
D
C
D
I drove by her house and sure e - nough that ain't my truck
cresc.
Chorus:
G
C(9)
in her drive, and this ain't my day to-night.
(truck.) (Instrumental solo ad lib. 3rd time . . .
f

D
G/B
C
D
Looks like she's in love and I'm out of luck.
That ain't my sha-
. . . end solo)
G
Em
C
G/B
C
-dow on her wall,
Lord this don't look good at all,
that's my girl,
1.
D
D.C.
2.
D
D.S. 𝄋
my whole world,
but that ain't my
but that ain't my
3.
D
G
C
G/B
C
but that ain't my truck.
That's my girl,

Verse 2:
I pulled over by the curb,
I've been sittin' here all night
Wonderin' what it was I did so wrong
That he did so right.
I've thought of breaking down the door
But there's nothin' left to say;
That Chevy four by four
Says it all sittin' in my place.
(To Chorus:)

THAT'S JUST ABOUT RIGHT

Words and Music by
JEFFREY ALLEN BLACK

Am
B♭
F
Hard lines___ and the sha - dows come eas - y, I see it all___ just as
mf
C
Am
B♭
clear as a bell. I just can't seem to set my ea - sel to please_ me,

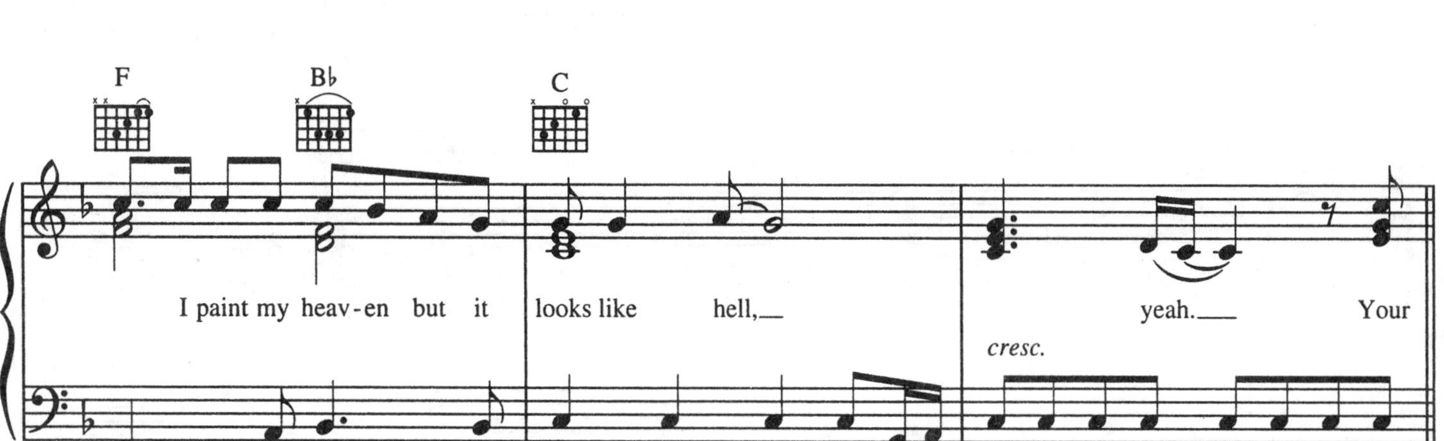
F
B♭
C
I paint my heav - en but it looks like hell,__ yeah.___ Your
cresc.

Chorus:
B♭
C
F
3
blue might be grey, your less might be more.______ Your
f

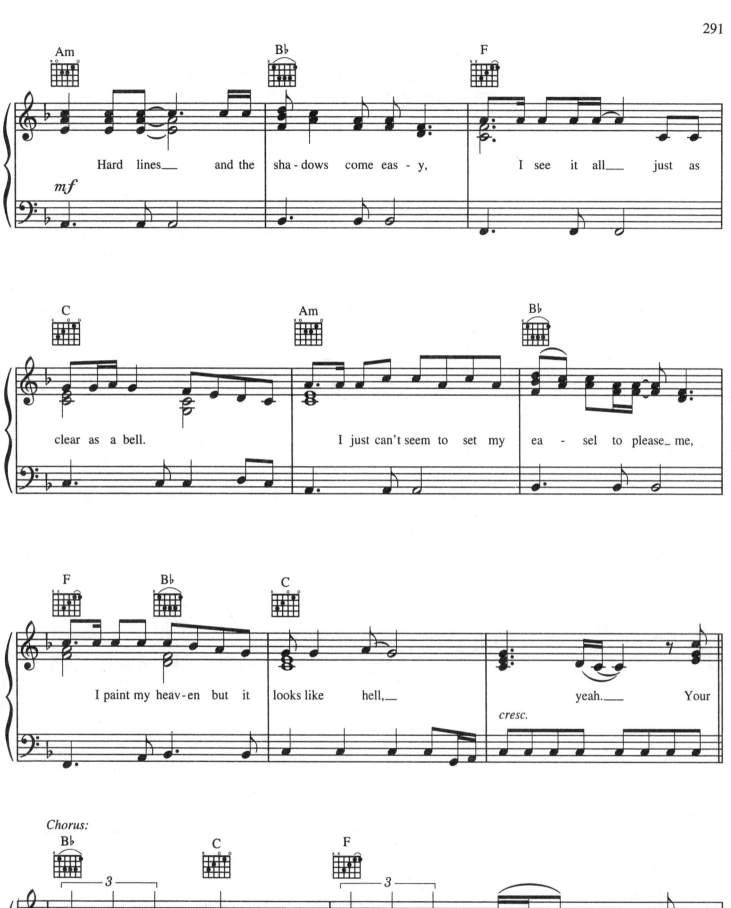

B♭
C
F
win - dow to the world might be your own front door. Your
B♭
C
F
B♭
shin - i - est day might come in the mid - dle of the night,
C
Dm
that's just a - bout right.
mf
1.
2.
D.S. 𝄋 al Coda
B
F
B♭
F
C
Dm
B♭
F
2. He says

Coda
Am
Bb
mf
You can go through life with the greatest intentions, but you

F
Bb
C
do what you do what you just got-ta do,
cresc.
yeah. Your

Chorus:
Bb
C
F
Bb
C
f
blue might be grey, your less might be more. Your win-dow to the world might be your own

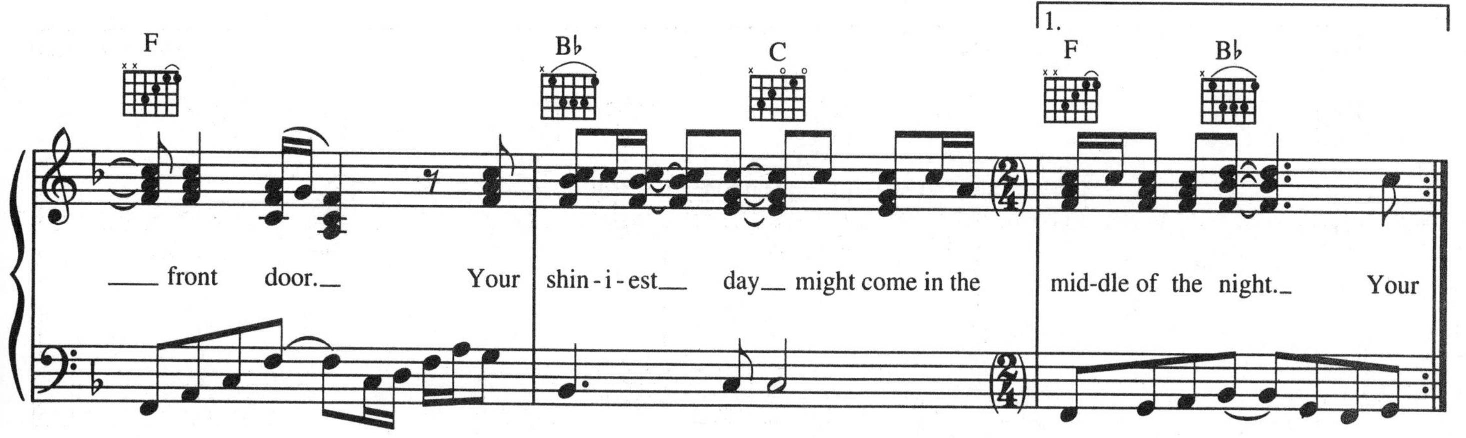
F
Bb
C
1.
F
Bb
front door. Your shin-i-est day might come in the mid-dle of the night. Your

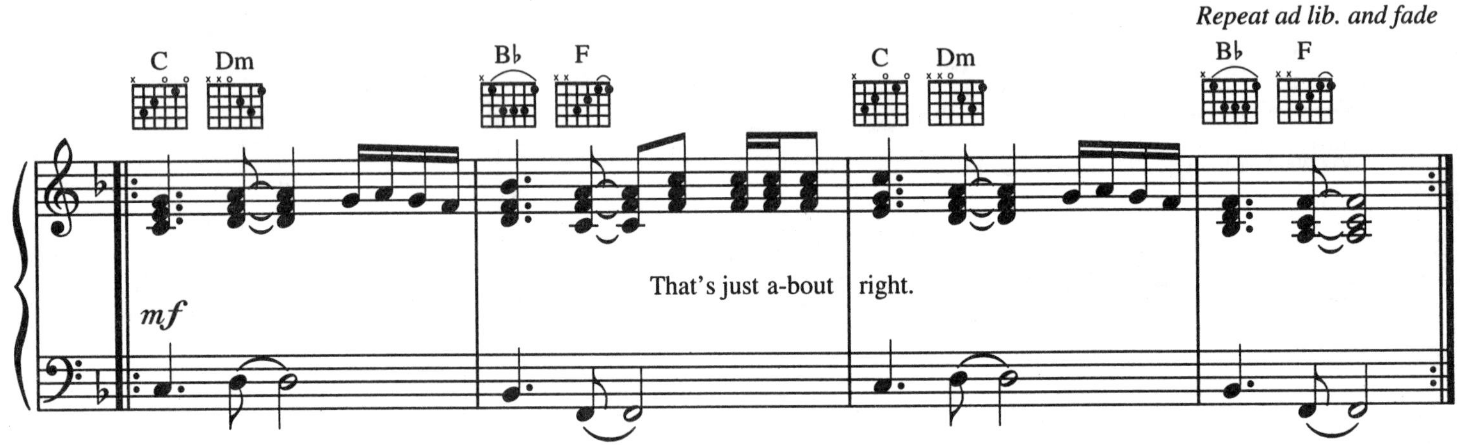

Verse 2:
He says that I ain't comin' down 'til my picture is perfect.
And all the wonders have gone from my eye.
Down through my hands and on to the canvas.
Still like my vision but still a surprise.
Real life, he says is the hardest impression,
It's always movin' so I let it come through.
That my friend I say is the glory of true independence,
Just to do what you do, what you do, what you do.
(To Chorus:)

Verse 3:
My old friend came down from the mountain;
Without even lookin', he found a little truth.
(To Coda)

THE WOMAN IN ME (NEEDS THE MAN IN YOU)

Words and Music by
SHANIA TWAIN and ROBERT JOHN "MUTT" LANGE

The Woman in Me (Needs the Man in You) - 3 - 1

Verse 2 & 3:
Eb(9)
Gm7
F
Dm7
be
3. See additional lyrics
the rock that you see,
when the nights get too long and I just can't go on.
Bb
Cm
Bb/D
The wom - an in
Chorus:
Eb
Ebsus
Eb/G
Dm/A
me needs you to be the man in my
Gm
arms to hold ten - der - ly.
'Cause I'm a wom - an in
love, and it's you I run to.
Yeah, the wom-an in me
Cm7

Verse 3:
When the world wants too much,
And it feels cold and out of touch.
It's a beautiful place
When you kiss my face.
(To Chorus:)

THEY'RE PLAYIN' OUR SONG

Words and Music by
BOB DIPIERO, JOHN JARRARD
and MARK D. SANDERS

Chorus:
G
C
play-in' our song on the ra-di-o. O-kay, Mis-ter D. J., at-ta
D
G
C
way to go. A mil-lion watts of love pow-er com-in' on strong. Dance
G
1.
D
G
G
with me dar-lin', they're play-in' our song.
C
G
D
G
2. Oh the

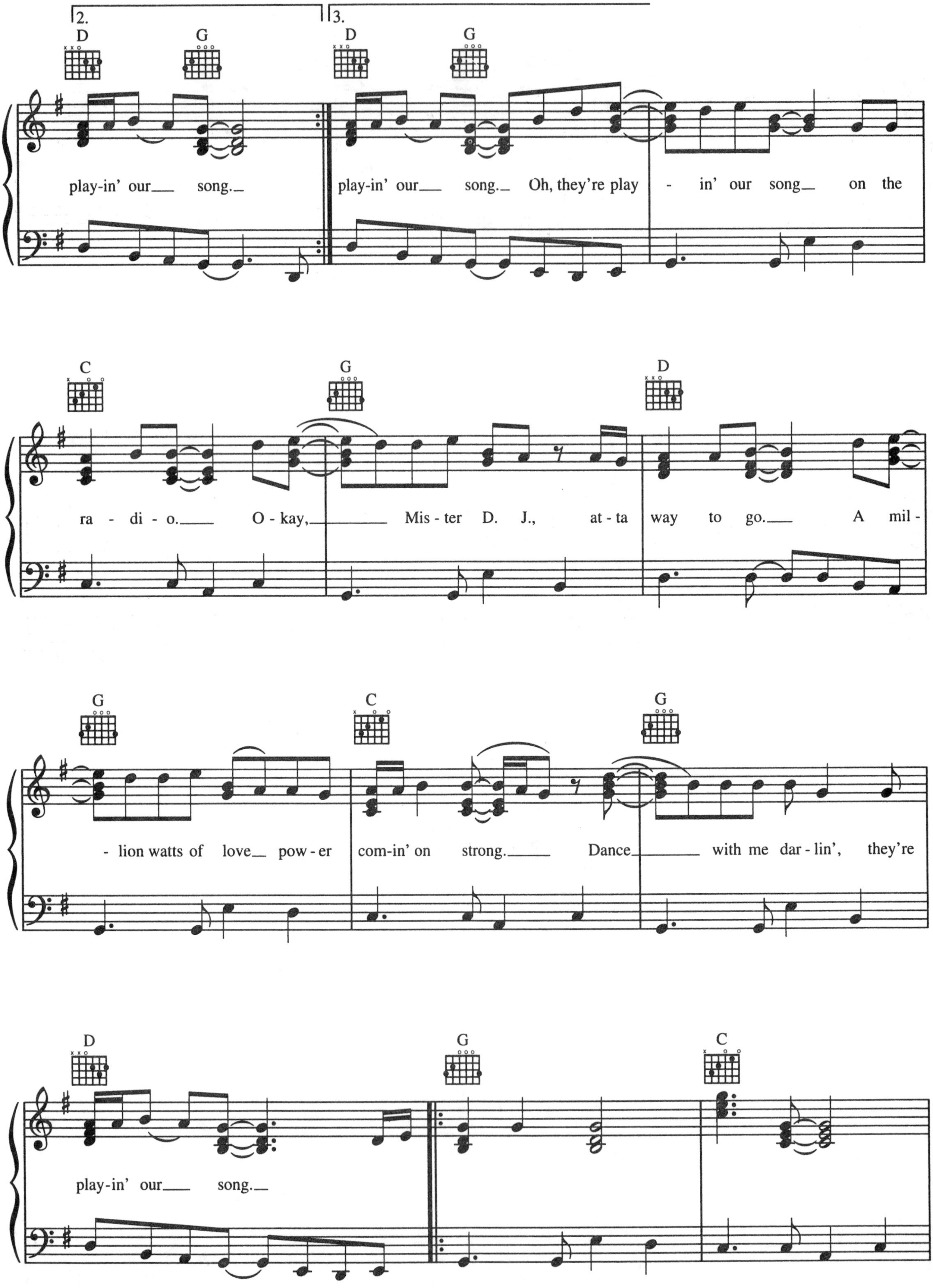

2. 3.

D G D G

play-in' our song. play-in' our song. Oh, they're play - in' our song on the

C G D

ra - di - o. O - kay, Mis - ter D. J., at - ta way to go. A mil -

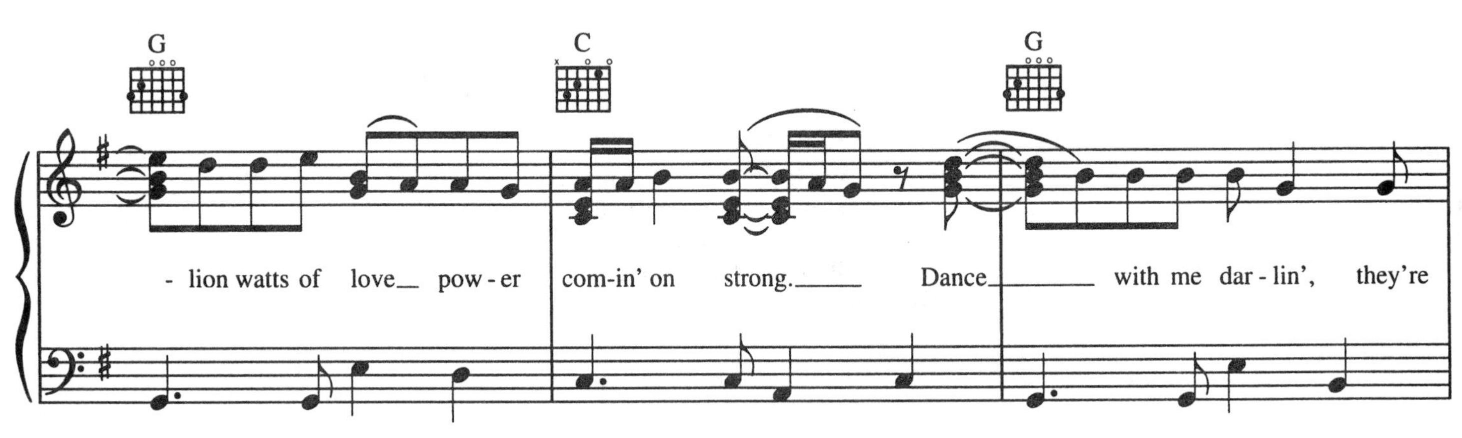

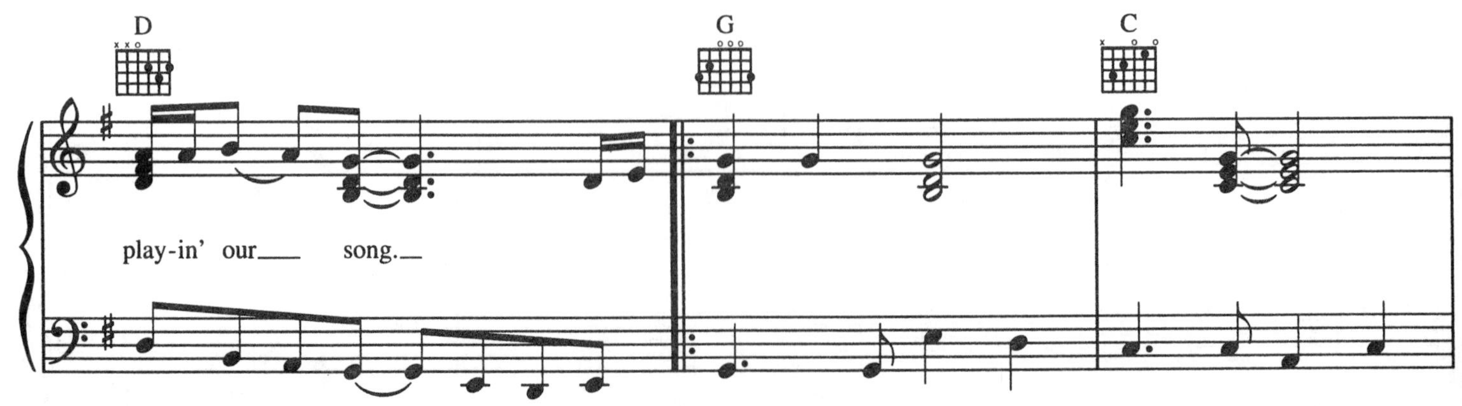

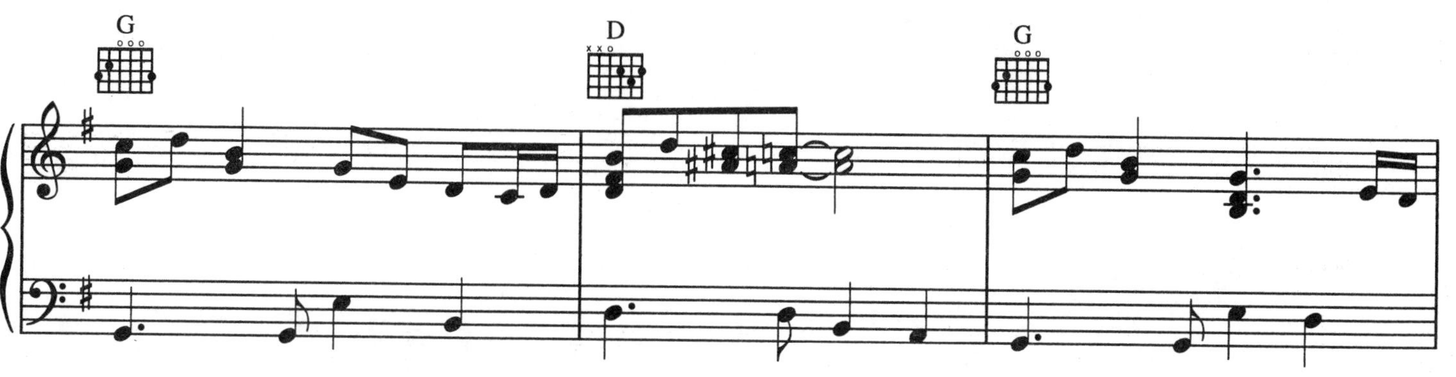

Repeat ad lib. and fade

Verse 2:
Oh, the house needs cleanin', the grass needs mowin',
We both got places that we need to be goin'.
Tomorrow's a big day, better get ready,
But tonight it's just you and me rockin' steady.
(To Chorus:)

THINKIN' ABOUT YOU

Words and Music by
TOM SHAPIRO and BOB REGAN

E
F♯
smile that way,
the sound of your voice
say - in' my name. I've been
B
E
C♯m7
F♯
B/D♯
E
think-in' a - bout you,
just keep
think-in' a - bout you.
Bridge:
G♯m7
F♯
B
G♯m
C♯m7
This sin - gle - mind - ed fas - ci - na - tion I've got,
F♯
B
F♯
B
G♯m
do you call it love?
If you don't, then what?
All I know is I don't know

C♯7
E
F♯
what you've done, and this train of thought ain't a-bout to jump the track that it's on.

Verses 3 & 4:
B
E
3. In the back of my mind, there's a se - cret place.
4. See additional lyrics
But the whole world knows by the

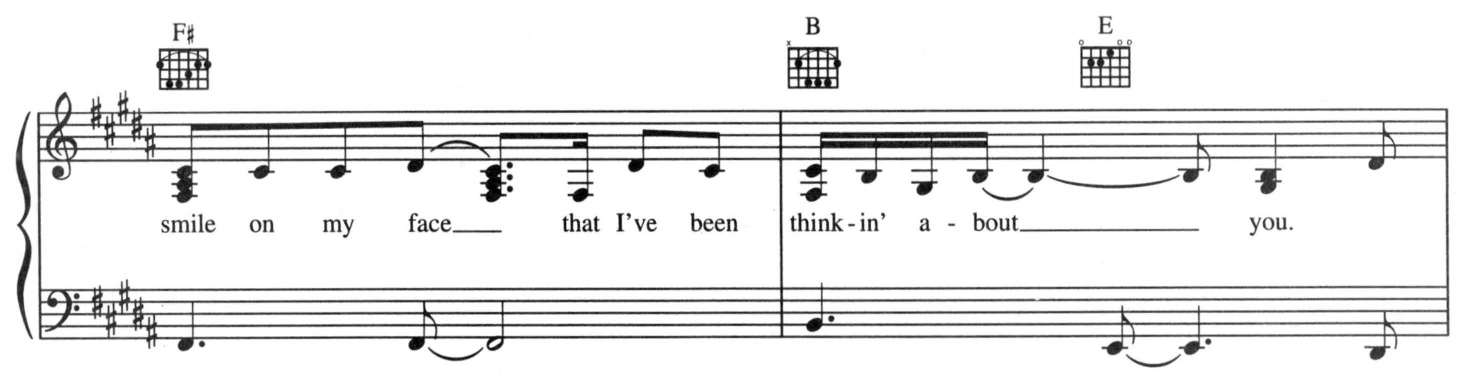
F♯
B
E
smile on my face that I've been think-in' a - bout you.

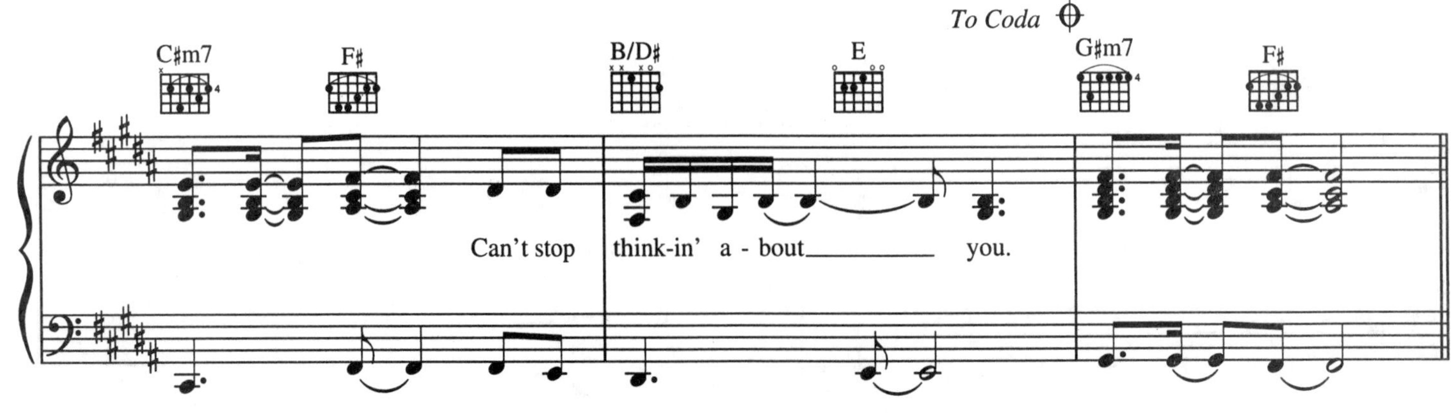
To Coda
C♯m7
F♯
B/D♯
E
G♯m7
F♯
Can't stop think-in' a - bout you.

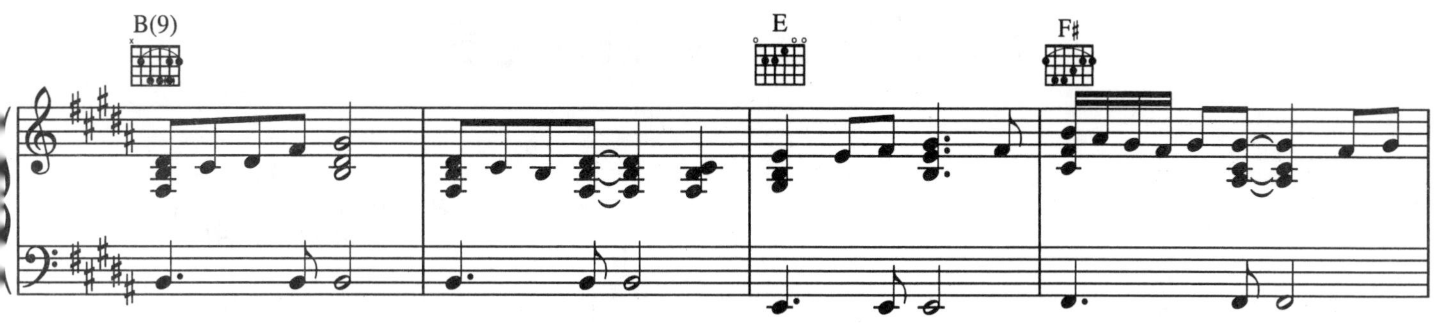

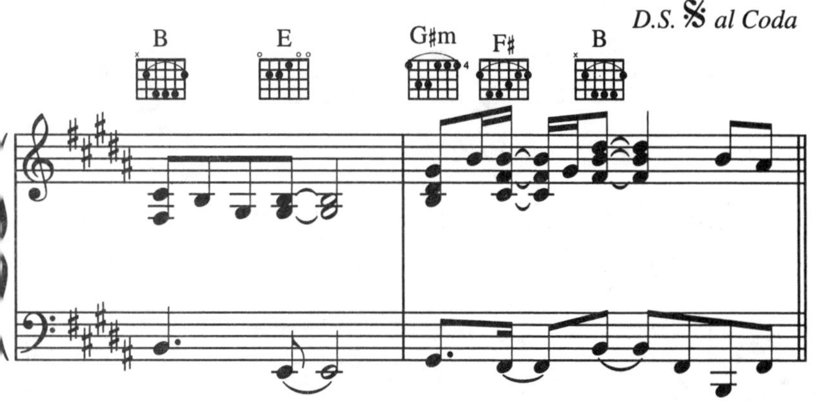

Verse 4:
I know it's crazy, callin' you this late,
When the only thing I wanted to say is that
I've been thinkin' about you,
Oh, just keep thinkin' about you.

SOUTHERN GRACE

Written by
PORTER HOWELL, BRADY SEALS
and STEWART HARRIS

Am7
D
me no oth - er love will ev - er do.
Her
cresc.
Chorus:
Em7
C(9)
G
voice is like the whis - per of a warm wind through the pines.
Her
f
Em7
C(9)
D
smile can reach the soul of an - y man.
Her
Em7
C(9)
G
D/F♯
heart is strong, her love is true, and her touch is soft as lace. There ain't noth -
dim.

C(9)
G/B
Am7
D
- in' like a wom - an
with South-ern
mf
dim.
1. C(9)
D
Grace.
mp
2. C(9)
G
Bridge:
C(9)
Grace.
cresc.
She's got me
fall - in' in her eyes a -
f
D
Am7
C(9)
D
gain to - night,
lost in lov-in' arms as the
world goes by.
C(9)
D
C(9)
D
(Instr. solo ad lib....
...end solo)
Her

Chorus:
Em7
C(9)
G
voice is like the whis - per of a warm wind through the pines. Her
Em7
C(9)
D
smile can reach the soul of an - y man. Her
Em7
C(9)
G
D/F♯
Em7
heart is strong, her love is true, and her touch is soft as lace. There ain't noth -
dim.
C(9)
G/B
Am7
G/B
C(9)
G/B
- in' like a wom - an, there ain't noth - in' like a wom - an,
p

Verse 2:
You should see the way she walks into a room;
It's almost like her feet don't touch the floor.
But when the chips are down, her feet are firmly on the ground.
I could never ask for any more.
(To Chorus:)

SUMMER'S COMIN'

Words and Music by
CLINT BLACK and HAYDEN NICHOLAS

E
first one stand - in' in line for my day in the sun, I've been
A
work - in' till the sun don't shine.
1. I'm tak - in'
Verse:
E
D
off my hat and leave it to the boys, get that old work mon - key down
2. See additional lyric
A
E
off my back. All I want's a lit - tle peace and noise, hit the

G
D
A
cruise con - trol, get me back on track, let my old Ford treat me like a
E
Chorus:
A
Cad - il - lac. Noth - in' on Earth that - 'll
(2nd time Inst. solo ad lib. . . .
get me hum-min' like a heat wave com - in'; I'll come run - nin', with her
D
mak - in' that tan in the broad day - light, and ev - er - y night is a Sat -

A
- ur - day night. And ev - ery - thing's_ right with the sum - mer com - in'; I'm the
E
first one stand - in' in___ line_______ for my day in the sun,__ I've been
A
1.
N.C.
work - in' till the sun don't shine.
2.
D.S. 𝄋
3.
E
2. When the
... end solo)
For my day in the sun,__ I've been

Verse 2:
When the day gets cookin', gonna grab my toys,
And it really doesn't matter which wave we're on.
Get to turnin' up them good old boys,
Crankin' into the night; by the break of dawn,
All the towns are red and I still see blond.
(To Chorus:)

THIS WOMAN AND THIS MAN

Words and Music by
JEFF PENNIG and
MICHAEL LUNN

Moderately slow ♩ = 72
A
F♯m7
E
D
mf
A
F♯m7
E
D(9)
Verses 1 & 2:
A
F♯m7
1. Been
try-in' so hard_ just to talk to you,_
2. See additional lyrics
E
D
A
F♯m7
E
D
have-n't heard_ half of what you want me___ to.____
A
F♯m7
E
D
A
F♯m7
Hurt so bad_ o-ver where we've been,_
don't know how_ not to go back there a - gain._

E
D
A
D
E
I know what I want to say. Can I
G
D/F♯
D
get it through to you, now, in some oth-er way? Like . . . there was this
Chorus:
A
E
F♯m7
wom-an, and there was this man. And there was this mo-ment they had a chance to hold
E
D
A
on to what they had. How could they be so in love, and still nev-er
E
F♯m7
E
D
see. Now noth-in' could be sad-der than this wom-an, this wom-an and this

1.
A
F♯m7
E
D(9)
2.
A
man.
2. A
man.
Bridge:
Dsus
D
Dsus
D
For all we've got__ to lose,
there's so much to gain._
Csus
C
G
If we come this far__ and leave it be - hind,__
there's on-ly you and me__ to blame._
D
Em7
Bm7/F♯
Em7
D
E
There was this

A E

wom - an, and there was this man. And there was this
(man.) *Instrumental . . .*

F♯m7 E D

mo-ment they had a chance to hold on to what they had. How could they be

A E

so in love. and still nev - er see. Yeah,

F♯m7 E D *Repeat and fade*

we can get it back a - gain, this wom - an, this wom - an and this

Verse 2:
A stranger's eyes in a lover's face,
See no signs of a better time and place.
Have we lost the key to an open door?
I feel the need to reach out to you even more.
It's a circle goin' 'round.
If we don't get us out from under,
It's gonna take us down.
(To Chorus:)

TAKE ME AS I AM

Words and Music by
BOB DIPIERO and KAREN STALEY

Gm7
B♭(2)
C7
not just prom - is - es and emp - ty fan - ta - sies. I don't
...end solo)
Chorus:
F
B♭
F/B♭
Dm7
C
need a bed of ros - es, 'cause
F
B♭
Dm
C
ros - es with - er a - way. All I
F
B♭
Dm7
C
real - ly need is hon - es - ty
B♭(2)
from some-one with a strong heart, a gen - tle hand,

Verse 2:
Baby, I need for you to know
Just exactly how I feel.
Fiery passions come and go.
I'd trade a million pretty words
For one touch that is real.
(To Chorus:)

TILL YOU LOVE ME

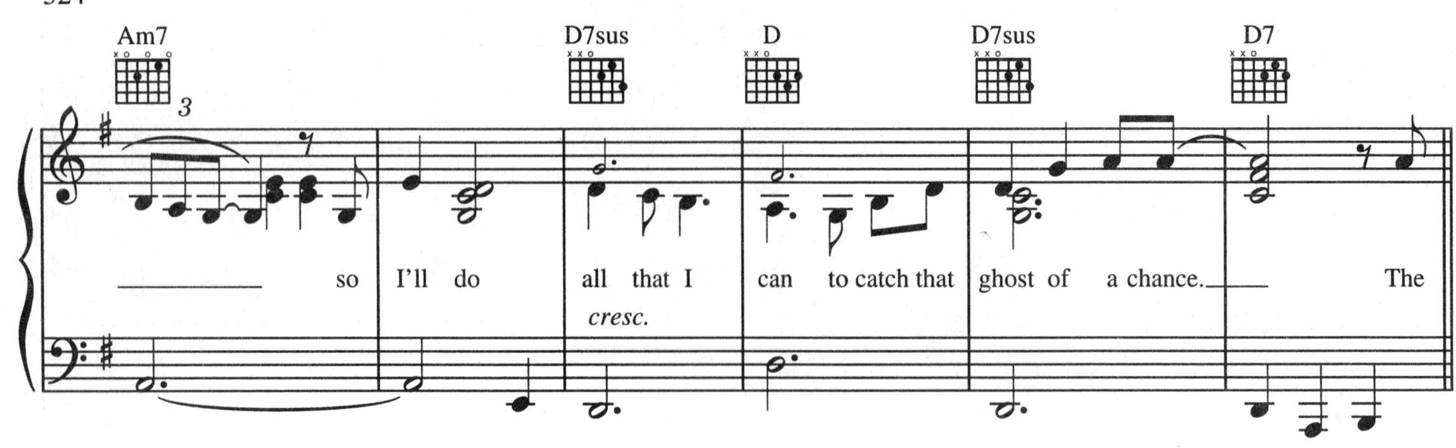
Am7
D7sus
D
D7sus
D7
3
so I'll do all that I can to catch that ghost of a chance. The
cresc.

Chorus:
C
G
3
3
sun - light, the moon-light are be - yond my con-trol. And there are stars in the heav -
f

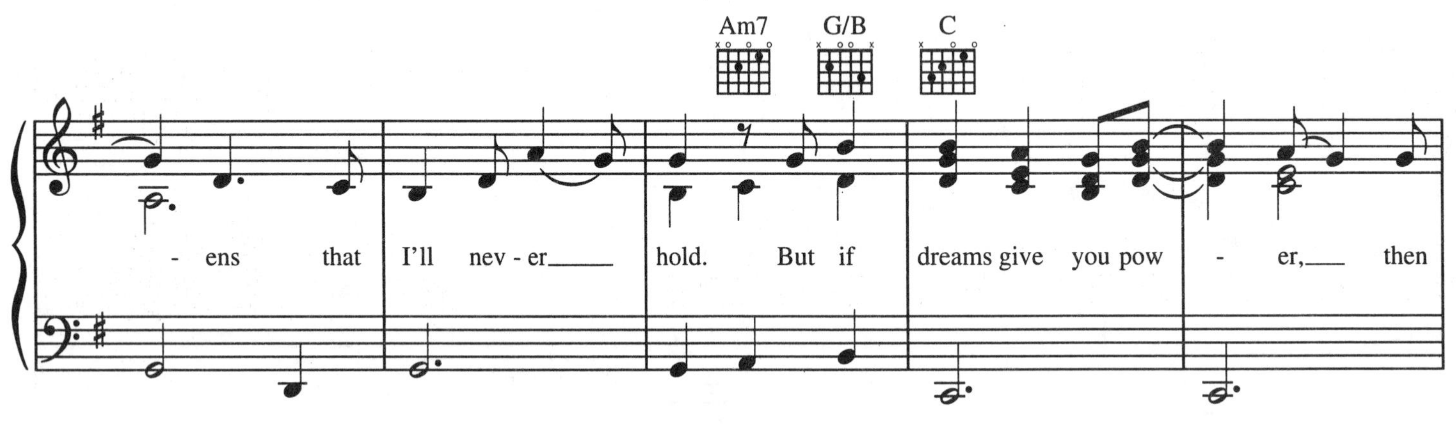
Am7
G/B
C
- ens that I'll nev - er hold. But if dreams give you pow - er, then

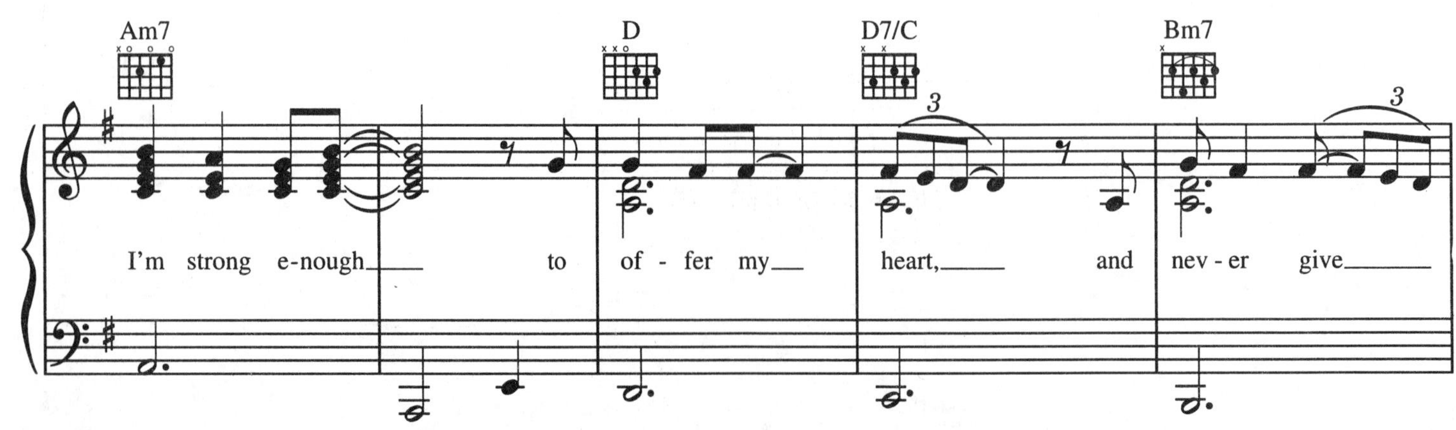
Am7
D
D7/C
Bm7
3
3
I'm strong e-nough to of - fer my heart, and nev - er give

Verse 2:
I looked in your eyes, so bright and so blue.
And that's when I knew that you could be mine.
If good things come to those who wait,
Well, I guess I can wait if that's what I have to do.
Oh, it's worth it for you.
(To Chorus:)

TRYIN' TO GET TO NEW ORLEANS

Words and Music by
STEVE RIPLEY, WALT RICHMOND,
and TIM DUBOIS

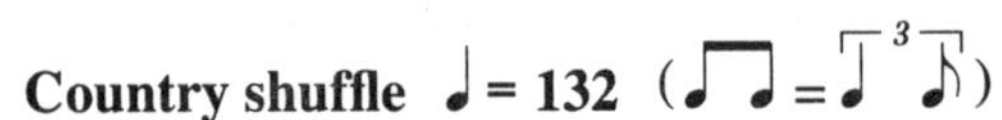

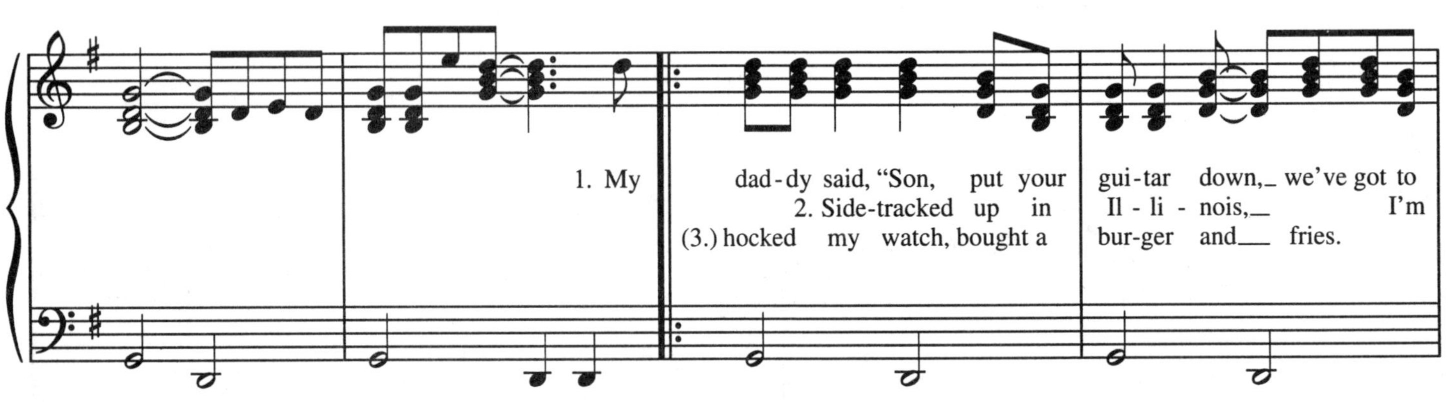

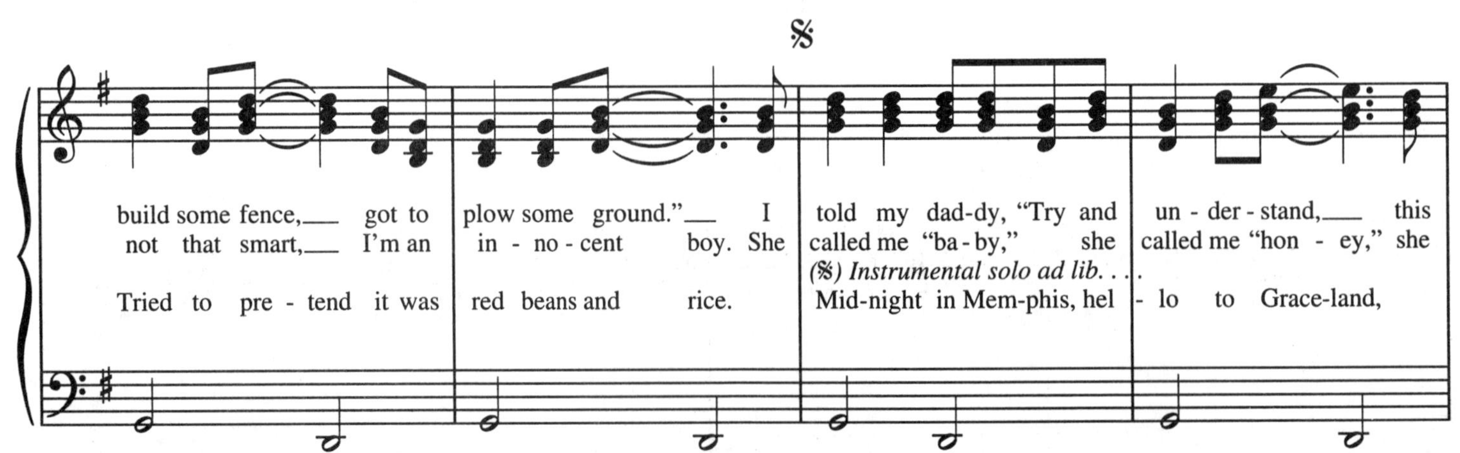

D7
John Deere trac-tor don't fit my plan." And I hit the road, chas - in' down a dream...
called me a cab and took a - way my mon - ey. On the road a - gain, some - where south of Mo -
next stop, Lou - i - si - an - a. And I'm on the road, chas - in' down a dream.
G
D7
line.
And I need a lit - tle help, see I'm try'n to get to New Or - leans.
And I need a lit - tle help, see I'm try'n to get to New Or - leans.
And I need a lit - tle help, see I'm try'n to get to New Or - leans.
G
To Coda
1.
2.3.
Bridge:
C
3
Don't know why
got - ta go,
F
if I don't try,
I'll nev - er know
C
a - bout e - touf -

G
fe and Ca - jun queens.
You know I
need a lit - tle help, you see I'm

1.
D.S. 𝄋
2.
D.S.S. 𝄋𝄋 al Coda
try'n to get to New Or - leans.
3. I

Coda
D7
G
Yeah, I
need a lit - tle help, you see I'm
try'n to get to New Or - leans.

D7
G
Well, I'm just an
old poor boy,
chas - in' down a dream.
And I

D7
G
need a lit - tle help, you see I'm try'n to get to New Or - leans.
D7
G
1.
2.
D7
And I
need a lit - tle help, you see I'm
G
1.
2.
try'n to get to New Or - leans.
And I

UNTANGLIN' MY MIND

Words and Music by
CLINT BLACK and MERLE HAGGARD

Slowly ♩ = 69
G
C
G
D
Bm
Em7
Asus
A
mp
(with pedal)
D
A7
D
A
Verse:
D
A
1. I
guess you're glad to see I'm fin - 'lly
D
Bm
F♯m7
leav - in'.
I know
things for you will change now for the
Em7
A7sus
A7
G
good.
But it's
all that I can do to pack my

D
E
suit - case
and walk a - way from you the way I
A
Em7
A7
D
A
should.
And
I can't seem to find the voice of rea -
D
Bm
F♯m7
- son,
ev - 'ry -
thing seems up - side down and right - side
Em7
A7sus
A7
G
wrong.
While
part of me is here and won't like leav-

D
A
- in',
the rest of me, the best of me is
Chorus:
D
Em7
D/F♯
G
C
G
gone. And I'm
cresc.
sure no one will won - der where I've gone
mf
D
G
F2
C
to, but if
an-y-one should ask from time to time,
G
C
G
D
tell 'em that you fin - 'lly drove me cra - zy and I'm

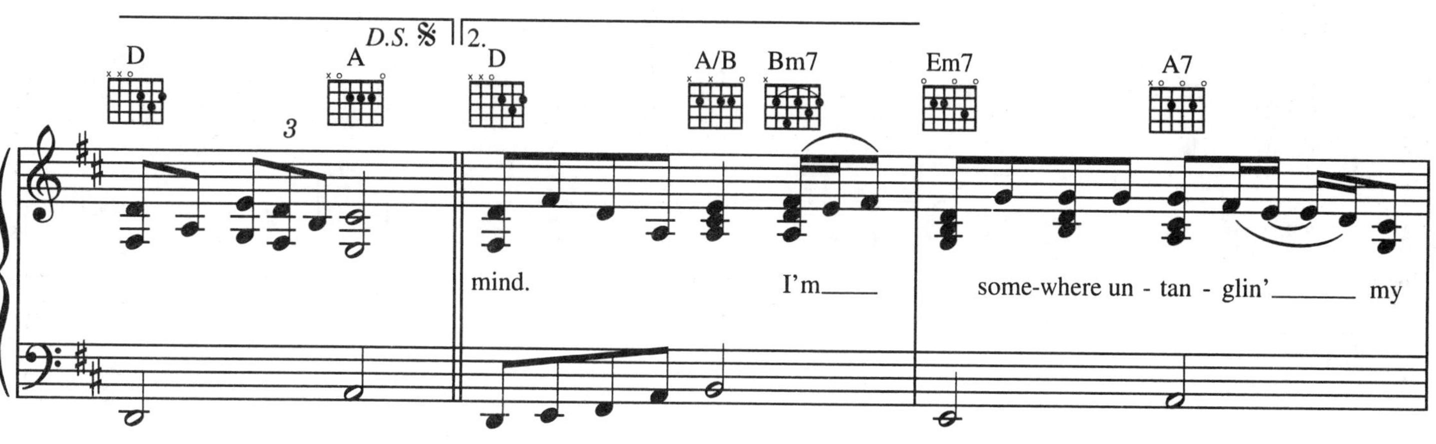

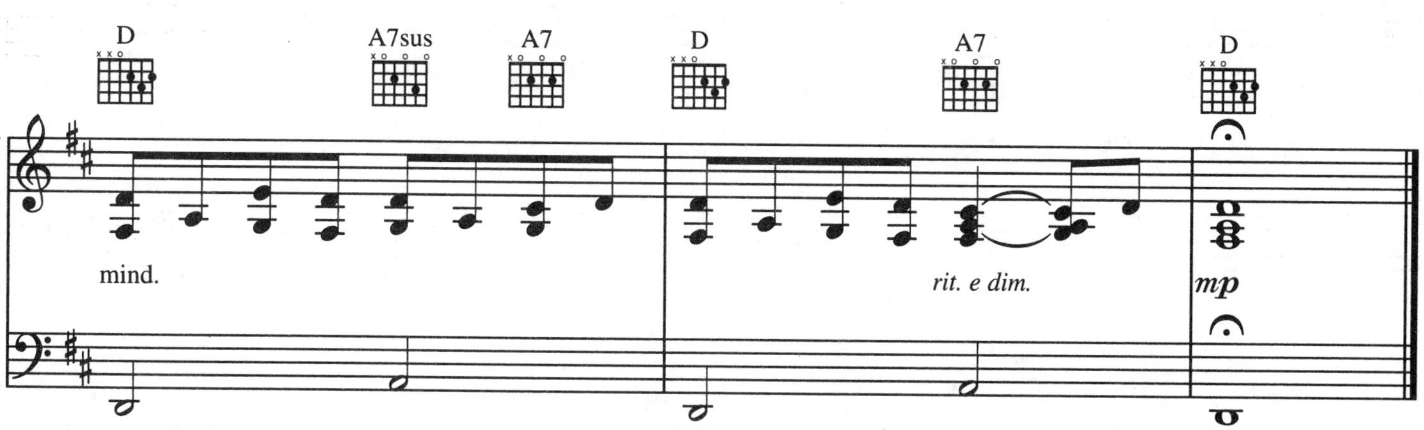

Verse 2:
Tell 'em I won't be ridin', I'll be walkin'
'Cause I don't think a crazy man should drive.
Anyway, the car belongs to you, now,
Along with any part of me that's still alive.
But there's really not much left you could hold on to,
And if you did, it wouldn't last here, anyway.
It'd head to where the rest of me rolled on to,
So, even if I wanted to, I couldn't stay.
(To Chorus:)

WALK ON

Words and Music by
MATRACA BERG and RONNIE SOMOSET

Walk On - 3 - 1

Am Em C D Am Em D
B♭m Fm D♭ E♭ B♭m Fm E♭

Side - walk, ba - by talk,_ don't get it with me_ no more._

Am Em C G D
B♭m Fm D♭ A♭ E♭

Next time a - round_ the block_ when you go by_ my door,_ ba - by:

𝄋 *Chorus:*

G D F C G
A♭ E♭ G♭ D♭ A♭

Walk on till you're gone_ a - way.

D F C D D2 D Dsus D D2 D
E♭ G♭ D♭ E♭ E♭2 E♭ E♭sus E♭ E♭2 E♭

Walk on till you find_ some day, oh hon - ey,

Verse 2:
Good-bye, baby cry, till you're singing the poor boy blues.
This time I don't mind if you're shining your walking shoes.
Fresh ink, in the pen, your papers are ready to sign.
They'll both be waiting for you, when you walk by, baby.
(To Chorus:)

(This Thing Called) WANTIN' AND HAVIN' IT ALL

Words and Music by
DAVE LOGGINS and
RONNIE SAMOSET

Now, he's sit - tin' at a ta - ble with his law - yer o - ver his
Bm
G
will, 'cause he's heeled. The kids don't call, they're
D
wait - in' on the man to die. He's gon - na
E
A7
leave 'em all a lit - tle some - thing, but they're gon - na be real sur - prised.
D
G
There's a poor man liv - ing on a bud - get at the bot - tom of that

D
hill.
He's got a wife and two kids and a
wor-ried mind_ 'bout
Bm
how he's gon-na pay the bills._
But
G
on-ly the rich man knows,
see,
D
that's where a lot of his mon-ey goes._ To a
E
man who brought wood in the win-ter, to take a lit-tle
A7
weight off_ of his shoul-ders. There's this
Chorus:
D
thing_ called_
G
want-in' and hav-in' it all._
D
But if you're

A7

gon-na get there, you're gon-na have to walk. But first, you'll have to crawl. You know

D G D G

you got-ta do it step by step. Miss one and you'll fall in-to this well

A A7 1. D G

called want-in' and hav-in' it all.

D G D G

D N.C.

3

2.
D
2. The
all.
See,
Bridge:
A
D/A
A7
A7sus
A7
life's full_ of chang - es_ and want - in'_ right now what
D
G
D
you on - ly see in_ your dreams. You
A
D/A
A7
A7sus
A7
know you_ don't like it_ and think it's_ the strang - est
E
B
thing you've ev - er seen._

N.C.
Spoken: There ain't nothin' you can do about it.
See, there's this
Chorus:
E
A
E
thing called wantin' and havin' it all.
But if you're gon-na get there, you're gon-na have to walk. But
B7
E
A
first, you'll have to crawl. You know you got-ta do it step by step.
E
A
B
1.
B7
Miss one and you'll fall in-to this well called wantin' and hav-in' this

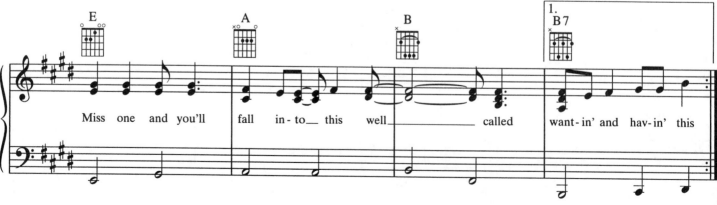

Verse 2:
The poor man has everything that the rich man wants.
He's got a love in his life and his heart.
He's got a house he calls home.
The rich man owns everything for miles around
But what he needs can't be bought, it has to be found.
His rich kids think that they're better
'Cause they're better off.
That's how they grew up thinkin'
And now, he thinks that's all his fault.
So while there's still time,
The daddy that they nickled and dimed is gonna
Make 'em learn to take a turn and stand in line for this...
(To Chorus:)

WHEN AND WHERE

Words and Music by
BRETT JONES, JEFF PENNIG and JESS BROWN

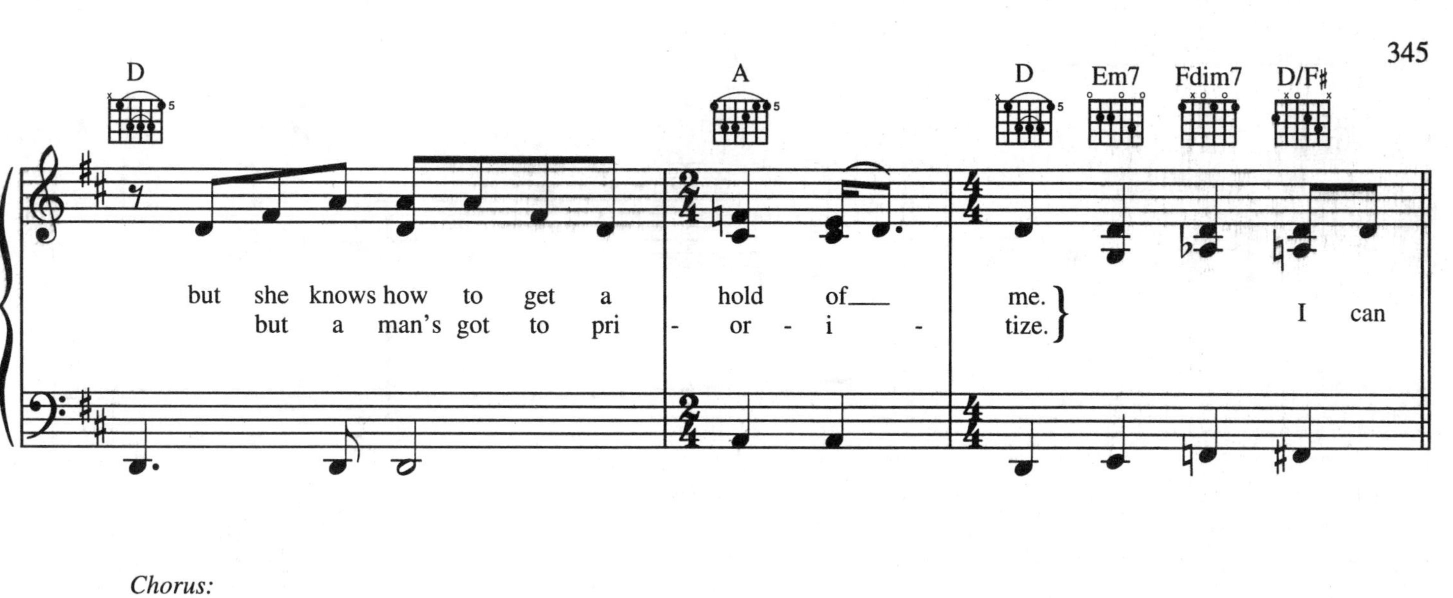
D
A
D
Em7
Fdim7
D/F♯
but she knows how to get a hold of___ me.
but a man's got to pri - or - i - tize.
I can

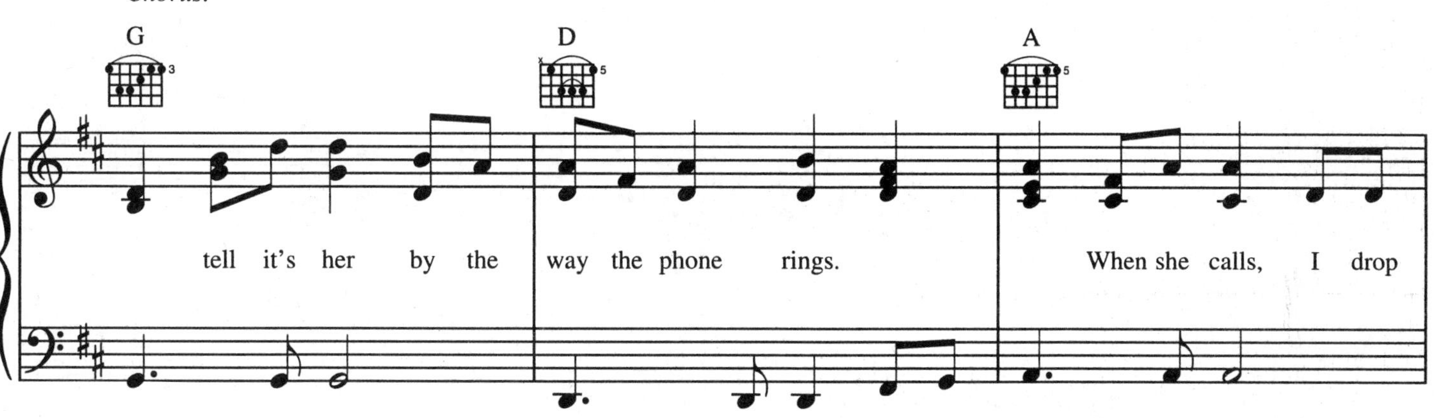
Chorus:
G
D
A
tell it's her by the way the phone rings.
When she calls, I drop

D
D7
G
D
G
ev-'ry - thing.____
Snaps her fin - gers________ and I'm
there.__________

D
N.C.
1.
A
D5
G7
"Hel-lo, dar-lin'.
When_ and_
where?"_

D5
C5
2.
A
When_ and_
D5
1.
where?"_ (1st time only)
Inst. solo ad. lib . . .
C5
G
2.
G
D5
A
D5
D/F♯
Bridge:
G
D
A7
An - y time,_
an - y place,
say the word and I'm
on my_ way. I can

Chorus:

G D A

tell it's her by the way the phone rings. When she calls, I drop

D D7 G D G

ev-'ry-thing.___ Snaps her fin-gers___ and I'm there.___

D5 N.C. A

"Hel-lo, dar-lin'. When_ and_

D5 G7 D5 A D5

where?"_

WHO NEEDS YOU

af - ter fight - ing with the traf - fic and the peo - ple on the in - ter - state.
F
B♭
Then I had an al - ter - ca -
E♭
tion with the wash - ing mach - ine,
C
F
so by the time that you got home, I guess I was a lit - tle mean.
B♭
And you and me, we got in - to a ter - ri - ble fight,

we stayed up yell - in' at each
F
oth - er 'til late last night.
You
B♭
crashed on the couch a - bout half past
E♭
two,
B♭
N.C.
F
N.C.
and I woke up this morn - ing think-ing who needs you.
B♭
E♭
Chorus:
Who needs you, steal -

B♭
ing my cov - ers, and tak - ing up half the bed? Who
F
needs all the cra - zy things you do?
E♭
Who needs you and all of your lov - in', no
B♭ E♭7 B♭ D♭6
mat - ter what I might have said? I'll give you just a lit - tle clue,
E♭7 B♭ D♭6 E♭7
I'm feel - ing might - y sad and blue, 'cause I'm
3
4

B♭
1.
F
N.C.
the on - ly fool who needs you.
2. So, dar -
2.
F
who needs you.
E♭
B♭
Who needs you and all of your lov - in', no mat - ter what I might have said?
E♭7
B♭
D♭6
E♭7
I'll give you just a lit - tle clue, I'm feel -

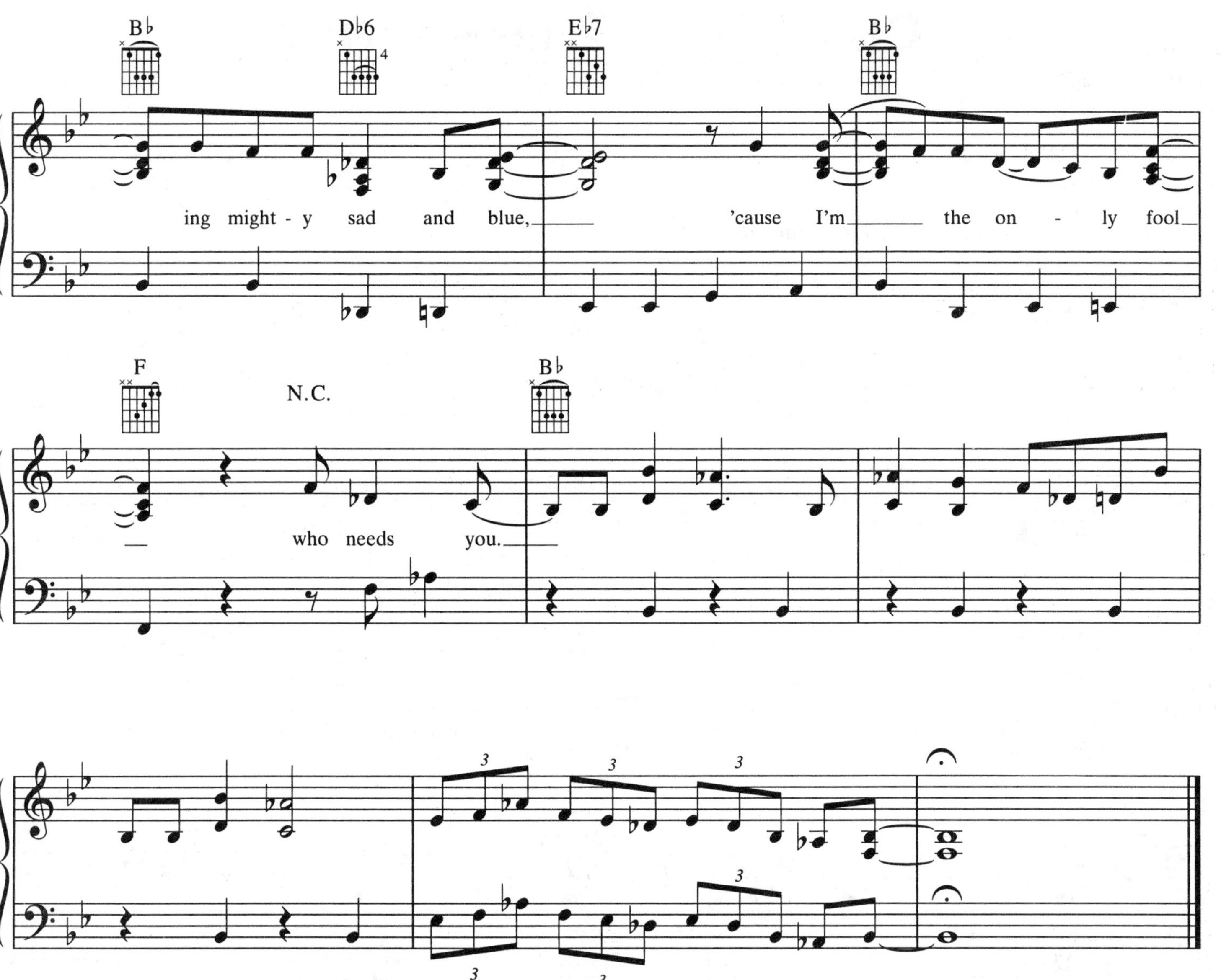

Verse 2:
So darlin', wipe the sleep out of your eyes,
Wake up and let me apologize.
I never should have said those things to you,
Now I swear that I still care,
And not a single word was true.
Let me get your favorite coffee cup,
Here's the cream, now sugar, can we please make up?
We're not due at work for an hour or two,
Why don't you lay back down
And let me show you just who needs you?
(To Chorus:)

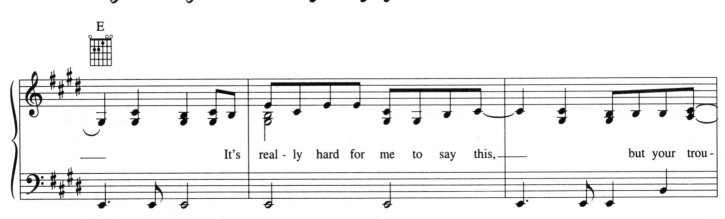

YOU BETTER THINK TWICE

Words and Music by
VINCE GILL and REED NIELSEN

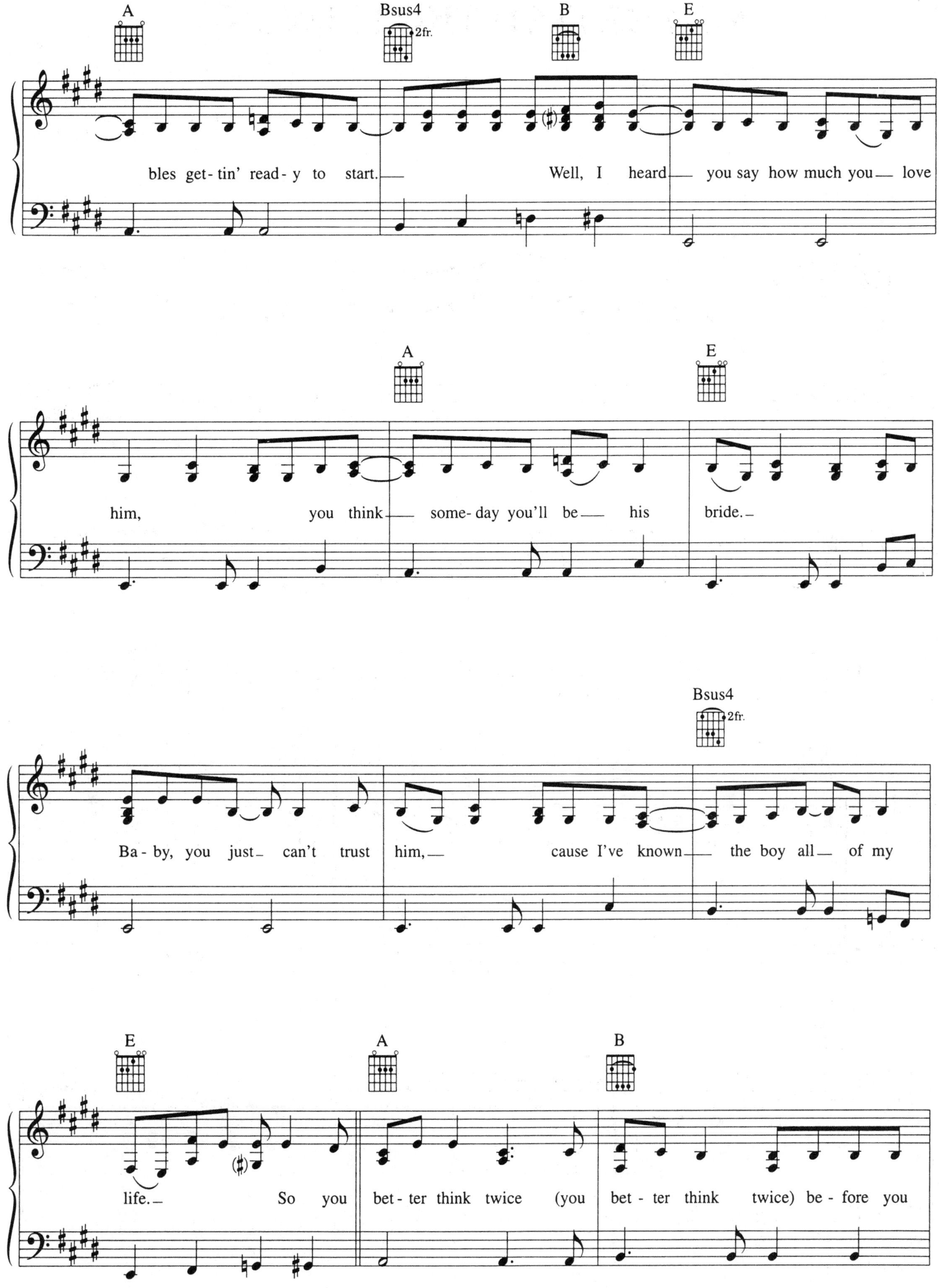

A Bsus4 2fr. B E

bles get- tin' read- y to start. Well, I heard you say how much you love

A E

him, you think some- day you'll be his bride.

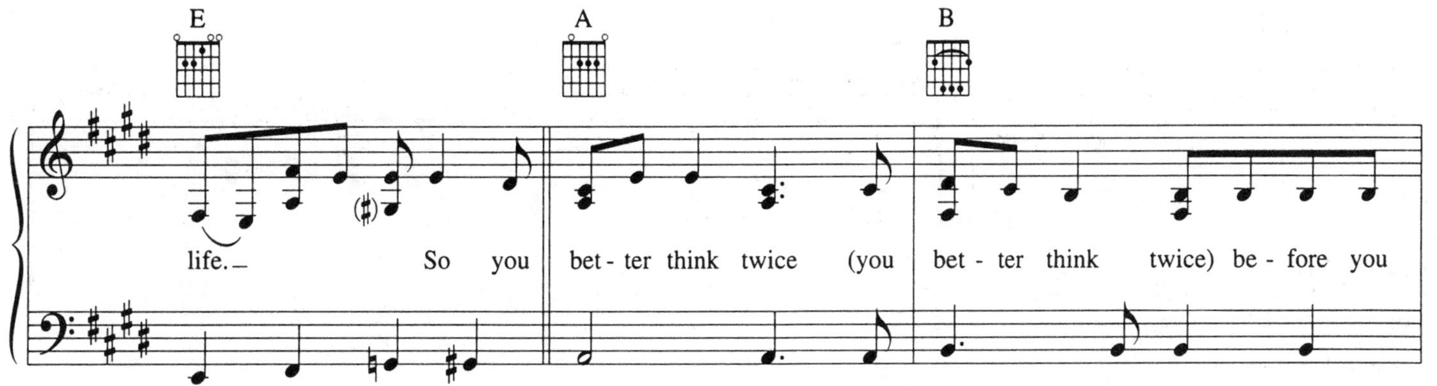

A
B
A
roll the dice (be- fore you roll the dice.) Yeah, you bet - ter think twice be - fore

Bsus4
2fr.
1.
E
you give your heart a - way.

2.
E
You real -

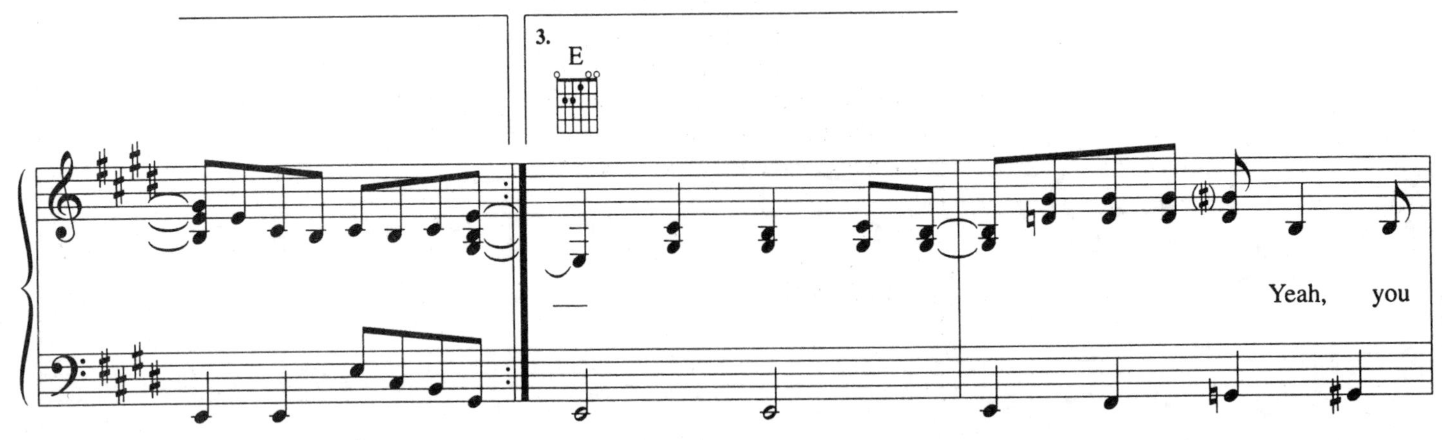
3.
E
Yeah, you

A
B
A
bet - ter think twice (you bet - ter think twice) be - fore you roll the dice (be - fore you
B
A/C#
B/D#
roll the dice.) Yeah, you bet - ter think twice be - fore you give your heart a - way.
Repeat and fade (vocal ad lib)
E

Additional lyrics

2. You really must think I'm something,
   Talkin' trash about my best friend.
   I just hate to see you wind up with nothing,
   'Cause you're way too good for him.
   I know that you don't believe me,
   But I've been with him when he's runnin' 'round.
   He don't mean to hurt nobody,
   He ain't never gonna settle down.
   (To Chorus)

3. *Instrumental*
   (To Chorus)

YOU CAN SLEEP WHILE I DRIVE

Lyrics and Music by
MELISSA ETHERIDGE

* Melody sung 1 octave lower

2.
C(9)
3.
C(9)
3. We'll go through
You know I've
G
F
C
seen it be - fore, this mist that
mf
cov - ers your eyes.
You've been
G
F
C
Bb
look-ing for some-thing that's not in your life. My in - ten-tions are true, won't you
Am
F
Bb
F
3
take me with you? And ba - by you can sleep wnile I drive.

C(9)
Dm
C(9)
Dm
C
Am
G
C
Am
G
Oh
is it oth - er arms you want to
hold
C
B♭
you,
the strang - er,
the
lov - er, you're free.
Can't you
Am
F
Dm7
C(9)
get that with me?
Come on
ba - by, let's get out of this
town.
3
I got a
mp
a tempo

Dm7
C(9)
full tank of gas___ with the top rolled___ down.___ If you won't
B♭
Am
F
take me with you,___ I'll go be - fore night is through,___ and
Slowly
B♭
F
C(9)
B♭maj7/C
ba-by___ you can sleep while I drive.___
rit.

Verse 2:
I'll pack my bag and load up my guitar,
In my pocket I'll carry my harp.
I got some money I saved,
Enough to get underway,
And baby you can sleep while I drive.

Verse 3:
We'll go through Tucson up to Sante Fe,
And Barbara in Nashville says we're welcome to stay.
I'll buy you boots down in Texas,
A hat in New Orleans,
And in the morning you can tell me your dreams.

WHEREVER YOU GO

Words and Music by
CLINT BLACK and HAYDEN NICHOLAS

E♭5
B♭5
whole oth - er world in the palm of your hand. Out of this world and
E♭5
out of your mind, just like it don't mat - ter what you're leav - in' be - hind. Try
B♭5
and change your life and change your whole point of view, but no
E♭5
mat - ter what you do, it's the same old you. Wher - ev - er you go,
f
E♭
Chorus:
F5
there you are.
B♭5
You can run from your - self,
E♭
F5

B♭5
A♭
but you won't get far.
You can dive to the bot-
F5
B♭5
-tom of your med-i-cine jar,
E♭
To Coda
1.
F5
but wher-ev-er you go,
there you are.
dim.
B♭5
E♭5
D.S.
mf
2.
B♭5
A♭5
B♭5
A♭5
B♭5
there you are.

Bridge:
E♭5
B♭5
A♭
Once you've been bit - ten, it's like crossing a line. It's a part of the plan, and all that's
F
B♭5
on your mind. Think that it-'ll help you find some - bod - y to be, but the
mf
E♭5
D.S.S. 𝄋𝄋 al Coda
man in the mir - ror is all you'll see. Wher - ev - er you go
f
Coda
F5
B♭5
E♭
F5
there you are. I said wher-ev - er you go,
B♭5
there you are.
dim.
mf

Verse 2:
Bottle of scotch whiskey, whatever you find;
When you're out on the wire, it's a matter of time.
Changing every moment when you're taking the fall;
There's everything to gain when you're losing it all.
Feel your head spinning with your feet on the ground;
You climb the wrong ladder, and it's keeping you down.
Think you're getting higher, but you're still laying low,
You don't want to be anyone you know.
(To Chorus:)

WHOSE BED HAVE YOUR BOOTS BEEN UNDER?

Words and Music by SHANIA TWAIN
and ROBERT JOHN "MUTT" LANGE

Verses 1 & 2:
F
B♭
lone - ly,
2. See additional lyrics.
don't act so
blue.
I know I'm not the
on - ly,
girl you run
to.
I know a-bout Lo -
Gm
E♭
li - ta,
See additional lyrics for D.S.
your lit-tle Span-ish flame.
I've seen you 'round with
Ri - ta,
the
red - head
down the lane.
Chorus:
N.C.
Whose bed have your
boots been un - der?
And whose heart did you
steal, I won - der?

To Coda
Cm
F
E♭
F
This time did it feel like thun - der, ba - by? And who did you run to?
B♭
E♭
And whose lips have you been kiss - in'?
And whose ear did you
Cm
F
make a wish in?
Is she the one that you've been miss - in', ba - by?
1.
A♭
E♭
B♭
N.C.
Well, whose bed have your boots been un - der?
2. I heard you've been
2.
A♭
N.C.
A♭
E♭
N.C.
B♭
Well, whose bed have your boots been un - der?

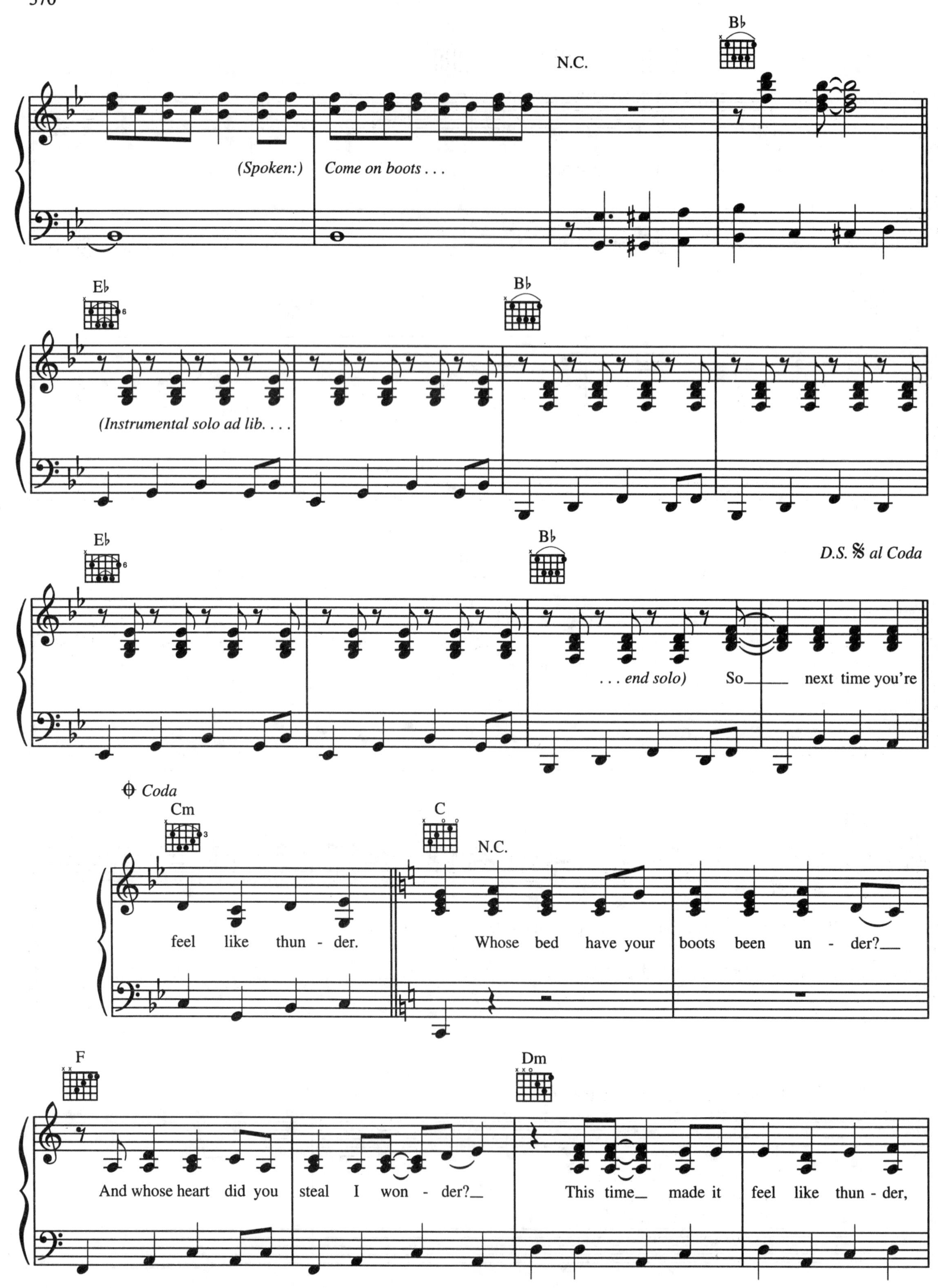
B♭
N.C.
(Spoken:)
Come on boots . . .
E♭
B♭
(Instrumental solo ad lib. . . .
E♭
B♭
D.S. 𝄋 al Coda
. . . end solo)
So
next time you're
Coda
Cm
C
N.C.
feel like thun - der.
Whose bed have your boots been un - der?
F
Dm
And whose heart did you steal I won - der?
This time made it feel like thun - der,

Verse 2:
I heard you've been sneakin'
Around with Jill.
And what about that weekend
With Beverly Hill?
And I've seen you walkin'
With long-legs Louise.
And you weren't just talkin'
Last night with Denise.
(To Chorus:)

Additional lyrics for D.S.:
So next time you're lonely,
Don't call on me.
Try the operator,
Maybe she'll be free.
(To Chorus:)

WHICH BRIDGE TO CROSS (WHICH BRIDGE TO BURN)

Words and Music by
VINCE GILL and BILL ANDERSON

B
F♯7
know how to love one and tell one we're
B
F♯
through. I can't sleep at night, I
B
C♯7
toss and I turn. I keep los - ing sight of the
F♯7
B
D♯7
les - sons I've learned. I'm stand- ing at the cross- roads with

G#m
4fr.
C#7
E
B
3
3
just one con - cern:
Which bridge to cross and
F#7
B
1.
F#7
2.
G#7
4fr.
3
which bridge to burn.
I
C#
4fr.
F#
C#
4fr.
G#7
4fr.
3
C#
4fr.
E#7

A♯m
D♯7
F♯
C♯
4fr.
G♯7
4fr.
C♯
4fr.
G♯
4fr.
I can't sleep at night, I
C♯
4fr.
D♯7
toss and I turn. I keep los - ing sight of the
G♯7
4fr.
C♯
4fr.
E♯7
les - sons I've learned. I'm stand- ing at the cross- roads with

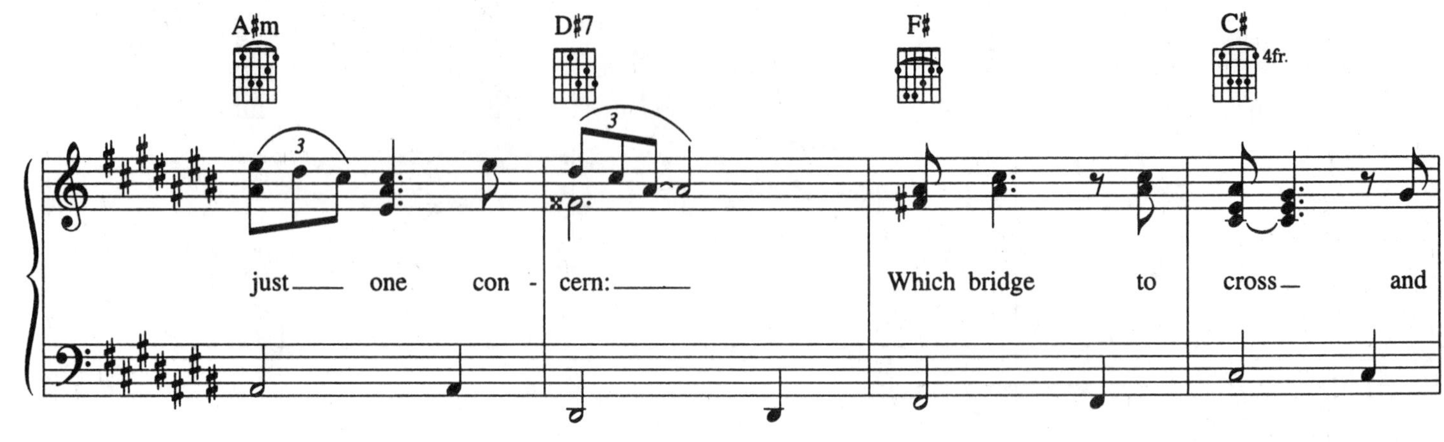

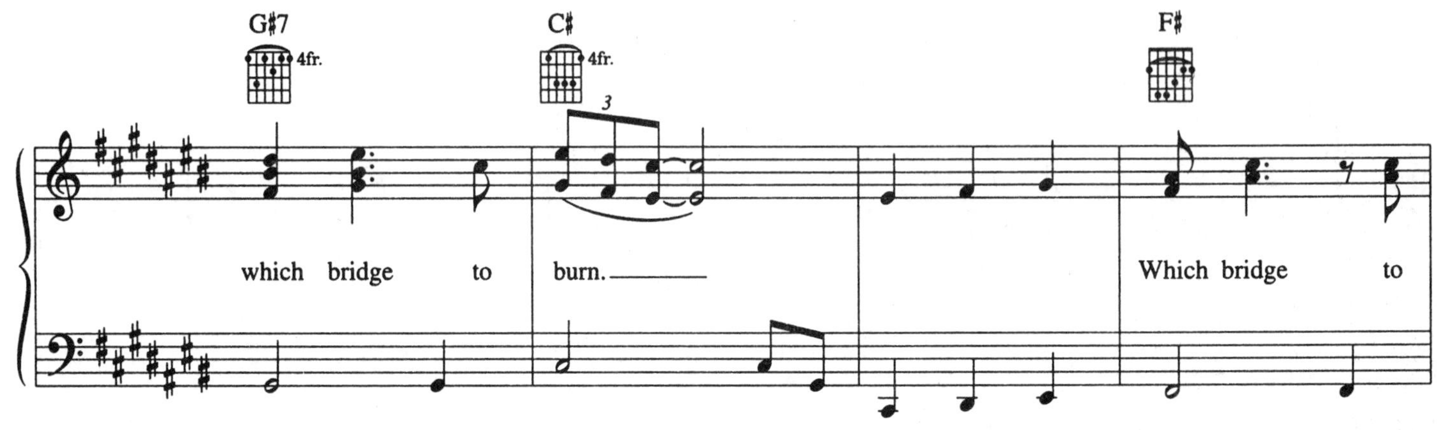

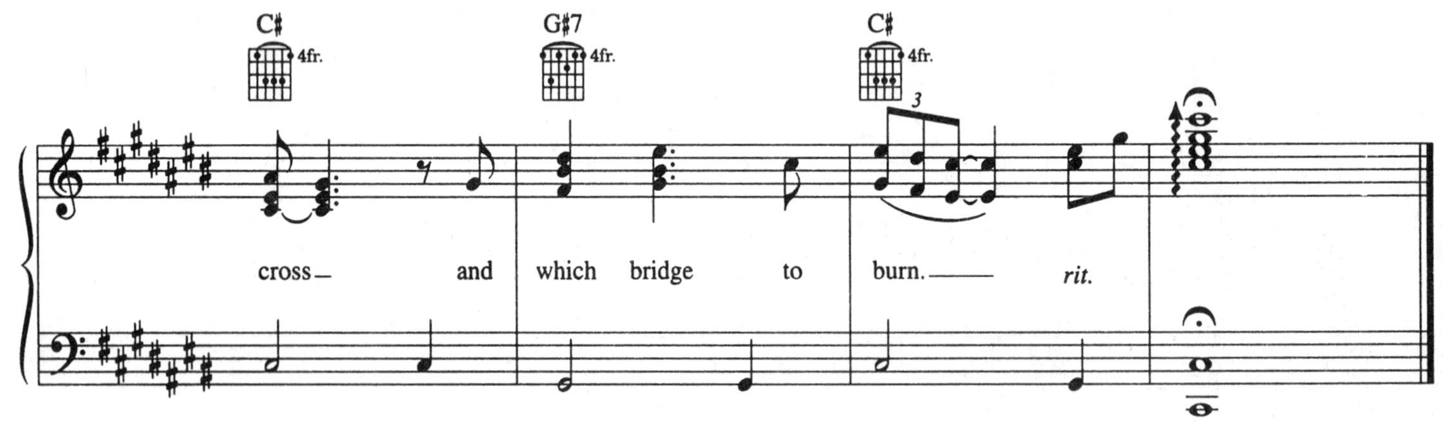

Additional lyrics

2. I knew this was wrong, I didn't listen,
   A heart only knows what feels right.
   Oh, I need to reach a decision,
   And get on with the rest of my life.
   (To Chorus)